USING ASSESSMENT RESULTS FOR CAREER DEVELOPMENT

4th Edition

USING ASSESSMENT RESULTS FOR CAREER DEVELOPMENT

4th Edition

VERNON G. ZUNKER

Brooks/Cole Publishing Company
Pacific Grove, California

I(T)P ™ The trademark ITP is used under license.

 A CLAIREMONT BOOK

Brooks/Cole Publishing Company
A Division of Wadsworth, Inc.

© 1994, 1990, 1986, 1982 by Wadsworth, Inc., Belmont, California 94002. All rights reserved. No part of this book may be reproduced, stored in a retrieval system, or transcribed, in any form or by any means—electronic, mechanical, photocopying, recording, or otherwise—without the prior written permission of the publisher, Brooks/Cole Publishing Company, Pacific Grove, California 93950, a division of Wadsworth, Inc.

Printed in the United States of America

10 9 8 7 6 5 4 3 2 1

Library of Congress Cataloging in Publication Data

Zunker, Vernon G., [date]
    Using assessment results for career development / Vernon G.
Zunker. — 4th ed.
        p.   cm.
    Includes bibliographical references and index.
    ISBN 0-534-21204-2
    1. Vocational guidance.   2. Occupational aptitude tests.
3. Vocational interests.   I. Title.
HF5381.Z87   1993
371.4'25—dc20   93-20947
                                                                CIP

Sponsoring Editor: *Claire Verduin*
Editorial Assistant: *Gay C. Bond*
Production Editor: *Nancy L. Shammas*
Production Service: *Scratchgravel Publishing Services*
Permissions Editor: *Elaine Jones*
Cover Design: *Robert Taylor*
Cover Photo: *UNIPHOTO, Picture Agency, Inc.*
Typesetting and Interior Design: *Scratchgravel Publishing Services*
Printing and Binding: *Malloy Lithographing, Inc.*

Preface

A few years ago several of my students expressed a need for a book that emphasizes the use of assessment results in career counseling. Most of these students had taken a typical graduate course in tests and measurement and were fairly well versed in the technical aspects of test development; they agreed that such a course was necessary for their professional development. However, a course that was more pragmatically oriented, one that would give them more information on how test results can assist clients in career development, was, in their opinion, of vital importance. Many of my colleagues agreed with this conclusion but also pointed out that a basic course in tests and measurement should be a prerequisite to a more pragmatically oriented course. With these thoughts in mind, I wrote the first edition of this book about 12 years ago.

During the last ten years more attention has been given to the use of test results, especially for students preparing to become career counselors. Publishers of tests are more alert to the need for providing counselors with profiles and accompanying information for using test results in the career decision-making process. Self-administered and self-interpreted procedures have been used by some publishers. Computer-assisted career guidance programs have also been innovative in providing test results in informative formats. I hope that courses designed to introduce tests as tools to foster self-understanding and growth will be forthcoming in the near future.

In the meantime, I have revised *Using Assessment Results for Career Development* to illustrate how assessment results can be used in career counseling to increase self-awareness and thus lead to rational career choices. The model for using assessment results that I formulated some 12 years ago remains intact and continues to be a relevant method for use in career decision making. I have included a number of tests that have recently been developed, and I have updated the chapters in an effort to deal more effectively with current issues in career guidance. This book may be used as a supplement in both career development and test and measurement courses.

In Chapter 1 a frame of reference for using assessment results in career counseling is established. A conceptual model for using assessment results is discussed in Chapter 2. Chapter 3 provides an overview of interpretive procedures; this chapter is designed to be a reference. Chapters 4 through 9 illustrate the use of results of ability tests, achievement tests, interest inventories, personality inventories, value inventories, and career maturity inventories. In Chapter 10 examples of how to use combinations of assessment results are given. Chapter 11 covers the use of assessment instruments especially designed for the handicapped and academically disadvantaged. Chapter 12 covers the use of nonstandardized self-assessment devices in career exploration.

The pages that follow are an expression of my appreciation to all those who influenced my values and enabled me to assess my own strengths and weaknesses in an ever-changing world. Many influenced my development through precept and example. Others revealed the stark realities of life directly. From all, I have learned something about myself. I hope that the systematic methods of enhancing individual development illustrated in this book will aid others in becoming self-aware.

I am grateful to many students and a number of my colleagues who offered words of encouragement and wisdom while I was putting these pages together: Donna Bender, San Jose State University; Joanne Chenault, National University; Marianne Gills, Georgia College; Carolyn Kern, University of North Texas; and Robert Reardon, Florida State University. I also acknowledge the assistance of manuscript reviewer Howard Splete of Oakland University in Rochester, Michigan.

Above all, I am most grateful to my wife, Rosalie, who encouraged, prodded, and kept her vivacious sense of humor throughout the entire writing of this text. Without her encouragement, the entire project would have been less meaningful.

Vernon G. Zunker

Contents

Chapter Eight
Using Value Inventories **104**

Chapter Nine
Using Career Maturity Inventories **119**

Chapter Ten
Combining Assessment Results **131**

Chapter Eleven
Using Assessment for the
Academically Disadvantaged and Disabled **150**

Chapter Twelve
Using Nonstandardized Self-Assessment Inventories **163**

Using Assessment Results for Career Development

4th Edition

Chapter One

Interpreting Assessment Results

This book begins where courses in assessment usually end. Instead of emphasizing the procedures used for standardizing tests and inventories and the methods used to develop them, this book illustrates the use of assessment results. The material is presented with the assumption that the reader has a substantial foundation in tests and measurements. In each chapter representative examples of tests, inventories, and self-assessment measures are reviewed with an explanation of how results are used. Fictitious cases further illustrate the use of many of these instruments. These cases resemble actual counseling encounters that I have had or that counselors I have supervised have had. The cases do not include descriptions of the entire information-gathering process and all counseling encounters. In each case only material relevant for illustrating the use of assessment results is presented. All standardized assessment instruments mentioned in this book are listed in Appendix A along with the names and addresses of the publishers.

Various approaches to assessment interpretation have been reported in the literature since Parson's (1909) seminal work. The trait-and-factor approach advocated by Parsons and later by Williamson (1939, 1949) was straightforward—it matched individual abilities and aptitudes with the requirements of a job. This approach has been drastically modified over the years toward considering, for example, many different individual characteristics and traits. In other words, individuals are being encouraged to consider many aspects of themselves in the career decision-making process, including their abilities, interests, personalities, values, past work and leisure experiences, and total lifestyles. In fact, more emphasis is being placed on integrating all life roles in the career counseling process. Specifically, individuals are encouraged to evaluate the effect work roles will have on other roles such as family, civic, and leisure roles.

This broad approach has been accompanied by computer scoring, new assessment instruments, and economic and societal changes, which have all complicated the issues of measurement and certainly the interpretation and use of assessment results. Computerized reports provide an almost unlimited amount of assessment information. The introduction of new measuring instruments and the refinement and revitalization of established tests and inventories provide further information to the career counselor. In addition, new technology has created a variety of new occupations, and the changing economic conditions and restructuring of organizations have caused many individuals to search for new, different occupations (Drucker, 1992). The stereotypes of the breadwinner father and the homemaker mother have undergone significant modification. A greater proportion of women are entering the work force (U.S. Department of Labor, 1992–1993), and it is predicted that six out of ten women will work for 30 years or more in the future (U.S. Department of Labor, 1978). The increasing number of workers in transition (Arbeiter et al., 1978; Drucker, 1992) has led to the development of assessment instruments to meet their special needs. The variety of clients may include a former executive who is a victim of downsizing in an organization, a homemaker and divorcee who is entering the work force for the first time, a high school dropout, and a college graduate who is unable to find an appropriate occupation. Special instruments have also been developed for individuals who are disadvantaged or who have disabling conditions. All these factors have made it necessary for counselors to reevaluate how they can most effectively use assessment results.

This chapter provides a general background for the interpretation of assessment results. First, it discusses assessment as a diagnostic and predictive tool, assessment as a means of comparing an individual with criterion groups, and the developmental use of assessment results. Second, this chapter discusses norms—when to use them, what kind to use, and how much weight to give to them. Third, it describes the interpretation of score profiles. Fourth, the chapter reviews the limitations of one-shot counseling. Finally, it provides a preview of the following chapters, which illustrate the use of assessment results in specific situations.

USE OF ASSESSMENT RESULTS

Assessment results are counseling tools for fostering career exploration. All theories, systems, and strategies underscore the inclusive and complex nature of the career-choice process. The process of deciding is indeed complex and unique for each individual, dependent on cognitive factors and the social structure of the individual's milieu. Individuals evaluate their choices internally by considering values, interests, achievements, and experiences and externally by seeking acceptance and approval within the work environment. They must deal with self-doubts concerning the appropriateness of their choice and in the process must make a careful examination of cognitive and affective domains. The significance of choosing a career parallels other major choices in an individual's life; the use of assessment results can provide useful information in the career decision-making process.

How, when, and whether to use assessment results are decisions shared by the counselor and the counselee. These decisions are based primarily on evaluation of the purpose for using measuring instruments. Can assessment results provide the information sought, and is that information relevant for the decisions that are to be made? This principle is followed when using assessment results for individuals as well as for groups. Tests are not to be given indiscriminately, and the same tests are not to be given routinely to everyone. Individuals in different phases of career development have different needs, which must be considered when determining whether to use assessment procedures. One individual may need assistance in developing an awareness of her interests. Another may need to clarify his values in order to establish priorities. Personality conflicts may be a deterrent for another individual who is considering a job change. Yet another may need assistance in clarifying her expectations about work in general.

A careful analysis of the purpose for using measurement devices would answer these questions: When is the most strategic time in the career decision-making process to introduce assessment? What are the alternatives the individual is considering? Does the information provided by the test correspond to the requirements of the particular jobs or training programs under consideration? Or, if a group is being counseled, will the results from the inventory introduce pertinent information for group discussion?

Because career exploration follows paths determined by individual needs, the use of assessment results in career counseling will vary and should be geared toward meeting specific objectives. Later chapters show how the use of assessment results in counseling can be designed to meet individual objectives. This chapter discusses assessment in a general way as a diagnostic and predictive tool, and as a means of comparing an individual to criterion groups, and most importantly, as relevant information for fostering career development over the life span.

Some overlap in the use of measuring instruments may occur. For example, a diagnostic test may be used to predict performance. However, a diagnostic test used to determine treatment for deficiencies may not be useful in predicting how well an individual will perform on a specific job. Likewise, a test used to predict performance may not be useful for determining treatment or for comparing an individual with criterion groups. For each client, a counselor must decide what kind of test or inventory to use.

Diagnostic Uses of Assessment

Achievement and aptitude assessment results in particular are often used to evaluate individual strengths and weaknesses in order to determine preparedness and potential for training and for beginning work. The identification of skills and aptitudes may broaden the individual's options for careers and education. In the same sense, the assessment of academic and skill deficiencies may help in the identification of the need for treatment, remedial training, or skill development.

Jake, a high school senior, was among a group of students participating in career exploration with his high school counselor. During the initial interview Jake told the counselor that he wanted to go to college but that he had a lot of interests and was not sure which one to pursue. Also, he expressed concern about his ability to succeed academically in college. After further discussion, the counselor and Jake agreed that he would complete an aptitude battery. The assessment results identified several academic strengths and a few specific deficiencies. Next, Jake and the counselor spent several sessions relating Jake's strengths to career fields and college majors that might be explored. Finally, they reviewed the curriculums of nearby colleges and decided, in light of Jake's academic deficiencies, which remedial courses he might take during his freshman year. By the end of counseling, Jake, though still not decided, had narrowed his ideas about a career choice. Moreover, he indicated that he felt positive about his initial academic plan.

Interest, value, personality, and career inventories may also be used diagnostically. Typically, these measures are used to raise an individual's level of self-awareness and to indicate to counselors when clients are lacking in self-awareness or have views of themselves that are inconsistent with assessment results.

Predictive Uses of Assessment

Assessment results may also be used to predict future academic and job performance. The probability of performing well on a job, in a training program, or in an educational program is relevant information on which to base further exploration. However, currently available ability measures primarily provide broad measures of an individual's experience and ability at the time of testing (aptitude tests) whereas achievement tests assess present levels of developed abilities. What is vitally needed is a measure of the occupational significance of abilities—that is, how important it is to have certain abilities to perform successfully in specific occupations. Until we have more data about prediction of occupational success and prediction of training and occupational performance, we should limit these references to more general terms in the counseling dialogue.

Herb wanted to know whether he could qualify for a machine operator's job in a local industrial plant. Fortunately, Herb's counselor had worked closely with the personnel division at the plant and, in fact, had assisted in gathering data for selection and placement. As a result, the counselor administered the test that had been used to develop cutoff scores for a variety of jobs in the plant. Herb's score was sufficiently high for him to qualify for a machine operator's job. In this case, Herb was provided with information that helped him evaluate his chances of meeting the requirements of a specific job.

Noel decided that she would like to attend the local community college. However, she was concerned about her chances of being a successful student in that college. Her counselor had developed an expectancy table (see Chapter 3) based on test scores and grades earned at the college by students who had attended the high school from which Noel was graduating. Noel agreed to take the test used in the study, and the counselor was able to assess her chances of getting a "C" or better at the college. The prediction of success based on local data was of vital importance in Noel's career exploration.

When assessment results are used to predict subsequent performance, the counselor should ensure that relevant predictive validity has been established for the tests that are used. For example, a test used to predict job performance should have a previously established high correlation with performance criteria for that job. Likewise, tests for predicting academic performance should be used only when relevant expectancy tables have already been established. Predictive validity is discussed further in Chapters 4, 10, and 11.

Comparative Uses of Assessment

Comparing one's personal characteristics (abilities, interests, values) with those of criterion groups is a stimulating part of career exploration. For example, it can be enlightening for individuals to compare their interests with the interests of individuals in certain occupational groups. The similarities and differences found can encourage discussion of the relevance of interests in career exploration.

The Strong Interest Inventory is an example of an interpretive report that compares an individual's interests with those of people in a wide range of occupations. Although an individual may be pleased to find that her interests are similar to those of social science teachers, she should also be encouraged to pay attention to interests that are dissimilar to those of other occupational groups.

Developmental Use of Assessment

Career development as a continuous process is enhanced by relevant assessment results used to increase awareness of career exploration opportunities over the life span. Learning to link measured aptitudes, interests, and values to work requirements and lifestyle preferences are good examples of using assessment results to foster career development. Meaningful assessment during all phases of career development involves the diagnostic, predictive, and comparative use of assessment results. At the elementary school level, for example, a career development objective focus may center on increasing self-awareness through the relationship of assessed personal characteristics to broad expectations of work in the future. A career development objective at the junior high school level stresses measured likes and dislikes and their influence on positive self-concepts. At the high school level students should understand the interrelationship between educational achievement results and work requirements. The college student is challenged with assessing personal aptitudes and preferences when determining a major and/or a career. The career development objective for an adult in career transition requires an evaluation of learned skills from previous work and leisure experiences in determining a new and different career direction. For the older adult, measured interests and leisure activities, skills needed in part-time or volunteer work, and assessment of established values are relevant developmental uses of assessment results. In all the examples of career development objectives, assessment results provide vital information for enhancing individual growth. The career counselor needs to be aware of a wide range of assessment instruments to meet individual needs at various stages of career development.

The role of assessment in career development counseling has also been emphasized by the National Occupational Information Coordinating Committee (NOICC, 1992) in national guidelines suggested for student and adult career development competencies. A summary of career development competencies by area and level has been reported by Zunker (1994). Some examples of specific competencies in which the developmental use of assessment results can be the major focus are as follows.

1. **For the elementary school student**

   Competency: Knowledge of the importance of a positive self-concept.
   The student will:

   • Identify personal interests, abilities, strengths, and weaknesses
   • Describe ways to meet personal needs through work

Competency: Awareness of the benefits of educational achievement.
The student will:

- Identify personal strengths and weaknesses in academic areas
- Identify academic skills needed in several occupational groups
- Describe school tasks that are similar to skills essential for job success

2. **For the junior or middle school student**

Competency: Knowledge of the influence of a positive self-concept.
The student will:

- Describe personal likes and dislikes

Competency: Knowledge of the benefits of educational achievement to career opportunities.
The student will:

- Describe individual strengths and weaknesses in school subjects
- Describe the skills needed to adjust to changing occupational requirements
- Describe the importance of academic and occupational skills in the world of work
- Describe how aptitudes and abilities relate to broad occupational groups

3. **For the senior high school student**

Competency: Understanding the influence of a positive self-concept.
The student will:

- Demonstrate an understanding of how individual characteristics relate to achieving personal, social, educational, and career goals
- Identify and appreciate personal interests, abilities, and skills

Competency: Understanding the relationship between educational achievement and career planning.
The student will:

- Describe the relationship of academic and vocational skills to personal interests
- Demonstrate transferable skills that can apply to a variety of occupations and changing occupational requirements

4. **For the adult**

Competency: Skills to maintain a positive self-concept.
The adult will:

- Identify skills, abilities, interests, experiences, values, and personality traits and their influence on career decisions
- Determine or clarify career and life goals based upon a realistic understanding of self.

More specific suggestions for developmental use of assessment results are included in Chapters 4, 5, 6, 7, and 8.

NORMS

The usefulness of assessment results in career counseling is determined by the types of norms available. In using norms, the counselor should keep the following questions in mind. When should norms be used? What kind of norms should be used? How much weight should be given to norms?

Norms represent the level of performance obtained by the individuals (normative sample) used in developing score standards. They may thus be thought of as typical or normal scores. Norms for some tests and inventories are based on the general population. Other norms are based on specific groups such as all 12th-grade students, 12th-grade students who plan to attend college, left-handed individuals, former drug abusers, former alcoholics, or the physically disabled.

The organization of norm tables varies somewhat from test to test. For example, the manual for the Differential Aptitude Test (Form S and T) lists separate norms for boys and girls by semester from fall of grade 8 to fall of grade 12. The Adult Basic Learning Examination (Level III) provides norms for adults by sex, age, race, last grade completed, and median Stanford Achievement Test score.

The description of the normative sample is of primary concern. In some manuals only a brief description is given, leaving counselors to assume that their counselees resemble the normative population. Others, such as the Kuder Occupational Interest Survey, provide specific definitions of normative groups. Such detailed descriptions of persons sampled in standardizing an inventory provide good data for comparing the norm samples with counselee groups. In many instances more information would be useful, such as score differences between age and ethnic groups and between individuals in different geographical locations. The more descriptive the norms, the greater their utility and flexibility.

When using norms, counselors must carefully evaluate the population from which the norms have been derived to determine whether that population resembles the counselees in background and individual characteristics. We would not want to use norms derived from a sample of Puerto Ricans in the Northeast to advise a group of Chinese students on the West Coast. However, norms derived from Puerto Ricans in the Northeast are more appropriate for use with Puerto Ricans living elsewhere in the country than are general-population norms.

National norms, sometimes referred to as general-population norms or people-in-general norms, are usually controlled in the sampling process to be balanced in regard to geographical area, ethnicity, educational level, sex, age, and other factors. National norms may be helpful in determining underlying individual characteristics and patterns. For example, an individual whose measured values suggest only an average need for achievement compared with that of business executives and entrepreneurs may exhibit a moderately high need for achievement when compared with people in general. This information suggests an underlying or secondary need for achievement that may not have otherwise been clarified. The identification of lower-order yet important personal traits affords greater depth for career exploration.

In many instances national norms should not be used. National norms based on a sample of 12th graders are of little value in predicting success in a particular university. Appropriate norms would be those derived from students who have attended the university under consideration. Likewise, norms based on a general population are not useful in predicting success in a certain job at a local factory. Selection and placement in an industry are usually based on norms derived from workers in a specific occupation or work setting.

Because operational and educational requirements vary from one location to another, the use of local norms is recommended. For example, you will recall that, for predicting Noel's chances of being successful in a particular college, the counselor had collected data from former students from Noel's high school to develop the norms.

Local norms are also useful for job placement. Although more weight can be given to local norms than to general norms and local norms should be developed whenever possible, counselors usually do not have the necessary time and resources to devote to such projects. Most counselors must rely on the published norms furnished in test and inventory manuals. Most of the counseling cases discussed in later chapters illustrate the use of assessment results with published norms.

SCORE PROFILES

In early counseling approaches the profile served as the primary tool for making one-shot predictions of vocational choice (Goldman, 1972; Prediger, 1980). Choices were considered definite and irreversible (Cronbach, 1984). Currently, the score profile is considered as only one source of information on individual characteristics.

To make assessment results as meaningful as possible, computer-generated narrative reports are increasingly being used as supplements to the profile. The computer interprets the score results in narrative form according to a planned program. These narrative reports are often sent directly to students and parents. Because score profiles alone do not always stimulate individuals to explore careers, such supplementary materials and follow-up exercises are needed to complement the interpretation process (Prediger, 1980). Although supplements to profiles may prove to be helpful in stimulating career exploration, the counselor should not completely abandon the role of interpreting the profile. In fact, the potential for increasing the number and variety of computer-generated score interpretations in the future is almost a mandate for counselors to sharpen their skills in this respect.

Regardless of the format of the score profile, three important principles of interpretation must be retained: Differences between scores should be interpreted with caution. Profiles should be interpreted with concern for the influence of norms. Scores should be expressed in ranges rather than points.

Differences between Scores

Caution must always be used when interpreting differences between scores on a profile. Small score differences are meaningless and should be attributed to chance effects. Counselees may be tempted to make much more of small score differences between subtests than is plausible. But one should not eliminate second-, third-, or fourth-order measured interests and consider only highest measured interests in career exploration. Likewise, when interpreting the score profile from a general abilities test, one should not consider only a career in mathematics because the score in mathematics was a few percentile points higher than the other scores. To point a person narrowly to a slightly higher measured characteristic is counterproductive in developmental counseling. (Score differences are discussed further in Chapters 3 and 4.)

Relation of Norms to the Shape of a Profile

An individual's profile must be carefully interpreted in light of the norm reference group. The position of scores on a profile (its shape) is determined by the norms used. For example, Everett, who is interested in architecture, has taken the Differential Aptitude Test. His score profile compared with that of men in general suggests that his general abilities are high enough for him to consider college. To obtain a reliable estimate of his chances of success in a school of architecture, his scores were compared to norms derived from architecture students. The shapes of the profiles were quite different. When Everett's scores were plotted against those for men in general, all were considerably above average. When compared with scores of architecture students, most of his scores were in the average range. This profile gives a much more valid estimate of his chances for success in a school of architecture than does the general profile. Whenever possible, score profiles used for predicting performance should be compared with those of competitors (Cronbach, 1984).

Scores as a Range

On some score profiles results are reported as points on a scale; on others scores are reported as a range that includes the error of measurement of each test. The range may be represented on a percentile graph by a bar, line, or row of *x*'s, with the obtained percentile at the center. This method reflects the individual's true score more accurately than does the single-point method.

Because career development is a continuous process, the score profile provides information from which only tentative decisions need be made. These decisions, not being binding or irreversible, provide information on which to base a further study of individual characteristics. Therefore, the range is more appropriate as a reference for individual decisions than is a single point. Because we are usually not able to obtain precise measures in career exploration, the error of measurement should be considered for all scores recorded as a single point on a scale.

USING HOLLAND'S CODES FOR INTERPRETATION

According to John Holland (1985), individuals are attracted to a given career by their particular personalities and numerous variables that constitute their backgrounds. Although Holland's work is centered on the development of interest inventories and their interpretation, his concepts are also related to skills, abilities, attitudes, and values that will be discussed in many of the following chapters. It is therefore important to introduce the basic assumptions of his theory (Holland, 1985, pp. 2–4):

1. In our culture, most persons can be categorized as one of six types: realistic, investigative, artistic, social, enterprising, or conventional.
2. There are six kinds of environments: realistic, investigative, artistic, social, enterprising, and conventional.
3. People search for environments that will let them exercise their skills and abilities, express their attitudes and values, and take on agreeable problems and roles.
4. A person's behavior is determined by an interaction between his or her personality and the characteristics of the environment.

Central to Holland's theory is the concept that one chooses a career to satisfy one's preferred personal modal orientation. For example, a socially oriented individual prefers to work in an environment that provides interaction with others, such as a teaching position. A mechanically inclined individual, however, might seek out an environment where the trade could be quietly practiced and might avoid socializing to a great extent. Occupational homogeneity—that is, congruence between one's work and interests—provides the best route to self-fulfillment and a consistent career pattern. Individuals out of their element who have conflicting occupational environmental roles and goals will have inconsistent and divergent career patterns.

A brief explanation of Holland's personal styles and occupational environments follows. For a more complete explanation, see Zunker (1994).

1. *Realistic:* This personal style includes individuals who prefer concrete versus abstract work tasks, work outdoors in manual activities, and like to work alone or with other realistic people. Most occupations are blue-collar ones, such as plumber, electrician, photographer, and service occupations.
2. *Investigative:* This personal style includes individuals who prefer to work in an environment where one is required to use abstract and analytical skills, are somewhat independent, and are strongly oriented to accomplishing tasks. Many of the scientific professions require high levels of education and are intellectually oriented, such as chemist, biologist, and researcher. Examples of other investigative occupations are laboratory technician, computer programmer, and electronics worker.

3. *Artistic:* This personal style includes imaginative and creative individuals who value aesthetics, prefer self-expression through the arts, and are rather independent and extroverted. Some occupations included in this category are sculptor, artist, designer, music teacher, orchestra leader, editor, writer, and critic.

4. *Social:* These individuals are very concerned with social problems, prefer social interaction, are religious, participate in community service, are interested in educational activities, and prefer working with people. There is a strong orientation toward working with others and using interpersonal skills. Occupational categories in this group include those in education, such as teacher, school administrator, and college professor. Others are social worker, rehabilitation counselor, and professional nurse.

5. *Enterprising:* Individuals of this personal style are extroverted, aggressive, adventurous, dominant, and persuasive and prefer leadership roles. Their behavior is also characterized as goal directed, and they like to coordinate others' work. Occupational categories are managerial, including workers in charge of production and in various sales positions.

6. *Conventional:* The personal style of these individuals is practical, well controlled, sociable, rather conservative, preferring structured tasks, and comfortable when working with details. Occupations include office and clerical workers, accountant, bookkeeper, receptionist, teller, and key-punch operator.

Many of the following chapters refer to Holland's types and codes, and, in fact, some of this information will be repeated for a better understanding of his typology. For in-depth coverage, read Holland's original work and the research that supports his occupational types.

ONE-SHOT COUNSELING

People have different expectations for career counseling. Some take a realistic approach and expect to spend considerable time in individual study and in counseling encounters. Others expect counselors to analyze their assessment results and prescribe a career in one counseling session (Cronbach, 1984; Prediger, 1980). To illustrate this second kind of expectation, imagine yourself as a counselor in the following two cases.

Ed, a high school senior, drops by the counseling office one week before graduation and tells the counselor that he would like to know what major he should select for his first summer session in college. "I would like to take the test that will tell me what to major in." As Ed sees it, the test holds the key to his future.

Ann, a second-semester college sophomore, makes an appointment in the college counseling center during mid-semester break. She explains, "I would like to take those tests that will tell me what career I should choose so I can register for the courses next semester." She has an entire half day to make this decision!

Often, in more subtle ways than these, parents and students expect one-shot assessment interpretations to resolve the issue of career choice. They feel that tests have a mystical power to foretell the future. As Thompson (1976, p. 31) puts it, "Psychological tests are supposed to unravel this mystery, and client expectations are usually high." Within this frame of reference a counselor's major responsibility is to test clients and place them in the right job.

The limitations of one-shot counseling are apparent. First, in career exploration, many decisions are tentative. One-shot counseling approaches give just the opposite impression. Second, there is little opportunity to confirm the decisions based on assessment results. One-shot counseling does not provide for follow-up through observation, continuous discussion of assessment results, or retesting. Third, a one-shot counseling approach affirms the individual's desire to make decisions without devoting time to gathering information and considering alternatives. There is little opportunity to develop a systematic method of decision making. In effect, the counselee is seeking the counselor's approval to approach career decision making from a single throw of the dice without considering alternative information.

Ideally, the use of assessment results should be only one phase of career exploration. Individual characteristics measured by tests and inventories should be only one facet considered in the career decision-making process. Assessment results should be combined with background information for making career decisions over the life span. Counselors and counselees can then periodically verify or reevaluate assessment results along with other material and experiences in the continuous process of career development. In the next chapter, I develop models other than one-shot counseling for using assessment results in career counseling.

PREVIEW OF THIS BOOK

A model for using assessment results described in Chapter 2 is illustrated by a contrived counseling case found on pages 18–22. Other case studies in Chapters 4 through 12 are excerpts of the model and are used primarily to illustrate the use of a variety of assessment instruments.

In Chapters 4 through 12, I review a variety of tests and inventories selected because they are widely used or provide innovative methods of presenting score results or both. They are representative of the tests and inventories available. For a general evaluation of tests, consult the following references: *Tests in Print III* (Mitchell, 1983); *The Mental Measurements Yearbook* (Conoley & Kramer, 1989); *Test Critiques* (Keyser & Sweetland, 1985); *Tests: A Comprehensive Reference for Assessment in Psychology, Education, and Business* (Sweetland & Keyser, 1991); and *Measures of Personality and Social Psychology Attitudes* (Robinson, Shaver, & Wrightsman, 1991).

Each review in this book follows approximately the same format, providing the following information: purpose of the instrument, description of subtests, description of reliability and validity studies when appropriate, description of profile and score results, and method for interpreting the results. Case studies illustrate how the instruments may be used for career development. The cases demonstrate the use of assessment in career counseling with those ranging in age from high school youths to middle-aged adults.

Finally, Chapters 4 through 8 provide suggestions for the developmental use of assessment results that are based on the National Career Guidelines established by the National Occupational Information Coordinating Committee (NOICC).

SUMMARY

Computerized narrative reports, the refinement and revitalization of tests and inventories, societal changes, and the development of new technology have caused counselors to reevaluate the use of assessment results in career counseling. As a diagnostic tool, assessment results identify individual strengths and weaknesses. As a predictive tool, assessment results forecast the probability of performing well on a job or in a training/educational program. By comparing an individual to criterion groups, assessment results are used to stimulate career exploration. The use of assessment results to build competencies for career development is emphasized.

Norms should be carefully evaluated to determine whether the population sample resembles the counselee in background and individual characteristics. Whenever possible, local norms should be developed. More weight can be given to norms that are established on the basis of successful performance in a particular educational/training program or an occupation than to general norms.

The score profile is the primary tool used to interpret assessment results. When using the score profile, the counselor must be cautious in interpreting differences between scores, must carefully evaluate the norms used, and must consider scores as ranges rather than as points on a scale.

Expectations of career counseling differ. Some counselees expect a one-shot counseling encounter to answer the questions of career choice. One-shot counseling provides little opportunity for developing methods of decision making.

QUESTIONS AND EXERCISES

1. What kind of norms should be used to predict an individual's chances of getting a "C" grade or better at a certain community college? Explain your answer.
2. How can national norms be most effectively used in career counseling? What are the limitations?
3. What kinds of tests are most often used for diagnostic purposes? Explain.
4. Describe one circumstance where assessment may be used as (a) a diagnostic tool, (b) a predictive tool, (c) a means of comparing an individual with a criterion group.
5. How would you answer the request of Ed, the high school senior used as an example of one-shot counseling?

Chapter Two
A Conceptual Model for Using Assessment Results

The increasing number of sophisticated assessment instruments requires career counselors to continually upgrade their skills in using assessment results to meet the demands of a wide range of individuals. More than ever, career counselors are challenged to convert the statistics associated with test data into meaningful information.

As an integral component of the career counseling process, assessment is also changing and growing in complexity. Crites's (1977) evaluation of five major career counseling approaches indicates that the use of assessment results in the counseling process has evolved from an analytical, diagnostic, counselor-dominated task to a developmental, client-centered task. This change has paralleled a general transition in career counseling from an emphasis on trait-and-factor identification and matching to an emphasis on life stages and developmental tasks. Super (1990), among others, has had a tremendous impact through the focus on the use of self-concept in the career decision process. Moreover, the relatively recent translation of Super's (1990) career maturity concept into career counseling and education objectives has focused attention on career decision making as a developmental process. The developmental approach, like the previous trait-and-factor approaches, sees assessment as essential in enhancing self-awareness. However, added emphasis is placed on client involvement in the selection and interpretation of assessment measures. More important, within the developmental framework, assessment results are considered as a tool to promote career exploration rather than as the primary or sole basis for decisions.

The increasing complexity and diversity of assessment results suggest the need for a systematic model that will permit counselors to make an effective analysis of the assessment procedures and results appropriate for specific counseling needs. This chapter discusses a conceptual model for using assessment results in career counseling. I first provide the rationale for using assessment results. Then I present a model for use in individual counseling. Finally, I illustrate how the model can be used to stimulate career exploration among groups of individuals.

RATIONALE

In this model, the use of assessment results is conceptualized as a learning process emphasizing the development of self-knowledge. Identification and verification of individual characteristics are the main information provided by assessment results. This information is used with other information in career decision making. Although assessment results are used in a variety of ways (as discussed in Chapter 1), career counselors are encouraged to look beyond the score report in order to facilitate meaningful learning experiences that will enhance self-awareness and lead to effective career exploration.

Thus, assessment results should be only one kind of information used in career counseling. Testing and interpretation of score reports should not dominate the counseling process. Other factors such as work experiences, grades, leisure activities, skills, and attitudes toward work should receive equal attention. Assessment results are best used when they can contribute information that is relevant within this overall context.

The process is complex in that individuals must consider their own values, interests, aptitudes, and other unique qualities in making decisions. Although the method of career decision making is a relatively easily learned skill, one's application of the scheme involves consideration of one's complex and unique characteristics. The process usually begins when an individual recognizes a need to make a decision and subsequently establishes an objective or purpose. Then the individual collects data and surveys possible courses of action. Next the individual utilizes the data in determining possible courses of action and the probability of certain outcomes. Estimating the desirability of outcomes centers attention on the individual's value system. The final step involves making and evaluating the decision—either a terminal decision or an investigatory decision. If a terminal decision is reached, the individual once again evaluates the possible outcomes. Individuals with the same objectives will undoubtedly reach decisions by different paths based primarily on personal values and knowledge.

Other examples of decision models have been reviewed by Brown (1990). Some models specifically use assessment results to identify and clarify individual characteristics in order to enhance the decision process. For example, Sandra, a high school senior, is attempting to decide which college to attend. She collects information concerning entry requirements, costs, faculty/student ratios, academic programs, and other data from five colleges. Using assessments of her skills and abilities, she weighs her chances of being accepted by the colleges under consideration and the probability that she will be able to meet academic requirements at those institutions.

In determining a major at the college chosen, Sandra considers results of value inventories. These are among the questions she asks herself: "How much do I value a high salary? And if I do value a high salary, which college major would most likely lead to a high-paying job?" Value assessment is essential for making satisfactory decisions here. After Sandra selects an institution and major, she once again evaluates the possible outcomes of the decision.

In sum, decision making requires the counselee's self-knowledge of abilities, interests, values, and relevant past experiences, and the application of this knowledge to the consideration of alternatives. The more informed an individual, the greater probability of a desirable outcome (Pietrofesa & Splete, 1975). In the case of Sandra, tests that measure scholastic aptitude and achievement were used with other data such as earned grades to make adequate predictions. These assessment results provided support information that is not easily attained through other means such as interviews or biographical data. Assessment data have the distinct advantage of stimulating discussion of specific individual characteristics that can be linked to educational and occupational requirements.

A MODEL FOR INDIVIDUAL COUNSELING

The effective selection and implementation of assessment devices in career counseling can best be attained through the use of a conceptual model. Such a model provides a systematic method for establishing the purpose of testing and the subsequent use of assessment results. To be operationally effective, a model must be flexible enough to meet the needs of a wide variety of individuals in different stages of their lives. In essence, a model should provide guidelines that are applicable to individuals at all educational levels, in all population groups, of both sexes, and of all ages.

Drawing from the works of Cronbach (1984), Anastasi (1988), and Super et al. (1992), I have conceptualized a model for using assessment results in developmental career counseling as having four major steps. As shown in Figure 2-1 (page 14), these steps are analyzing needs, establishing the purpose of testing, determining the instruments, and utilizing the results. The process is

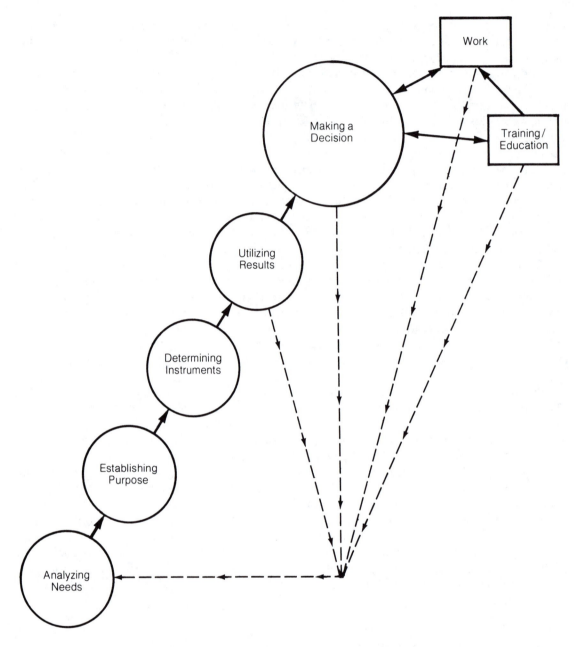

Figure 2-1.
Cyclical and continuous model for using assessment results in career counseling.

cyclical and continuous. One may return to the first step during career exploration, after a period of being employed, or after completing an educational/training program. For example, an individual who is exploring careers has discussed general interests with a counselor and, after reviewing occupational requirements, has identified a need for an assessment of abilities. An individual who is dissatisfied with his current career wishes to begin the process anew and to select a different career based on his increased understanding of needs that are not being met. After completing a training program for licensed vocational nurses, another individual has decided that this occupation is not what she wants; she wishes to meet with a counselor to analyze why she is dissatisfied and to reassess her career decision. Because career development is a continuous process, assessment may prove to be useful at any point in the life span.

Super et al. (1992) consider career maturity to be an important index to an individual's readiness for making career decisions. In an assessment model labeled the Career-Development Assessment and Counseling model (C-DAC), Super et al. suggest that expressed preferences, such as interest inventory results, should be viewed as basic status data or level of career maturity. Other measures, such as value inventories and life role importance questionnaires, should be used as moderator variables in the career counseling process. The basic logic underlying this approach is to measure developmental stages according to Super's (1990) scheme and the tasks or concerns of the individual to determine the needs of clients plus their readiness to make career commitments. With this information additional data gathered through interview and self-reports, counselors can determine developmental counseling intervention strategies for each client. Developmental strategies are recommended throughout this text.

Analyzing Needs

To assure that a counselor is on the correct course for meeting individual needs, a needs analysis may be accomplished by using interviews, a biographical data form, education and work records, or a combination of these. The underlying goal is to encourage counselee participation. Counselees who recognize their needs are likely to participate actively and enthusiastically in all phases of preparing for and using assessment results. For example, when Beth recognizes that she needs a structured approach for career exploration, she can be shown how assessments results can assist her. Likewise, when Ron recognizes the need for help in predicting his chances of success in an educational program, he should be motivated to do his best. Thus, the first key to effective use of assessment results is the counselor's skill in aiding the counselee in identifying needs and in relating needs to the purpose of testing.

The following four objectives are designed to assist the counselor in identifying needs: establish the counseling relationship, accept and adopt the counselee's views, establish lifestyle dimensions, and specify the needs. The accomplishment of these objectives may extend beyond the initial interview.

To establish a counseling relationship is to foster a sense of trust and mutual respect. To accomplish this goal the counselor communicates a sincere desire to help the counselee, provides hospitality by being friendly, arranges for personal introductions of staff members, and is on time for the appointment. A warm, friendly atmosphere is particularly essential during the initial interview. Every attempt should be made to communicate to the counselee that he or she has the undivided attention of the counselor.

To launch the initial counseling session the counselor may start with a simple question: "How can we help you?" The counselor listens for clues to continue the session. Although individual needs vary, the counselor should attempt to answer some of the following questions: What are the counselee's expectations of career counseling? Where is the counselee in the career decision-making process? Are tests indicated or contraindicated? Will the counselee be willing to invest the time necessary for career counseling? Does the counselee understand the role of the counselor and his or her own role as a counselee?

To accept and adopt the counselee's views requires the counselor to recognize that individuals are unique and have the right to their own commitments, self-awareness, and priorities. The counselor's role here is to assist counselees in becoming aware of their viewpoints and in recognizing how their viewpoints may affect career decision making. The following questions may be used to structure this part of the counseling session: Does the counselee have realistic expectations about the world of work? What is the counselee's level of sophistication in regard to career considerations? Has the counselee established short-term and long-term goals? How committed is the counselee to his or her viewpoints? Would value clarification be helpful?

Because career decisions can greatly influence an individual's style of life, the counselor should attempt *to establish the dimensions of lifestyle* when identifying needs. Place of residence, work climate, family responsibilities, use of leisure time, leadership opportunities, financial needs, mobility, and the desire to contribute to society are dimensions of lifestyle that warrant considerations in career decision making.

For example, an individual expresses a strong orientation toward achieving financial independence but is considering careers that may not be suitable for meeting this objective. The counselor can encourage this individual to clarify priorities for lifestyle, and through this process realistic alternatives and options can be developed.

Questions such as these help establish lifestyle dimensions: Does the counselee recognize that career choice will affect lifestyle? Has the counselee set lifestyle priorities? Would an interest, value, or personality inventory help this individual clarify needs? Are there significant discrepancies between lifestyle dimensions and the needs most likely to be met by the careers under consideration?

Finally, *to specify needs*, the counselor can maximize the counselee's participation by using statements and questions such as these: "Tell me more about your desire to explore interests." "You mentioned earlier that you are interested in knowing more about your aptitudes." "Can you explain how you could meet your personal goals by selecting this career?" "Why do you think you would like this kind of job?" "How would you describe an individual who chooses jobs that help others?" "Would you like to know more about your interests?" As the counselee states needs, the counselor summarizes and records the statements for later use in reinforcing the purpose of testing.

After doing a needs analysis, counselor and counselee may decide that assessment is not needed. Individuals seek career counseling for a variety of reasons. For example, an individual who has decided on a job may come to a career counselor for educational/training information, not for testing. Individuals who have given considerable thought to selecting a career and have narrowed their choices to a particular field are probably best served by providing them with an opportunity to discuss that field and with sources of information about it.

Establishing the Purpose

Following the needs analysis, the counselor and counselee decide on the purpose of testing. Both should recognize that testing cannot be expected to meet all identified needs. As stated in Chapter 1, testing can be used for diagnosis, prediction, and comparison of individuals with criterion groups. The results can be used to stimulate further study of individual characteristics in relation to potential career choices. In some instances, the purpose of testing is to answer a specific question, as in predicting chances of success in a training program or an occupation. In other instances, the purpose of testing may be less specific, as in establishing a direction for career exploration for an individual who is floundering. In cases such as this, where the purpose of testing is less tangible, the counselor may be tempted to prescribe a battery of tests without obtaining agreement on the purpose of the tests from the counselee. To avoid this pitfall, the counselor should establish the policy of explaining the purpose of each measuring instrument selected.

The purpose of each test and inventory should be explained in terms that the counselee can comprehend. For example, the purpose of an interest inventory may be explained to a high school student as follows: "This inventory will help us identify your interests. We can then compare your interests to the interests of groups of individuals in certain jobs." A high school student who is in the process of determining which college to apply to and who has inquired about an aptitude test will find the following explanation appropriate: "These test scores will give us some idea of your chances of making a 'C' or better at the college you are considering." The purpose of a test may have to be explained in simple terms to an individual who has a limited educational background: "This achievement test will show us how well you can read, spell, and do arithmetic problems. We can use the scores to help us choose a job or a training program for you."

In all instances, in order to make assessment results meaningful, we should attempt to relate the purpose of testing to the needs the counselee has identified (Cronbach, 1984). The counselee should also be made aware of how assessment results are used with other data in the career decision-making process. The following dialogue illustrates how a counselor can accomplish these objectives.

Counselor: As you will recall, we agreed to record your needs for information, materials, programs, and tests. Let's review our comments on testing possibilities. Do you remember any of the testing needs agreed on?

Counselee: Yes, I want to take an interest inventory.

Counselor: Do you remember why?

Counselee: I am not sure about what I want to do. I believe knowing more about my interests would help in choosing a career.

Counselor: Do you recall specifically how the results of an interest inventory would help the career decision-making process?

Counselee: Yes, I believe that I will be able to compare the interests of people in different occupations with my own interests.

Counselor: Go on.

Counselee: This will give me information about personal traits that I can use with other things I've learned about myself.

Determining the Instruments

A considerable amount of literature has accumulated concerning the selection of measuring instruments. The central consideration is meeting the standards for educational and psychological tests established by the American Psychological Association (1974). As you will recall, this book is to be used following or in conjunction with courses in tests and measurements. Therefore, technical methods of evaluating measuring instruments for selection will not be covered. Practitioners must be thoroughly familiar with the basic standards of test reliability and test validity before an effective evaluation of tests can be made. The types of reliability and validity that should be established for a test are determined by the purpose and use of the test. A review of the procedures for determining and comparing different types of reliability and validity may be found in several texts including Anastasi (1988), Cronbach (1984), and Kaplan and Saccuzzo (1993).

In this book I concentrate on tests of ability and achievement and on inventories that measure career maturity, interests, personality, and values. Ability tests can also be used to determine assignment to appropriate remediation levels.

Achievement tests aid the counselor in the evaluation of educational strengths and weaknesses. These tests may also be used for selection and classification in the same way that ability tests are used.

Career maturity inventories are used to assess vocational development in terms of self-awareness, planning skills, decision-making skills, and other equally important variables. Parts of career maturity inventories are self-report measures, on which individuals describe their characteristics and traits (Cronbach, 1984).

Interest measures, long associated with career counseling, provide a means of comparing an individual's interest patterns with those of reference groups. Personality inventories provide clues to individual traits that influence behavior. Value inventories also reflect individual traits; they identify value constructs that influence behavior. Results from interest, personality, and value inventories promote discussion of the counselee's relationship to the working world and the satisfaction the counselee may derive from a career.

In the chapters that follow, each of the test categories mentioned here is discussed in detail.

Utilizing the Results

Because individual choice patterns are unique and can be influenced in part by economic conditions and experiences over the life span, the utilization of assessment varies greatly. More than likely, individuals will find that assessment results can assist them at various stages of their lives, particularly in clarifying needs and in developing self-awareness. Contemporary thought places considerable importance on the individual's responsibility for finding satisfaction in the ever-changing world of work. This concept was succinctly stated by Shakespeare in *Julius Caesar*: "The fault, dear Brutus, is not in our stars, but in ourselves, that we are underlings."

The use of assessment results in career counseling is to be carefully calculated and systematically accomplished through established operational procedures. In general, assessment results identify individual characteristics and traits, which in turn point to possible avenues for career exploration. The counselor and the counselee discuss potential career fields using assessment results to facilitate the dialogue.

Beyond this pragmatic and operational procedure for using assessment results are considerations that place testing and the use of test results in perspective—that help counselees use test results to view themselves as total persons. So far, I have dealt with some specific uses of assessment, and in the chapters that follow I illustrate these uses in detail. In all this reporting and confirming of assessment data, counselors are in effect helping counselees build and generate a broad concept of themselves as total persons. Counselors segregate and clarify individual differences in order to formulate plans for the present and lay the foundations for planning in the future. Counselees integrate their individual traits and characteristics to stabilize their sense of direction in an ever-changing society.

The concept of career development as being continuous over the life span suggests that individuals change. There is, therefore, a tentativeness to many career decisions. One consistency in career decision making is a conceptual framework that provides for in-depth and effective use of assessment results because clarification of an individual's traits will always involve, at least to some extent, the measuring instruments available at the time.

USING THE MODEL FOR INDIVIDUAL COUNSELING—AN EXAMPLE

The following counseling case illustrates the use of a conceptual model utilizing assessment results in a senior high school counseling center. Each step in the model is illustrated by dialogue between counselor and counselee and by occasional notations made by the counselor. Standardized assessment instruments used in this case were not identified. In later chapters, other counseling cases describing the use of models employing assessment results are described citing specific standardized assessment instruments.

In the following illustration of the conceptual model, both major and minor components of the model are identified to demonstrate a sequential order of events. Notations and dialogue between counselor and counselee are created for the purpose of illustration.

Amy, a self-referred 17-year-old female high school senior, reported to the counseling center that she was undecided about plans after graduation. She filled out a questionnaire and was introduced to Gretchen, her counselor.

Step 1. Analyzing Needs

A. Establish the counseling relationship

Counselor: Amy, I'm Gretchen, welcome to the Counseling Center. I believe you have met Carla, our secretary, who will help us with appointments and records. Please call either one of us if you need any information as we go along. My office is the first door to the left, here. Please come in and have a seat.

After a brief discussion of current events, the counselor explained the order of procedures and assured Amy of client confidentiality. The conversation shifted easily to Amy's indecision concerning her plans after high school.

Amy: I'm not even sure I'm capable of going to college. Besides, I don't know what I want to be and I can't decide about a major. All my friends have this settled, but not me.

The counselor assured Amy that the counseling center could help her make these decisions. She also informed her of their career counseling time commitment of five to six counseling sessions with some additional time for testing, if appropriate. The counselor also established a counseling goal by asking Amy if a possible goal to work on would be for her to decide if she should go to college.

B. *Accept and adopt the counselee's views*
The counselor encouraged Amy to discuss her academic background, general interests, leisure and work experiences, and values. Amy informed the counselor of her previous work experience, which consisted of two months as a swimming instructor and four months as an assistant program director in a home for the elderly. Amy indicated that she liked both jobs.

Counselor: Could you explain how the experiences of these two jobs might influence your future choice of a career?

Amy: Well, I never thought about it, but I do enjoy working with people. I like to teach, also, but I don't believe I would like to be a schoolteacher.

Counselor: I would be interested in knowing how you've come to those conclusions.

Amy: I'm not sure I could handle all the discipline problems that teachers have to deal with. Besides, I want to do other things helping people. I really enjoyed the work I did with the elderly.

Amy continued to express interests and aspirations while the counselor made the following notations:

Good rapport has been established . . .
Amy feels free to express herself . . .
likes working with people . . .
has some limited exposure to careers . . .
has developed tentative expectations of the future, but needs help in clarifying interests . . .

C. *Establish the dimensions of lifestyle*

Counselor: Now, let's take a look at the future. In fact, I would like you to project yourself into the future. For example, think about where you would like to live five or ten years from now and what kind of leisure activities such as travel you would like.

Amy: Okay, let me see (pause). . . . Hmm, someday I would like to be living in an apartment on my own, of course, with my own car right here in the city, I think. I would like to have a nice place, but I really don't want a fancy car, just a fairly new one. I guess one of the most important things to me is having good clothes and being able to eat out in nice restaurants. I also like to travel. I've been overseas on vacation with my parents, and I would like to go back some day. About money . . . I want enough to be able to do these things.

Counselor: That's a good start, Amy. We will be discussing lifestyle preferences again. I think we can sort out more specific aspects of your lifestyle choices and how they may influence career decisions in one of our future sessions.

During the course of the counseling session, the counselor thought that the following assessments might be helpful:

1. Measure of college aptitude —
   Information for predicting success in selected colleges.
2. Measure of interests —
   General interest patterns are needed to stimulate dialogue about future goals.
   Specific interests will be used to link college majors with potential careers.
3. Measure of lifestyle preferences —
   Lifestyle measures will introduce another dimension for consideration in the decision-making process.

The counselor's overall goal was to provide Amy with relevant information that could be used in the decision-making process.

Step 2.   Establish the Purpose

Counselor: Our discussion has been very productive and before you leave today, let's summarize some of the needs you have expressed. One of the first topics we discussed was your indecision about college. Remember you questioned whether you should attend or not.

Amy: Yes, that's right. Maybe I was just blowing off steam; I know I should probably go to college.

Counselor: Would you like to take an aptitude test to see how prepared you are for college?

Amy: Yes . . . okay . . . (pause) . . . I did take one of the required exams for college a few months ago.

Counselor: Good, we probably have the results in our files and we can use these to help us with our decision. I'll check the files and if we need another test, I'll let you know at our next appointment.

Amy nodded approval.

Counselor: Another need you mentioned is choosing a college major.

Amy: Yes, I don't really know what I want to do. I've had subjects I like, but nothing grabs me.

Counselor: We have several interest inventories that could be helpful. Would you like to take one?

When Amy agreed that an interest inventory would be fine with her, the counselor turned her attention to the last of the list of indicated needs—lifestyle preferences.

Counselor: Today I also asked you to project yourself into the future and you were able to express some of your goals. Do you think it would be helpful to further clarify your lifestyle preferences?

Amy: That's something I really haven't thought about very much. I think it might help, but I'm not sure just how.

Counselor: Okay, that's a good question. Let me briefly explain that career and lifestyle are closely related. For example, your career choice will determine to some extent the kind of lifestyle you will have in the future. One illustration involves the financial returns you get from a job. Remember, you said you wanted a new car, have the opportunity to travel to Europe, and have a nice apartment. In order to be able to have and do these things you will need a job that provides the necessary resources.

Amy: I see. Well, yes, I probably should talk more about my future.

After the counselor was certain that Amy understood the purpose of each assessment instrument, an appointment for the next counseling session was set.

Step 3.   Determine the Instrument

The counselor discovered that Amy had taken a nationally administered college aptitude test and the results were on file in the counseling center. Composite scores indicated that Amy was well above the national norm for college-bound students. These test scores were current and could be used to predict chances of making a "C" or better at several colleges, so the counselor decided that another aptitude test was unnecessary.

The counselor chose an interest inventory providing measures of general and specific occupational interests. The goal was to stimulate discussion of general interests and to verify preferences Amy had previously expressed. Moreover, the counselor's primary objective was to stimulate dialogue that could help Amy clarify her interests.

Finally, the counselor chose a lifestyle measure that would assess Amy's preferences for a variety of lifestyle factors. The counselor was particularly interested in assessing Amy's preferences for work achievement and leadership, work environment and leisure orientation. As with the interest inventory, the counselor's objective was to stimulate discussion for the purpose of helping Amy clarify values and lifestyle preferences.

Step 4.   Utilize the Results

During Amy's next appointment the interest inventory and lifestyle preference survey were administered. After they were scored, the results of these inventories and aptitude tests were carefully reviewed by the counselor during pre-interpretation preparation. The counselor made notes on several items she felt would stimulate discussion. For example, on the interest inventory she made a notation that Amy had a very high score on the general occupational theme—social—and on such specific occupations as social worker and guidance counselor.

Highest scores on the lifestyle preference survey were educational achievement, work achievement, and structured work environment. The counselor was particularly interested in having Amy link lifestyle preferences to high-interest occupations and general occupational themes. Priorities for lifestyle preferences would be used to introduce another dimension of Amy's values in the decision-making process.

Finally, the counselor obtained studies of students' expectancies of making a "C" or better at several community colleges and universities. This information would provide an index to predict Amy's chances of matriculating in several two- and four-year institutions of higher learning.

The counselor began the utilization-of-results session by explaining the purpose of the college aptitude test Amy had taken. The scores were explained as follows.

Counselor: Since you have said you want to go to college, we will interpret your scores by using National College Bound Norms. These norms are derived for students who have indicated that they intend to enroll in a college or a university. Your total score places you in the 86th percentile among college-bound students. This means that 86 out of 100 college-bound students who took the test scored lower than you did and 14 out of 100 scored higher than you did.

Amy: Wow! That's better than I thought I would do on that test. Does this mean that I could do okay at City College?

The counselor was able to answer Amy's question by referring to an expectancy table that had been provided by City College. Based on Amy's total test score, the counselor was able to inform Amy of her chances of making an overall "C" average during her freshman year at City College. In Amy's case her chances of making a "C" or better at City College were very good.

The counselor was also able to point out the chances of making a "C" or better in specific courses offered to freshmen at City College. These data not only provided an index for predicting Amy's chances of matriculating in City College, but also could be used for suggesting an academic major.

The counselor's next step in utilizing assessment results was to outline the organization of scores on the interest profile. She explained the various scales on the test, including general occupational-interest scores and scores on specific occupations. The scores were interpreted as follows.

Counselor: Amy, you scored in the high category on the general occupational theme—social. People who score high on this theme like to work with people, share responsibilities, and enjoy working in groups. Do you feel that this is an accurate representation of your interests?

Using this procedure the counselor encouraged Amy to discuss other scores on the general occupational theme part of the profile. Likewise, this procedure was used to enhance the discussion of scores measuring specific occupations. Amy was encouraged to jot down occupations of interest for further exploration in the career library and on the computerized career information system. A discussion of lifestyle orientation related to interests helped Amy to crystallize her projections of future needs and desires.

Step 5.   Make a Decision

Amy eventually decided that she should attempt to get a college education. She decided to attend City College and tentatively major in human resource development.

STIMULATING CAREER EXPLORATION IN GROUPS

In the early 1970s a new concept of education emerged that emphasized career development, attitudes, and values as well as traditional outcomes of career choices (Hoyt, 1972). The career education concept is a comprehensive one that focuses on relationships between traditional education programs and the world of work. The major objective of career education is to prepare individuals for living and working in our society (Zunker, 1994). The impact of career education programs on career counseling has not been fully determined. But there is little doubt that career education programs will increase the need for counselors to turn to group procedures when using assessment results to stimulate career exploration because of demands on their time and the ratio of students to counselors.

The model proposed for utilizing assessment results in the previous section can easily be adapted to groups. The same steps apply. However, methods used in applying the model may have to be altered. For example, a needs analysis can be accomplished through group discussion, with each individual noting his or her own needs. Some will find that testing is not necessary at this point in their career development. Those who decide that testing is appropriate will move to the next step of establishing the purposes of testing. After purposes are identified, different types of tests and inventories can be selected. Small groups may be formed for administering the tests and sharing results. Individuals or entire groups may then go back to the first step, to reestablish needs, at any time in career exploration.

A modification of the model for groups could include the following procedures: Introduce the concepts of career development. Explain the use of assessment. Introduce the types of measuring instruments. Interpret the results. Introduce support material. Interest inventories are especially effective in promoting group discussions and are usually less threatening than aptitude or achievement tests. However, other types of measuring instruments may also be effectively used to generate activities for groups. The following example illustrates the use of an interest inventory in a classroom setting.

Ms. Smith, a high school counselor, was invited to a high school class in the process of working through a career education program. She was asked to present the types of measuring instruments available and to explain how the students could use the career resource center. Before the presentation Ms. Smith asked the teacher's permission to introduce the steps in career decision making and to make some comments on the basic elements of career development. As she presented this material she emphasized the purpose and use of assessment results.

The students requested that an interest inventory be administered. Afterward, the counselor explained how to interpret the score profiles. Considerable time was given to individual questions concerning the results. The counselor emphasized that interests are one of the important considerations in career decision making.

Following the interpretation of results, the counselor introduced the next step in the career decision-making process. Some of the students decided to take additional tests and inventories.

Others took different courses of action. Several decided to collect information about selected careers in the career resource center, and some members of the group chose to visit work sites.

In this case interest inventory results stimulated students to generate further activities within the framework of a decision-making model. This example illustrates the importance of clarifying the role of assessment within a career decision-making model. The counselor emphasized that career decision making involves a sequence of steps and the use of support materials. By placing assessment in proper perspective, the counselor was able to enhance the group's utilization of assessment results.

SUMMARY

Assessment results may be effectively used to enhance the development of self-knowledge. Within a career decision-making model, assessment results are used to clarify individual characteristics and to generate further activities. A model for using assessment results has the following steps: analyzing needs, establishing the purpose of testing, determining the instruments, and utilizing the results. Counselees should be actively involved in all steps of the model, which may be utilized for individual or group counseling.

QUESTIONS AND EXERCISES

1. What evidence can you give for the rationale that assessment results are used to enhance self-awareness?
2. With an example illustrate how the model for using assessment results described in this chapter is cyclical.
3. Why is the model of using assessment results only one part of the career decision-making process?
4. Why may it be necessary to retest an individual after two or three years?
5. How are assessment results used in the total-person approach to career decision making?

Chapter Three

Some Measurement Concepts

In this chapter several measurement concepts and methods of interpreting assessment results are discussed for the purpose of improving the career counselor's skill in the selection and utilization of standardized instruments. Later chapters will make numerous references to the material in this chapter in describing specific tests and inventories. Generally, the information found in this chapter is contained in separate chapters in most textbooks. The purpose for combining this information here is, first, to provide an overview of the common elements used in assessment interpretation; second, to provide the information necessary for comparing the strengths and weaknesses of currently used methods of score reporting; third, to provide definitions of measurement concepts for easy referral.

The first section of this chapter emphasizes methods of interpreting assessment results. Specifically, it describes the normal bell-shaped curve and then discusses percentile equivalents, standard scores, grade equivalents, and criterion-referenced measures. The second section discusses important measurement concepts: standard error of measurement, standard error of differences between two subtests, and expectancy tables.

TRANSFORMATION OF SCORES

Bell-Shaped Curve

Two of the most prominently used methods of interpreting assessment results are percentile equivalents and standard scores. In order to obtain an understanding of the relationship between these two reporting procedures, refer to the well-known normal, or bell-shaped, curve in Figure 3-1. M represents the mean, or midpoint (50th percentile), with four standard deviations on each side of the mean. Starting at M, go to the right to +1 standard deviation and note the percentile equivalent of 84 (in rounded numbers). Likewise, go to the left of M to –1 standard deviation and find the percentile equivalent of 16. You will notice that other percentile points can be obtained for each standard deviation. Understanding the relationship of percentile equivalents to standard deviations and their relative positions on the bell-shaped curve helps in the interpretation of test scores. For example, a percentile score of 98 is 2 standard deviations from the mean. A score equal to 2 standard deviations below the mean is approximately at the 2nd percentile.

Referring to Figure 3-1 you can see also that a GATB score of 120 is 1 standard deviation above the mean, or at the 84th percentile. An ACT score of 25 is at the same relative position. These two scores are not to be regarded as equal. The standard scores for each test were developed using samples from different populations, and each test may be quite different in content. However, two standard scores can be compared by their relative position under the normal bell-

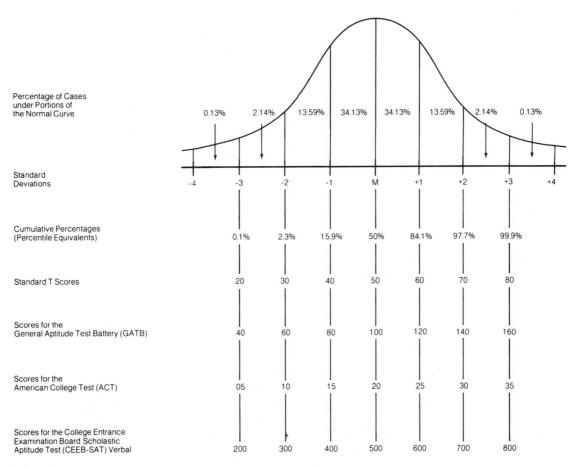

FIGURE 3-1.
Bell-shaped curve.

shaped curve. For example, an ACT score of 25 is at the same relative position within its reference group as a GATB of 120.

Percentile Equivalents

In Figure 3-2 a typical test profile is constructed to depict percentile equivalents. Note the heavy line representing the midpoint and the thinner lines representing the 25th and 75th percentiles, the average range for this particular achievement test. The difference in scores between the 25th and 75th percentiles is not as great as may appear. Refer to the bell-shaped curve in Figure 3-1 and notice that to move several percentile points within the average band does not take as great a performance as it does to move the same number of percentile points beyond the 75th percentile. Thus, the counselor needs to be cautious when interpreting differences in scores within the average range; the difference in performance within this range may not be as significant as it appears.

Percentile equivalents are direct and relatively easy to understand, which is the primary reason for their popularity. However, it is important to identify the norm reference group from which the percentile equivalents have been derived. Norm-referenced tests can be based on local, state, regional, or national data or on data for selected groups such as all seniors (nationally) who are attending college or all college seniors in the western region of the United States. Thus, in

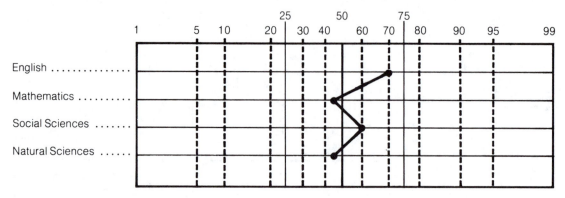

FIGURE 3-2.
Profile depicting average band of percentile equivalents.

order to effectively communicate test results, the norm frame of reference should be established. For example: "From a national sample, 60 out of 100 high school seniors who attended college scored lower than you did while 40 out of 100 scored higher."

Standard Scores

Normalized standard scores used in tests and inventories are based on standard deviation units in a normal distribution. Figure 3-1 shows the percentage of scores within each standard deviation unit and standard scores used by selected standardized tests. The first, the standard T score, has a range of 20 to 80, extending three standard deviations above the mean and three standard deviations below the mean. For all practical purposes, the entire range of scores of 99.72% of the cases will fall within +3 and –3 standard deviations. The middle 68% of the scores are within –1 and +1 standard deviations. Approximately 95% of scores will fall between ±1.96 standard deviation units. A T score of slightly less than 60 is in the top 20% for a given test. Such points of reference make the standard score a valuable tool for interpretation of assessment results. For example, a meaningful interpretation can be made of a score that is 1.5 standard deviations from the mean when normalized standard scores and their relationship to standard deviations are understood. Thus, the relative position of the standard score under the normal distribution provides a discernible point of reference for that score's variation from the average.

A frame of reference can easily be established for standardized tests by thinking of their scores in the same way. For example, a GATB score of 120 is 1 standard deviation from the mean, or at the 84th percentile. Likewise, 1 standard deviation below the mean (16th percentile) is equal to a GATB score of 80. The middle 68% of the scores are between the standard scores 80 and 120. A meaningful interpretation can thus be given to any standard score when the mean and standard deviation are known.

A *stanine* is a standard score on a scale with nine approximately equal units. The mean stanine is 5, and the standard deviation is 2. The advantage of the stanine is that scores are presented as a range rather than as points on a scale, as shown in Figure 3-3. In a normal distribution the lower level, 1, represents the bottom 4% of the cases; stanine 5 represents the middle 20%; and stanine 9, the highest level, represents the top 4%. Thinking of a range rather than a point for score interpretation is more descriptive and deters emphasizing small differences. To be of practical significance the difference between stanine scores must be 2 or more.

Stanine scores may also be thought of in broader categories, as Figure 3-3 illustrates. For example, stanine scores 1, 2, and 3 are considered below average; stanine scores 4, 5, and 6 are considered average; and stanines 7, 8, and 9 are above average. Cumulative percentile points (Figure 3-3) provide further possibilities for interpreting stanines as lower quarter, middle half, and upper quarter.

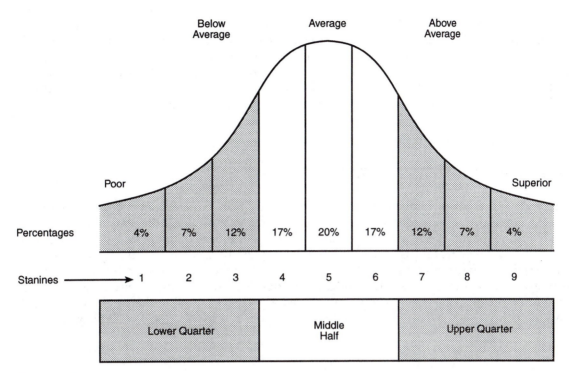

FIGURE 3-3.
Stanines.

Grade Equivalents

Because of the familiarity of grade placement and its frame of reference, grade equivalents are often used to interpret achievement test scores. Norms for grade equivalents are derived from average raw scores of students in each grade level. These equivalents are expressed by a number representing grade level and the ten months of the school year, September through June. For example, 10.0 represents the beginning of the tenth grade in September; 10.5 represents average performance in February of that academic year.

Because of the idea of placement within a grade, misinterpretation of grade equivalents can occur. For example, a score of 8.5 on a science test for a student currently in the sixth grade should not be interpreted to mean the student has mastered the science courses taught in the seventh grade and the first half of the eighth grade and can now be placed in the second half of the eighth-grade science class. No doubt, the student has performed admirably on the science test, but grade equivalent scores are not to be regarded as performance standards. Also, grade equivalents are not to be considered comparable for all scales. For example, in the fifth grade growth in learning a particular subject such as mathematics will be much greater than it will be in the ninth grade.

Criterion-Referenced Measures

In criterion-referenced measures an individual's score is interpreted by relative position within the distribution of scores obtained by the standardization sample or other groups of special interest. In other words, the interpretation of criterion-referenced test scores is based on how well the individual's performance matches a set of standards or external criteria judged by the test user to be suitable for the individual's grade level. The focus is on levels of performance within a limited range of specific skills or content. For example, criterion-referenced scores provide an index of how well an individual has mastered arithmetic computations or certain reading skills. In criterion-referenced tests specific information is provided as to what the individual is capable of doing: "The subject was able to subtract numbers with decimals." "The subject used the correct verb form in a sentence." Scales from a criterion-referenced test are used to determine an individual level of performance with reference to a specified content criterion.

ACCURACY OF MEASUREMENT

This section presents several concepts regarding the accuracy of measurements that should also aid the counselor in transforming assessment results into meaningful interpretations. First, in order to understand the relative position of a score, the counselor must be aware of inherent error, which is specific for particular tests. Second, significant differences that may exist between subtests on any one test greatly affect the interpretation that may be given to the test results as a whole. Finally, inaccuracy in interpreting assessment results for educational and vocational planning can be reduced by constructing locally based expectancy tables. In the paragraphs that follow, these concepts and their application to test interpretation are discussed and illustrated.

Standard Error of Measurement (S.E.M.)

A score on a test should not be considered an exact point without any error. It is much more accurate to think of test scores as estimates of true scores. Thus, an individual's performance on a test can best be thought of as falling within a range or a band rather than as a point on a scale. The S.E.M. is an estimate of the amount of error in a particular test score; it is often provided in the test manual.

The traditional approach to using the S.E.M. is illustrated by the following example. An individual receives a score of 105 (observed score) on a test that has a reported S.E.M. of 5. We now want to obtain an estimate of the person's true score. Because of errors of measurement, observed scores are assumed to be normally distributed around the true score. Hence we can refer to standard deviation units to give us the limits of observed scores. In this example, the S.E.M. is used as a standard deviation (S.D.). Therefore, 105 ±1 S.D. (5) = 100–110. Over all individuals, according to the normal distribution, true scores lie within this band 68% of the time. With an S.D. of 2, however, 105 ±2 S.D. (10) = 95–115. Over all individuals, true scores lie within this band 95% of the time. Therefore, the probability is high that the true score for the student in the example is between 95 and 115 and the probability is somewhat lower that the true score is between 100 and 110.

Standard Error of Differences (SED) between Two Subsets

In career counseling it is often necessary to be certain when differences in subtest scores are of particular importance. The differences between scores can be ascertained by computing the SED. The following example illustrates this method.

A multiaptitude test battery reports T scores (mean = 50 and standard deviation = 10) for interpretation of subtest scores. On the abstract reasoning subtest scale a reliability coefficient of .89 is reported. Another scale has a reported reliability coefficient of .95. To find the SED between the two tests, the following formula is used:

$$SED = \sqrt{2 - r1 - r2}$$

$$SED = 10\sqrt{2 - .89 - .95}$$

$$SED = 4$$

where r1 = reliability of test 1; r2 = reliability of test 2.

To determine whether the difference between the individual's scores on the test is a real difference and not due simply to chance, the SED is multiplied by 1.96. Because ±1.96 standard deviation units on the normal distribution will include 95% of the cases, scores within that range will occur by chance only 5% of the time. In this case the result is obtained by multiplying 4 by 1.96, which is 7.84, or approximately 8 points. Thus, we can interpret a difference of 8 points or more between the two subtests in our example as being meaningful.

Expectancy Tables

In educational planning a counselor often has to advise a student of chances of success in a particular college or university. An expectancy table constructed from the records of previous graduates and their performance at the university being considered provides relevant information. In Table 3-1 a sample expectancy table has been constructed from the first-semester grade point averages and ACT composite scores.

TABLE 3–1.

Sample Expectancy Table

American College Test (ACT) Composite Scores	First-Semester Grade Point Averages							
	0.00–0.49	0.50–0.99	1.00–1.49	1.50–1.99	2.00–2.49	2.50–2.99	3.00–3.49	3.50–3.99
32–35						(100) 1	(67) 1	(33) 1
29–31					(100) 1	(91) 2	(73) 4	(36) 4
26–28				(100) 2	(89) 7	(50) 4	(28) 3	(11) 2
23–25				(100) 5	(81) 9	(48) 6	(26) 6	(4) 1
20–22			(100) 6	(88) 13	(61) 15	(31) 12	(6) 3	
17–19		(100) 5	(92) 6	(83) 24	(46) 22	(12) 5	(5) 3	
14–16		(100) 5	(86) 9	(62) 13	(27) 8	(5) 2		
11–13	(100) 2	(92) 5	(72) 8	(40) 62	(16) 3	(4) 1		
8–10	(100) 2	(85) 4	(54) 5	(15) 2				
5–7	(100) 1							

The numbers that are not in parentheses are the number of students whose grade point averages are in the designated range. For example, two students whose ACT composite scores were in the range 26–28 earned grade point averages between 1.50 and 1.99. Seven students in this same ACT score range earned grade point averages between 2.00 and 2.49.

The numbers in the parentheses are the cumulative percentages of individuals within a particular ACT score range whose earned grades are in the corresponding grade point average cell or higher. For example, 88% of the individuals whose ACT composite scores were in the 20–22 range earned grade point averages between 1.50 and 1.99 or higher. Likewise, 92% of the individuals whose ACT composite scores were in the 11–13 range earned first-semester grade point averages of .50–.99 or higher.

To demonstrate the chances of success at the university being considered, the ACT composite score provides an index of academic success. For example, 81 out of 100 individuals whose ACT composite scores were 23–25 made a 2.00 grade point average or higher. The chances that individuals with the same ACT scores would make a 2.50 or higher grade point average are 48 out of 100.

SUMMARY

In this chapter several methods used to interpret assessment results have been discussed. These methods illustrate how assessment results can be transformed into meaningful information on characteristics and traits—information that can be used in career counseling. The concepts of measurement accuracy discussed illustrate further how tests must be interpreted to enhance the usefulness of information provided in career counseling.

QUESTIONS AND EXERCISES

1. From Figure 3-1, what are the approximate percentile equivalents for the following standard scores? GATB: 140, 61, 85. ACT: 15, 23, 36.
2. From Figure 3-1, what is the closest standard deviation to a standard score of 108 for a test that has a mean of 100 and a standard deviation of 10?
3. Why is it important to identify the norm reference group when using percentile equivalents to interpret assessment results? Illustrate your answer with an example.
4. What are the advantages of stanine scores over percentiles and grade equivalents?
5. Use the sample expectancy table (Table 3-1) to answer the following questions: (a) What would be the chances of Bob's making a 2.00 grade point average or better with an ACT score of 30? (b) What would be Joan's chances for a 2.00 grade point average or higher with an ACT score of 16? (c) What advice would you offer to Bob and Joan?

Chapter Four
Using Ability Tests

Ability measures have been associated with career counseling since the time of the early trait-and-factor approach to career guidance (Parsons, 1909). Simply stated, the trait-and-factor approach matched the individual's traits with the requirements of a specific occupation. The key assumption of the trait-and-factor approach was that individuals have unique patterns of abilities or traits that can be objectively measured and that are correlated with the requirements of various types of jobs. Thus, appraising traits was the major task of the counselor. Williamson (1939, 1949) advocated the use of psychological testing in vocational counseling specifically for the purpose of analyzing an individual's potential in relation to requirements of training programs and occupations. Williamson considered a major role of the career counselor to be aiding individuals in assessing their assets and liabilities through an evaluation of test results. These early approaches to career counseling inspired the study of job descriptions and job requirements in an attempt to predict success on the job from the measurement of job-related traits.

The attention to specific job requirements revealed the need for multitrait measures. In particular, there was a need for a differential assessment of an individual's abilities. Multiaptitude test batteries evolved to fill this need. The statistical technique of factor analysis provided the tools for measuring individual abilities, and thus provided the foundation for multiaptitude test batteries. The growth of career counseling and the need for selection and classification of industrial and military personnel increased the demand for differential measures. The use of aptitude test results to select applicants for colleges and professional schools increased significantly with the growth in college enrollments after World War II. The armed forces have sponsored ongoing research programs to develop aptitude test batteries for their use. A number of multiaptitude tests have also been developed for career counseling (Drummond, 1992). The use of aptitude test results remains a prominent part of career counseling.

In this chapter I concentrate on the use of aptitude tests for career development. I discuss three multiaptitude batteries and give examples of their use. I also describe the limitations of multiaptitude test batteries. Finally, a list of developmental strategies for aptitude test results is provided.

PURPOSE OF APTITUDE TESTS

An *aptitude test* is a measure of a specific skill or ability. There are two types of aptitude tests: multiaptitude test batteries and single tests measuring specific aptitudes. Multiaptitude test batteries contain measures of a wide range of aptitudes and combinations of aptitudes and provide valuable information that may be used in career decision making. Single aptitude tests are used when a specific aptitude needs to be measured, such as manual dexterity, clerical ability, artistic ability, or musical aptitude.

An *aptitude* is a specified proficiency or the ability to acquire a certain proficiency (Super & Crites, 1962). It also may be defined as a tendency, capacity, or inclination to do a certain task. A common misconception is that aptitudes are inherited, unchangeable characteristics that need to be discovered and subsequently matched with certain job requirements. Such an assumption is misleading for the interpretation of aptitude test results (Bennett, Seashore, & Wesman, 1974). Rather, aptitude should be viewed as the result of both heredity and environment; an individual is born with certain capacities that may or may not be nurtured by the environment. In essence then, aptitude tests reflect the interaction of heredity and environment and predict the capacity to learn.

Within this frame of reference aptitude scores provide a broad measure of an individual's experience and ability at the time of testing. For example, academic aptitude reflects the entire array of skills needed to meet the demands of an academic curriculum. Mechanical aptitude reflects all the skills needed to do mechanical work.

Because aptitude scores are used to predict future performance in educational and vocational endeavors, they are a major element in career counseling. The probability of performing well on a job, in a training program, or in college is the kind of information the career counselor usually seeks. The matching of the individual's abilities to job requirements has long been the subject of research by government, industry, and job-planning specialists.

IDENTIFYING ABILITIES BY HOLLAND'S TYPES

In this section abilities associated with Holland's types will be identified. Significant dialogue between client and counselor can be encouraged with examples of abilities that are type related. Although each work environment requires specific tasks, the counselor can enhance an individual's career development by relating general abilities to work requirements. Discussion of abilities along with other data such as measured interests and personality traits should serve to broaden the client's scope and focus in career decision making.

Holland has identified six types of abilities:

1. *Realistic abilities:* Jobs associated with this type are those relating to things rather than people. Realistic occupations are likely to be blue-collar jobs requiring physical, mechanical, and spatial abilities. White-collar realistic jobs include engineering and navigation.

2. *Investigative abilities:* This type encompasses the scientific professions, therefore requiring the highest educational level and highest level of intelligence of the Holland types (Gottfredson, 1980). Intellectual skills such as verbal and nonverbal reasoning are most important for success in occupations associated with this type.

3. *Artistic abilities:* This type includes several dimensions of abilities. For example, creative ability depends on the specific type of creative work (Guilford, 1957). Musical talent is quite diverse in abilities—consider the vocalist, the conductor, and the composer. However, some tests are designed to measure specific areas of musical talent. Because predictive studies of artistic talents are not promising (Lowman, 1991), available screening tests should be followed by further evaluation by specialists in the diverse occupations associated with this type.

4. *Social abilities:* Different occupations require different patterns of social and interpersonal skills. For example, machine operators need social skills to establish rapport with co-workers and supervisors, whereas a receptionist in the same plant requires interpersonal skills to deal with customers and strangers. As with other types in the Holland system, identified social abilities present rich sources of information to be used in career decision making. The counselor is in a good position to evaluate a client's social abilities that might be applicable to a specific occupation, especially when standardized tests offer little help in measuring social skills.

5. *Enterprising abilities:* This type is associated with managing others and with leadership skills. Ghiselli (1963) has suggested that managerial jobs require an ability to direct others, moderate to high intelligence, self-assurance, and initiative. Other researchers such

as Klemp and McClelland (1986) have identified such generic enterprising competencies as good planning skills, synthetic thinking, and the ability to conceptualize information and procedures. Although some of these abilities may be measured by standardized instruments, the skilled interviewer helps identify these abilities in discussions of work and leisure activities.

6. *Conventional abilities:* This type is primarily associated with clerical and numerical duties and the ability to understand and manipulate data. Lowman (1991) has suggested that specific conventional abilities include perceptual speed and accuracy, perceptual speed of figure identification, and numerical computational ability. In the higher-level jobs, such as accountant, general intelligence and reasoning ability are important.

Counselors must recognize that many of the abilities measured by current standardized tests are not job specific; that is, the requirements of jobs vary from one work environment to another. Whereas there are similarities in job duties and responsibilities within a particular occupation, there are also distinct differences in the requisite skills necessary for appropriate performance. For example, an accountant in one firm may be required only to manage data, while an accountant in another firm may need to manage employees as well.

The first step in career decision making may be started in part by a recognition of identified abilities that are associated with occupations within the Holland types. Counselors need to point out to the client that identified abilities may be related to a number of careers and types, making it necessary to gather more information for specific job requirements.

DIFFERENTIAL APTITUDE TEST (DAT)

The DAT is one of the better known and most widely researched aptitude tests on the market. There are four versions available, including a computerized adaptive version and a shorter version for employee selection and placement. The other two forms are full-length versions and contain separate norms for males and females for grades 8 through 12. Vocational technical school adult norms were made available in early 1990.

There are eight subtests: verbal reasoning consists of analogies for measuring verbal thinking and understanding; numerical ability consists of arithmetic computation problems; abstract reasoning consists of problems requiring nonverbal reasoning ability; clerical speed and accuracy consists of clerical problems requiring a rapid response; mechanical reasoning consists of pictorial items requiring mechanical solutions; space relations consists of items requiring visualization of completed objects from parts and of how objects would appear if moved or rotated; spelling consists of items requiring recognition of correctly spelled words; and language usage consists of items requiring recognition of errors in grammar.

Separate sex norms were derived from a stratified random sample of over 60,000 students. An impressive amount of validity data correlate test scores with a variety of course grades and achievement test scores. Sufficient evidence indicates that the test is a good predictor of high school and college grades. However, there are limited data concerning the ability of the test to predict vocational success. Consistently high reliability coefficients are reported by sex and grade level. Long-term consistency is supported by various studies, including a follow-up of 1700 high school students four years after graduation and a seven-year follow-up of a smaller sample. Cronbach (1984) suggests that differential ability patterns are fairly well stabilized by mid-adolescence.

Interpreting the DAT

The DAT provides individual reports for interpretation. One type is a computer-produced profile, shown in Figure 4-1; the other is a hand-plotted profile, shown in Figure 4-2. Both are interpreted in the same manner. The bar graph or row of X's represents the range of percentiles (the individual's true score). The first step in interpreting the DAT is to observe whether the ends of bars or rows of X's overlap. There is a significant difference between any two that do not overlap. Two bars or rows of X's having an overlap of more than one-half their length are not significantly different. If the overlap is less than half their length, a difference should be considered as probable and should be specifically determined by retesting (Bennett et al., 1974).

The combination of verbal reasoning and numerical ability is a good index of scholastic aptitude. The verbal reasoning score is highly correlated with grades in a number of academic courses, especially English courses. The numerical ability score is highly correlated with grades in mathematics courses. Extensive research has been done with other combinations of DAT scores for predicting success in academic subjects and vocational courses (Bennett et al., 1974).

The DAT manual provides extensive information concerning individual DAT scores and predictors of course grades. Using this information, the counselor can ascertain which aptitudes are required for certain courses and which aptitudes are useful in certain occupations. In addition, a regression equation for predicting College Entrance Examination Board Scholastic Aptitude Test scores from a combination of DAT scores is provided for counseling individuals considering college. These interpretive materials provide excellent guidelines for using the results of the test. A

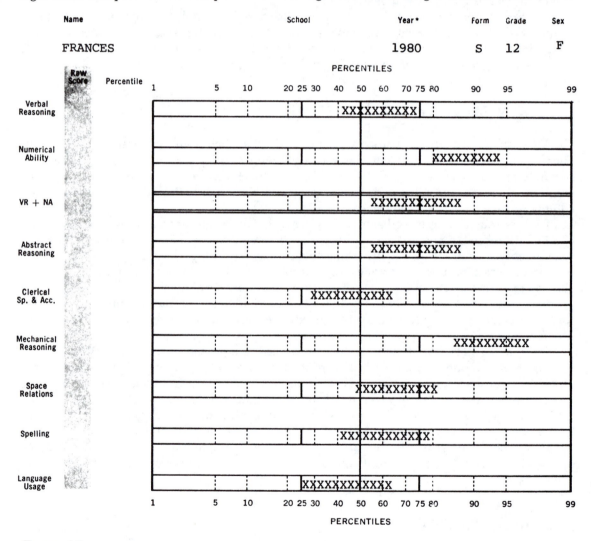

FIGURE 4-1.
DAT computer-produced profile.
From *Differential Aptitude Test* by G. K. Bennett, H. G. Seashore, and A. G. Wesman. Copyright © 1974 by The Psychological Corporation. Reprinted by permission.

number of reviews on the DAT have been published, including Linn (1982), Anastasi (1988), and Pennock-Roman (1988).

Case of a Female High School Student Interested in Jobs Typically Held by Men

Frances, a high school senior, came to the counseling center undecided about a career. Frances had three older brothers who had attended college and were fairly successful. Her academic record was good. Although she was not an honors student, she had excelled in mathematics and science courses. The counselor soon discovered that Frances had a background different from that of most female students with whom she had talked. Frances was interested in working on automobiles; her brothers had taught her the fundamentals of auto mechanics, and she was known as one of the best mechanics in the school. She had rebuilt parts of her car with her older brothers' help. She listed auto mechanics as a hobby of greatest interest, and she listed the sciences and mathematics as her favorite subjects. The counselor and Frances decided that it would be worthwhile for her to take tests that would provide specific information about her skills. They selected the DAT primarily because it provides both an index of scholastic aptitude and measures of specific skills.

The results of the test are shown in Figure 4-1. In discussing the results with Frances, the counselor discovered that Frances was almost embarrassed by the outcome of her test. She

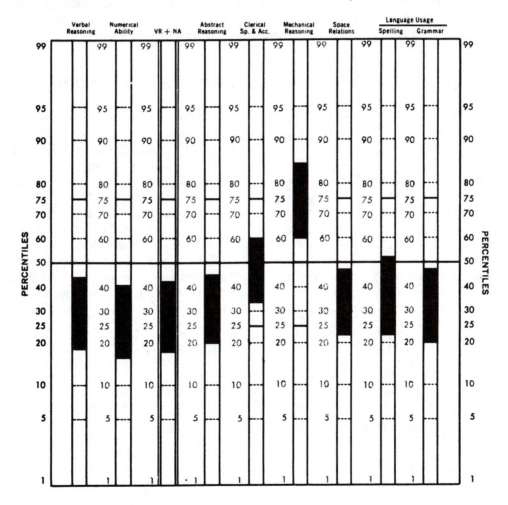

FIGURE 4-2.
DAT hand-plotted profile.
From *Differential Aptitude Test* by G. K. Bennett, H. G. Seashore, and A. G. Wesman. Copyright © 1974 by The Psychological Corporation. Reprinted by permission.

admitted that she did not consider herself as having interests typical of most girls her age. She stated that she should have done better in English and shouldn't have strong interests in auto mechanics and high scores in science and math. Frances also hesitated to express an interest in jobs typically for men.

Counselor: This profile indicates that you have very high scores in numerical ability and mechanical reasoning. Have you ever considered careers that require these skills?

Frances: (hesitantly) But don't just boys go into those fields?

Counselor: Many boys do, but this does not mean that you shouldn't consider these areas as possible career choices. More and more women are going into careers that usually only men went into in the past.

The counselor encouraged Frances to consider any career she was interested in during this part of career exploration. She emphasized the increasing acceptance of women in positions that were once thought to be only for men. Frances began to express interest in a number of careers requiring numerical and mechanical skills. She seemed relieved that she was able to express herself freely. The counselor assured her that it was legitimate for her to have an interest in any career.

Frances zeroed in on the fact that most of her scores on the DAT pointed to an engineering degree. She became particularly interested in mechanical engineering. She mentioned that she had always been interested in machinery and what makes machines run. She decided to explore the requirements and particulars of this occupation in the career resource center.

Differential Aptitude Test-Career Planning Program (DAT-CPP)

The DAT-CPP is a method of combining DAT scores with an individual's educational goals, expressed interest in specific school subjects, and expressed interest in specific jobs for the purpose of vocational planning. The program includes the use of the DAT (form S or T) and a Career Planning Questionnaire (CPQ). Both the DAT and the CPQ are computer scored for this program.

On the CPQ the student checks liked school subjects and activities listed under 18 different categories. Excluding the group for school sports, the student then picks the three groups liked best and records them on the form provided. Next, the student provides information concerning future educational plans or training plans and reports rank in class. Finally, the individual reviews 20 groups of jobs and occupations and picks the three groups most liked.

The final report contains two parts: a profile of DAT scores and a narrative report addressed directly to the student. The narrative report is designed to confirm the student's career choices or to suggest alternative plans. It reviews the data reported on the CPQ. Each occupational group indicated as a preference by the student is evaluated in the following way:

> You indicated that your first choice of career goals was in the group called: Medically Related.
> People who choose this kind of work usually like the school subjects and activities you like; however, they get more education than you are planning to get. Also, they have higher scores on some of the related aptitude tests.
> In view of these facts, you probably ought to reconsider this occupational choice and think about other occupational fields more in line with your abilities and educational plans.

The narrative ends with the summary statement such as this one:

> Considering primarily your tested aptitudes, and to a lesser extent your school subject and activity preferences, you may want to look also into the following occupational groups: attendants, helpers, loaders. This is only a partial list of the occupational areas which coincide with your abilities and school subject preferences.[1]

---

[1]From *Differential Aptitude Test* by G. K. Bennett, H. G. Seashore, and A. G. Wesman. Copyright © 1974 by The Psychological Corporation. Reprinted by permission.

General Aptitude Test Battery (GATB)

The GATB is made up of 12 tests measuring nine factors. This test was originally developed by the U.S. Employment Service. It requires approximately two and one-half hours to administer the entire battery. A standard score (mean = 100, S.D. = 20) is used for interpretation.

The U.S. Department of Labor has conducted continuous studies on the validity and reliability of the GATB. The manual reports on more than 450 studies involving over 25,000 individuals. Separate validity coefficients are given for minority group members. Reliability, ranging from the .80s to the low .90s, has been determined primarily by equivalent-form and retest methods.

The GATB measures these nine aptitudes. Intelligence, or general learning ability (G), is measured by three tests (vocabulary, arithmetic reasoning, three-dimensional space). Verbal aptitude (V) is measured by a vocabulary test in which the individual is required to identify words that have the same meaning or opposite meaning. Numerical aptitude (N) is measured by problems requiring computation and arithmetic reasoning. Spatial aptitude (S) is measured by a three-dimensional test requiring the individual to visualize how an object would appear when moved or rotated. Form perception (P) is measured by a combination of two tests, one of which requires tool matching, the other matching of geometric forms. Clerical perception (Q) is measured by a test requiring the matching of names. Motor coordination (K) is measured by one test requiring coordination of eyes, hands, or fingers in making precise movements. Finger dexterity (F) is measured by two tests, the first requiring the individual to assemble rivets and washers and the other requiring the individual to disassemble them. Manual dexterity (M) is measured by two tests, the first requiring the individual to place pegs on a pegboard and the second requiring the individual to invert the pegs while transferring them to another board.

One of the limitations of the GATB is that all the tests must be completed quickly (Anastasi, 1988). The strength of the GATB is in the research that has been conducted in establishing validity and reliability. The GATB is one of the most thoroughly researched test batteries. However, there is significant concern that the GATB may be out of date because of the rapid and vast changes in technology. Also and more importantly, there are charges of test bias, especially against racial and ethnic minority groups. As a result of these concerns, there is speculation that the GATB may be discontinued until additional research can be completed (Kaplan & Saccuzzo, 1993). The GATB has been reviewed by Borgen (1982) and Anastasi (1988).

Multiple Cutoff Strategy

The U.S. Employment Service utilizes multiple cutoff points on the GATB in occupational counseling programs. To determine the cutoff points for specific occupations, combinations of GATB factors are converted into standard scores. This strategy was developed by studying test scores, criterion correlations (job output, course grades, and so forth), and job analyses. The use of multiple cutoff points has been developed by extensive, ongoing research since 1947. Occupations found to have similar patterns of scores are combined into the work groups listed in the *Guide for Occupational Exploration* (U.S. Department of Labor, 1979a). The GATB aptitude scores found to be most significant are listed with the established cutoff scores (for adults, students in grade 10, and students in grade 9) for each of 66 work groups. The score patterns are known as Occupational Ability Patterns (OAPs). The OAP structure is used to guide individuals in career exploration. For example, an individual who is considering occupations in air and water operations should have the following minimum GATB scores: G 105, N 100, and S 100 (U.S. Department of Labor, 1979b, p. 31). OAP numbers are cross-referenced with the *Dictionary of Occupational Titles* (DOT) codes. This handy reference can thus be used for almost all kinds of work and for entry into professional careers.

A major criticism of the multiple cutoff method is that correlations are given for prediction of success by validity coefficients, but no data are reported on the probability of predicting an individual's success in an occupation.

Case of a Migrant Farm Worker Seeking a Stable Job

Jose had been a migrant farm laborer most of his life. His family left south Texas during harvest seasons and migrated to various sections of the country, working in the farm fields. Jose dropped out of school when he was in the seventh grade. By the time he was 19 years old, his parents were no longer migrating to the farm fields because of age and illness.

Jose came to the rehabilitation counseling office to find a permanent job. He reported to the counselor that many times he attended school for only a few months out of the year because it was necessary for the family to move from one location to another. However, Jose did state that he had been able to obtain a reader and a math book from his older brothers and had studied on his own. He mentioned that his family relied on his skills in mathematics on many occasions. His knowledge of occupations was limited because he had been exposed to only a few.

To determine his skills Jose took a battery of tests, including the GATB. Jose's score report for the GATB is shown in Figure 4-3. This profile reports the raw scores for each of the 12 parts of the test. Scores for the nine aptitudes are derived from these 12 scores. For example, raw scores from parts 3, 4, and 6 are converted to standard scores and totaled to give the G score. The standard error of measurement is provided for each of the aptitude scores. On the far right of the report form the OAP numbers for high ratings are circled.

Part B-1002 / B-1001	Raw Score	G	V	N	S	P	Q	K	F	M
1 B	22						80			
2 D	15			76						
3 H	10	10			98					
4 J	13	52	70							
5 A	27					53				
6 I	10	20		15						
7 L	15					39				
8 K	50						62			
9 M	68									25
10 N	80									62
11 O	27								16	
12 P	23								47	
Aptitude Scores		82	70	91	98	92	80	62	63	87
1 SEm		6	6	6	8	9	9	7	12	11
Aptitude Scores + 1 SEm		88	76	97	106	101	89	69	75	98

GATB INDIVIDUAL APTITUDE PROFILE

Name: Jose Date: 9/18/81

Adult ☑ B-1001 ☐
Grade 9 ☐ B-1002 ☑
Grade 10 ☐ Form: A (B) C D

OAP NUMBERS*

All H's
23 46
12 (35) 58
1 24 47
13 36 59
2 25 48
14 37 60
3 26 49
15 38 61
4 27 50
16 39 62
5 28 51
17 40
6 29 52
18 41
7 30 53
19 42
8 (31) 54
20 43
9 32 55
21 44
10 33 56
(22) 45
11 34 57

*CIRCLE IN RED FOR GRADE H
CIRCLE IN BLACK FOR GRADE M
CROSS OUT FOR GRADE L

FIGURE 4-3.
GATB profile for Jose.

The counselor reported to Jose that his highest scores were in spatial aptitude, form perception, and manual dexterity. The counselor explained spatial aptitude as follows: "Jose, spatial aptitude measures how well you could visualize or form mental pictures of objects before they are built or how you might look at drawings that are used to guide people in the building trades, for example. This ability is used by architects and engineers and by anyone who needs to visualize work before building it. This skill is good for machinists, carpenters, and in many other types of occupations." The counselor also presented an explanation of form perception and manual dexterity. Jose listened intently, but it was evident that he did not grasp the full meaning of these measures.

The counselor then decided to look at the combination of the three high scores in relation to occupations. The counselor found that Jose had a high rating on OAP-31, production technology. After talking about this general occupational area, the counselor listed specific occupations: "These skills are used by assemblers, machine operators, and solderers." This list of jobs had little impact on Jose other than to confuse him further.

The counselor then decided on a different approach: "What this really means, Jose, is that you have aptitudes in certain areas that are necessary for a number of jobs that we can explore. I would like you to think about jobs other than those you are familiar with at the present time. For example, a local industry needs machine operators. This is one of the jobs I mentioned before. We also have a number of other firms that hire people with the same kinds of skills you have. The next step should be to read descriptions of these jobs so that you will have a little better understanding of them. This should help you in deciding what you would like to do and will also introduce you to some jobs that you have never considered before."

Jose seemed delighted with the prospect of exploring different kinds of jobs. He still seemed uncertain about his future but was willing to investigate the jobs: "I never thought about any of these jobs before, and I didn't even know what went on in all those places. I always thought that I would have to be something like a janitor or a laborer. But this is what I really want, something that I can learn and be trained to do so that I can have a good job in one place for a long time."

Jose spent considerable time during the following weeks researching various careers. He eventually was placed as an apprentice machine operator in a local firm. He also wanted a high school equivalency diploma, so he enrolled in a local program to obtain it. His goal was to attend the local community college. In this case the aptitude test results provided a link to occupational information and to career options Jose had never considered before.

ARMED SERVICES VOCATIONAL APTITUDE BATTERY (ASVAB)

The ASVAB was developed to replace the separate Army, Navy, and Air Force classification batteries for selecting and classifying personnel. This battery is designed primarily for high school seniors. The armed services have developed cooperative programs with school systems for administering this battery, and they furnish test results at no cost.

The ASVAB form 19 consists of nine tests: Coding Speed, Word Knowledge, Arithmetic Reasoning, Tool Knowledge, Space Relations, Mechanical Comprehension, Shop Information, Automotive Information, and Electronics Information. These tests combine to yield three academic scales, Academic Ability (word knowledge, paragraph comprehension, and arithmetic reasoning), Verbal (word knowledge, paragraph comprehension, and general science), and Mathematical (math knowledge and arithmetic reasoning). Four other scales are occupational scales: Mechanical and Crafts (arithmetic reasoning; mechanical comprehension; and auto, shop, and electronics information), Business and Clerical (word knowledge, paragraph comprehension, mathematics knowledge, and coding speed), Electronics and Electrical (arithmetic reasoning, mathematical knowledge, electronics information, and general science), and Health, Social and Technical (word knowledge and paragraph meaning, arithmetic reasoning, and mechanical comprehension).

Because the ASVAB has been so widely used (by 1.3 million students each year), it has been closely scrutinized. The early editions were greatly criticized by Cronbach (1979) and Weiss (1978). Cronbach suggested that the subtest scores were too unreliable to be used separately and that the use of the test in general should be limited. Weiss argued that the reliabilities of subtest scores were low primarily because the subtests were too short. More recent reviews are more positive in terms of both the test battery's psychometric characteristics and its interpretative materials (Hanser & Grafton, 1983).

The composite scores of this test significantly correlate with success in the areas for which they were designed. However, there are insufficient data to prove that the subtests measure what they claim to measure. Likewise, internal consistency for composite scores are high whereas the reliability coefficients for the individual scales are low. Prediger (1987) has suggested that there are still serious limitations for career counseling in the newer forms of the ASVAB. Anastasi (1988) has pointed out that there is no evidence that military and civilian occupations with the same titles require the same abilities for success. Murphy (1984) has suggested that subtest scores should not be considered as distinct abilities.

According to Jensen (1988), the ASVAB measures general ability along with interests rather than differential aptitude. This conclusion fits well with the future versions of the ASVAB that will include one general (G) score and two factor scores of verbal and math. Also included in the plans for future editions are the use of the Self-Directed Search (Holland, 1987b) and more useful information for exploring civilian careers (Kaplan & Saccuzzo, 1993).

Case of a High School Student Interested in the Armed Services

Corrina resided in a small rural community. The nearest city was 50 miles away. She had considered a career in the Army and took the ASVAB during her junior year in high school. Later, she decided she didn't want to leave home and dropped her plans.

When she was a senior, however, Corrina reported to the counselor that she was reconsidering the armed services because of a lack of jobs in her community and the nearby city. Because an Army recruiter was not available in the community, the counselor had been provided with ASVAB materials for counseling purposes. The counselor explained each of the scores in the following manner: "Your score on the verbal composite is at the 51st percentile. This means that 51 females out of 100 in the eleventh grade scored lower than you did, while 49 out of 100 scored higher than you did. The dashes on the profile indicate the range of your score. In other words, your true composite score for verbal is somewhere within this range. The verbal composite is a measure of your vocabulary, understanding of scientific principles, and ability to understand written materials. The tests used to measure the verbal composite are word knowledge (meanings of selected words) and general science."

Corrina wanted to know more about the significance of her high score in perceptual speed. Before responding directly to her question, the counselor explained that most jobs require a combination of abilities, and even though she should consider jobs that depend heavily on speed and accuracy, she should consider other factors also. "Your perceptual speed score is related to occupations that require detail, accuracy, and numerical work. The occupations associated with this composite are administrative specialist, clerk-typist, court reporter, file clerk, and supply clerk. These occupations are usually found in the clerical, supply, and general administrative occupational groups."

After spending considerable time reviewing the sample occupations and occupational groups, Corrina decided she would like to consider the clerical groups. Specifically, she planned to visit an Army recruiter for more information about a career as a clerk-typist, file clerk, or supply clerk.

In Corrina's case the ASVAB results were used to stimulate career exploration. Associating several occupational groups with the results provided her with examples of occupations she could consider for a career. This information encouraged Corrina to relate her skills and interests to job opportunities in the armed services.

LIMITATIONS AND SUGGESTIONS FOR USE

Although multiaptitude tests provide differential measures of ability, expectations for the predictive value of the results may be too high. The scores from multiaptitude test batteries should not be expected to pinpoint careers. The tests cannot answer specific questions such as "Will I be a good architect?" "Will I be a good mechanical engineer?" "Will I be a good surgical nurse?" Only partial answers to these questions may be expected. For example, a space relation score on an aptitude battery should provide an index of the individual's ability to visualize the effect of three-dimensional movement, which is one of the aptitudes required of architects. However, many other factors, all of which cannot be measured by a multiaptitude battery, need to be considered by the prospective architect. It is therefore important to determine the individual's objectives before testing is accomplished.

"Should I consider being a mechanic?" "Do I have the aptitude to do clerical work?" "Is my finger dexterity good enough to consider assembly work?" Reasonable answers to these questions can be obtained from the results of aptitude tests. More important, however, a meaningful career search may begin once test results are evaluated. The results of multiaptitude test batteries provide valuable suggestions and clues to be considered along with other information in career decision making.

Many of the following suggestions for fostering the career development of students and adults can be modified and used interchangeably to meet the needs of both groups. These suggestions should not be considered exhaustive of all possibilities of using assessment results to enhance career development but rather as examples from which exercises can be developed to meet local needs and needs of other groups.

For Schools:

- Ask students to write a short paragraph on the subject of their personal strengths and weaknesses. Ask students to explain how they can improve their weaknesses.
- Divide students into groups and ask them to identify occupations that match their measured ability scores. Share their findings.
- Conduct a contest to determine who can find the most occupations that match ability subtest scores.
- Play "My Strengths" by having students make a list of the courses in which they do best. After reviewing ability test results, have them determine whether there is a good match.
- Ask students to share "These Are My Skills," in which selected ability scores are used as a basis for describing their skills. Match the skills with occupations.
- Construct a job box or a service file that has pictures of various occupations. Ask students to match and identify job skills with their ability test results.
- Construct displays that contain listings of occupations under categories such as verbal aptitude, numerical aptitude, spelling, and mechanical reasoning. Ask students to go to the display that contains occupations that match their test results. Find one or more and discuss.
- Ask students to read a vocational biography of someone in an occupation selected on the basis of ability test results.
- Using an ability test profile, ask students to make a list of several occupations to be considered for further evaluation.
- Ask students to construct resumés that outline their measured abilities.

For Adults:

- Ask adults to compare requirements of occupations with their ability test score results. Share with others.
- In groups discuss skills needed for certain occupations. Use test results as examples.
- Ask adults to discuss individual strengths and weaknesses. Use test results as examples.
- Ask adults to develop personal profiles of developed abilities.
- Ask adults to discuss the relevance of identified abilities in the career decision-making process.
- Ask adults to share how abilities were developed from previous work and leisure experiences.
- Ask adults to share identified abilities that can be linked to emerging and changing occupational requirements.
- Ask adults to discuss the relevance of developing abilities in learning over the life span. Use current test results as examples.

OTHER APTITUDE TESTS

In addition to the multiaptitude batteries discussed in this chapter, a number of other batteries are on the market. Here are six examples.

Primary Mental Abilities Test. This was one of the first factored aptitude batteries; it was restandardized in 1962. It can be scored for general intelligence and provides five specific factors for kindergarteners through adults: verbal meaning, number facility, reasoning, perceptual speed, and spatial relations. Scores are expressed as mental age, IQ, and percentile rank.

Academic Promise Test. Four tests provide information for predicting course grades and achievement test scores. The verbal test measures verbal reasoning and understanding of words. The numerical test measures quantitative ability. The abstract reasoning test measures nonverbal reasoning. The language test measures grammar usage.

Flanagan Aptitude Classification Test. This test consists of 16 subtests: inspection, coding, memory, precision, assembly, scales, coordination, judgment/comprehension, arithmetic, patterns, components, tables, mechanics, expression, reasoning, and ingenuity. Each test measures behaviors considered critical to job performance. Selected groups of tests may be administered. The entire battery takes several hours. This test is designed primarily for use with high school students and adults.

The Guilford-Zimmerman Aptitude Survey. This test consists of seven parts: verbal comprehension, general reasoning, numerical operations, perceptual speed, spatial orientation, spatial visualization, and mechanical knowledge. The tests are relatively independent and homogeneous. However, the norm population is not fully described in the manual.

Career Ability Placement Survey. This test is used to measure abilities of entry requirements for jobs compiled by the authors in 14 Occupational Clusters. It can be self-scored or machine scored for junior high school, senior high school, college, and adult populations. National normative data provide comparisons of scores for mechanical reasoning, spatial relations, verbal reasoning, numerical ability, language usage, word knowledge, perceptual speed and accuracy, and manual speed and dexterity.

Occupational Aptitude Survey and Interest Survey (OASIS). This instrument was developed to assist students in grades 8 through 12 in making career decisions. Specifically, the results provide information about relative strengths through the following subtests: verbal, numerical, spatial, perceptual, manual dexterity, and general ability. Total testing time is 35 minutes. Scores are expressed by percentile, stanine, and a five-point score that can be compared to similar scores necessary for 120 occupations.

SUMMARY

Early trait-and-factor approaches to career counseling utilized ability measures. Multiaptitude batteries evolved from a growing interest in intraindividual measurement. Ability measures may be used to stimulate discussion of personal characteristics and traits relevant for career decision making.

An aptitude is a specific proficiency or an ability to acquire a certain proficiency. The aptitude tests discussed in this chapter measure a variety of skills and abilities.

QUESTIONS AND EXERCISES

1. Define aptitude and illustrate how aptitude scores are used in career counseling.
2. What are the major differences between the DAT and the GATB? Give an example of a

case and specify why you would choose one of these tests over the other to assess the individual's abilities.

3. Is it important for aptitude tests to provide separate sex norms? Why or why not?

4. Why are aptitude test scores generally better predictors of high school and college grades than of occupational success?

5. How would you prepare high school students to interpret the results of the ASVAB? Develop a list of major points you would cover for a presentation to a group or to an individual.

Chapter Five
Using Achievement Tests

The career counselor has to be concerned with the academic achievement of each client. Levels of competence in reading, language usage, and mathematics may be the key to rejection or consideration of certain educational and vocational plans. In fact, most career planning in one way or the other is related to academic proficiency. The decision to obtain education and training beyond high school is often based directly on developed abilities as measured by achievement tests. Many vocations that do not require college training do require that the individual be able to read, do arithmetic, and write. Thus, achievement tests provide results that can be linked to most occupational requirements.

Career counselors should understand the difference between achievement tests and aptitude tests. Both measure learning experience. However, the achievement test measures learning of relatively restricted items and in limited content areas—that is, learning related to an academic setting. The aptitude test measures a specific skill, ability, or achievement learned from a variety of experiences.

The choice of an aptitude test or an achievement test may be crucial in career counseling. Assessment of the purpose of the testing is the key. Both aptitude and achievement test results may be used as predictive and diagnostic information. However, aptitude tests are designed primarily as predictive tests, whereas achievement tests assess the present level of developed abilities. Thus, achievement tests measure the end product; they evaluate what the individual can do at the present time.

TYPES OF ACHIEVEMENT TESTS

Numerous achievement tests are on the market today. They are usually either general survey batteries covering several subject areas or single-subject tests. They can be criterion-referenced or norm-referenced or both. Achievement tests are usually identified by grade level. It is important to establish the specific purpose for giving an achievement test to decide what type to use.

The general survey battery should be chosen when comparisons of achievement in different content areas are needed. The survey battery provides a relatively limited sampling of each content area but, as the name implies, covers a broad spectrum of content areas.

The single-subject test should be chosen when a precise and thorough evaluation of achievement in one subject is needed. More items and more aspects of the subject are usually covered in a single-subject test than in a survey battery. In educational planning, it is often desirable to choose a single-subject test when detailed information is necessary. The saving in testing time is also a major consideration in the decision to use a single-subject test.

Both types of tests can be used as diagnostic instruments when measurement of specific skills or abilities and proficiencies can relate them to occupational requirements. Detection of a specific deficiency is also valuable for referral to remedial programs.

This chapter first reviews and discusses one survey battery and gives an example of the use of the survey battery in career counseling. It then reviews an achievement test designed to measure basic skills in arithmetic, reading, and spelling and gives an example of its use. A criterion-referenced diagnostic achievement test is then reviewed with an example of its use. A single-subject test of a basic skill is reviewed, and its use is illustrated. Finally, more strategies for the developmental use of achievement tests are listed.

STANFORD ACHIEVEMENT TEST (SAT)

The Stanford Achievement Test is a good example of a survey battery. This test was first published over 50 years ago and has undergone numerous revisions. The test may be hand scored or computer scored. The publisher provides a comprehensive, computerized reporting service to assist local administrators with instructional planning and reporting to the public.

The first high school battery of the Stanford Achievement Test was published in 1965. Developers of this test thoroughly reviewed textbooks and many different curriculum patterns. Items were edited by individuals from various minority groups and were evaluated in try-out programs involving 61,000 students in 1445 classrooms in 47 different school systems. Frequent revisions of the test have been made to stay abreast of changing curriculum patterns. The general use of the test is enhanced by several guides designed to aid in the interpretation of results. Because of the high level of the skills assessed, this test is particularly useful for helping individuals in making plans for college. Reviews by Drummond (1992), Brown (1993), and Stoker (1993) provide additional information for evaluating the development and use of this instrument.

Reliability established by split-half estimates for each subtest range from .87 to .95. Reliability estimates based on KR-20 range from .86 to .94. Content validity is well documented by a thorough explanation of the evaluation and editing process for test items. Construct validity is based on correlations with prior editions of the test, internal consistency of items, and evidence of the decreasing difficulty of items with progress in school.

Interpreting the Stanford Achievement Test

Figure 5-1 illustrates how stanine scores and percentile equivalents are to be interpreted; their position under the normal distribution is a good frame of reference. The 7th edition of the Stanford Achievement Test Score Report presents raw and scaled scores, national and local percentiles, grade equivalents, and national grade percentile bands for each subtest and total score. A multiple-score report such as this one lends itself to meaningful interpretations for career counseling because the combination of scores displayed provides the counselor and the counselee with an overview of achievement by subject.

Particular attention should be given to the scaled scores, which provide an index for comparing growth from one grade level to another. Table 5-1 contains fictitious scores for illustrating how raw scores are converted to scaled scores on a math computation test. By using such a table, one can compare performance in grade 9, for example, with the score in math computation in grade 12. However, the table should not be used to compare performance in one subject with performance in another. The advantage of scaled scores is that they provide equal units on a continuous scale for making comparisons.

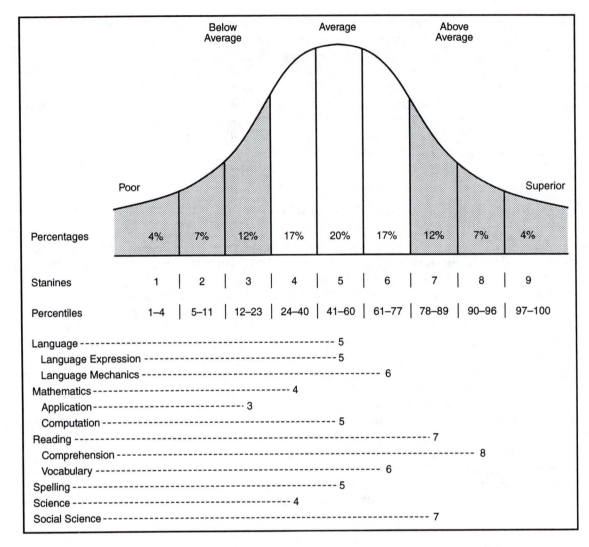

FIGURE 5-1.
Using stanines and percentiles.

TABLE 5-1.
Interpreting Scaled Scores for Any Achievement Test

Number Right (Raw Score)	Reading Comprehension Scaled Score	Number Right (Raw Score)	Reading Comprehension Scaled Score	Number Right (Raw Score)	Reading Comprehension Scaled Score
40	284	26	258	13	226
39	284	25	257	12	221
38	283	24	255	11	216
37	282	23	254	10	214
36	280	22	251	9	210
35	279	21	249	8	205
34	276	20	248	7	201
33	275	19	245	6	195
32	274	18	242	5	193
31	273	17	238	4	188
30	269	16	237	3	184
29	268	15	231	2	181
28	262	14	228	1	178
27	261				

Case of High School Student Referred to a Counselor Because of Poor Grades

Li, a junior in high school, was referred to the career counselor by his English teacher, who reported that Li was a poor student in English and, even with tutoring, had difficulty maintaining the level of performance necessary to pass the course. Earned course grades and comments from previous teachers reflected the same concerns. The teacher reported that Li's parents were insisting that he attend college, and Li was trying to meet their expectations of him. According to the teacher, Li was making a maximum effort, but with little success.

The counselor reviewed the results of an achievement test survey battery that had been administered during the current semester. A summary of Li's scores is shown in Table 5-2.

TABLE 5-2.
Achievement Test Survey Battery Results for Li

Test	National Percentile Equivalent	National Stanine
Reading comprehension	17	3
Vocabulary	20	3
Math reasoning	38	4
Math computation	57	5
Language usage		
Spelling	09	2
Grammar	11	3
Social Science	19	3
Science	32	4

The counselor concluded that the reported weaknesses in language usage were certainly verified by the recent achievement test results. The counselor found that previous test data for Li followed the same pattern—a weakness in language skills and average or better performance in mathematical computation.

Li spoke softly and volunteered little information. He seemed proud of and at the same time somewhat threatened by the fact that his two older brothers were attending college. He reported that his father owned and operated a manufacturing firm. Both his parents were college graduates.

When the counselor asked Li about his plans for the future, he answered with a well-rehearsed "I want to be an accountant." The counselor acknowledged Li's response positively and explored in more detail Li's interest in the field of business. During the course of the conversation it became apparent that Li possessed little knowledge about the activities of an accountant. To Li, the job was the same as bookkeeping. However, the counselor had established rapport with Li and had been able to get him to project into the future and to talk about what he perceived as a good job.

Prior to the next counseling session, the counselor consulted Li's math teacher. "Li has good computational skills and really tries hard; he certainly is not my top student in mathematics, but he does well in applications." This information confirmed the results of the previous test data and of the recently administered achievement test. The counselor was encouraged, for now he could include some positive facts when giving Li the test results.

At the next session, after a brief period of small talk designed to reinforce the rapport already established, the counselor suggested that they discuss the achievement test results. "Your score is at the 17th percentile on reading comprehension. This means that 17 out of 100 11th graders nationally scored lower than you while 83 out of 100 11th graders scored higher." The counselor explained the other scores in the same manner and then discussed groups of scores.

Li was particularly sensitive to his low scores in language usage. He commented that he had always had problems with English courses. The counselor asked that he explain how this problem could affect his plans for educational training and a career. Li acknowledged that he would have problems in college; his brothers had told him the English courses were difficult.

The counselor sensed that it was the right time to introduce encouraging information and an alternative potential career goal. "The field of business is broad and has many opportunities for you, particularly with your good math skills. We can explore some careers that require math skills, but that do not necessarily require a college degree. A couple of occupations that I can think of offhand are bookkeeping and bank teller." Li was delighted with this information and in subsequent counseling sessions made reports on several careers he had researched in the career resource center. He seemed most interested in bookkeeping.

In a meeting with the counselor, Li's parents expressed their appreciation for Li's enthusiasm and interest in career exploration. They said they had hoped that Li could attend college as his brothers had, but they recently came to the realization that Li was not as academically inclined. They now planned to encourage and support Li's interest in alternative careers.

In this case the achievement test results were linked easily to educational planning and occupational information. Li and his parents recognized that his weak English skills would make it difficult for him to be a successful college student, but that his relatively higher skills in mathematics opened other occupational opportunities.

WIDE RANGE ACHIEVEMENT TEST—REVISED (WRAT-R²)

The WRAT-R^2, first standardized in 1936, and revised in 1984, is an example of an abbreviated achievement test measuring arithmetic, reading, and spelling. The arithmetic section can be given in approximately ten minutes. The examiner is required to present orally up to 46 words for the spelling section. The reading section requires the individual to pronounce from a list words that become progressively more difficult. The test can be given in a relatively short time when the arithmetic and spelling sections are given in a group setting. Each subtest is divided into two levels. Level I is for children ages 5 to 11 years. Level II is for individuals 12 years through adulthood.

Reliabilities for the WRAT subtests were obtained by the split-half method based on odd-even scores. The reported coefficients are high, ranging from .94 to .98.

Validity was established by comparing WRAT subtest scores with scores on several widely used intelligence and achievement tests. However, Reid (1986) has suggested that the validity of this test is poorly documented and there is concern about what it really measures. He has advised caution in using the test with the exception of clinical and research applications. Other reviewers such as Reynolds (1986), Witt (1986), and Clark (1989) are also quite critical of its general use.

Interpreting the WRAT

The results are reported in percentiles, grade equivalents, stanines, standard scores, T scores, and scaled scores by age groups. The normative tables have a wide range; they are grouped by age from 5 years to 55–64 years. The standard scores have a mean of 100 and a standard deviation of 15.

The chief advantage of the WRAT is that it can be given in a relatively short time and can be used as a screening instrument for educational planning. It is particularly useful for testing individuals whose educational achievement is low; it gives an estimate of their developed abilities that can be used for vocational placement. Several case studies are reported in the manual to illustrate the use of the WRAT.

Cunningham (1986) points out that the WRAT-R^2 is useful as a quick screening instrument, but there is evidence to suggest that the results underestimate achievement in the basic skills, particularly in reading. If more reliable data are needed for determining achievement in arithmetic, reading, and spelling, the WRAT-R^2 should be followed with administration of other standardized achievement tests.

Case of a School Dropout Interested in Changing Jobs

Diana, 24 years old, dropped out of school when she was in the seventh grade. She had worked at a number of odd jobs but mainly as a nurse's aide and came to the career counseling center to find out what the requirements were for licensed vocational nurse (LVN). After reviewing the requirements, she asked the counselor whether there was some way of determining how she would do in LVN training and in classes that prepare individuals to obtain a high school equivalency diploma. The counselor suggested that she take an achievement test to give a rough estimate of her educational level in arithmetic, reading, and spelling. The WRAT was selected because it specifically measures basic achievement in those areas and can be quickly administered and scored.

The results of the WRAT for Diana are listed in Table 5-3. The counselor recognized Diana's disappointment in her performance. However, she pointed out that a high school diploma was not necessary to enter the local LVN training program. In discussing why she wanted to be an LVN, Diana expressed a sincere desire to help people.

TABLE 5-3.
WRAT-R^2 Results for Diana

Test	Stanine	Percentile	Standard Score
Arithmetic	3	12	82
Reading	2	09	80
Spelling	2	08	79

Before Diana returned for her next appointment, the counselor reviewed the items that Diana had missed on the test. It was obvious that Diana's spelling skills were poor, but item analysis of the arithmetic test revealed that she made a number of careless mistakes. A review of the reading test revealed that Diana's word attack skills were poor but probably because she had not been exposed to many of the words she missed.

At the next counseling session, the counselor reviewed her item analysis of Diana's test results by pointing out careless mistakes and a lack of self-confidence in attempting words on the oral reading test. Diana appreciated being given concrete examples of her mistakes; she realized that she might do better with greater exposure to academic materials.

In subsequent meetings Diana agreed to enter a remedial program sponsored by the high school learning assistance center. When Diana was asked about the decision, she stated "I've always been afraid of tests. Now—could you believe it?—the test scores helped me see the light!"

Diana's career exploration was enhanced in a number of ways by the test. First, she was encouraged to upgrade her vocational skills by further academic training. Second, she gained self-confidence by diagnosing the mistakes on her test. By encouraging her to upgrade her skills through educational programs, the counselor helped to make other work opportunities available to Diana.

MASTERY: SURVIVAL SKILLS TEST (SST)

The SST is a criterion-referenced test designed to measure mastery of essential reading and math skills. The reading test assesses performance of such tasks as reading telephone books, following simple directions, and reading a street map. The mathematics test assesses performance of such tasks as determining correct change, calculating budgets, and itemizing expenses. Each test can

SRA CRITERION-REFERENCED MEASUREMENT PROGRAM

mastery: an evaluation tool

REPORT FOR WESTRICK EDWARD   /FAIRVIEW HIGH
GROUP SOPHOMORE
GROUP 2232

SUBJECT SURVIVAL SKILLS-MR   GRADE 10-1
GROUP I.D. 180HURON   DATE 05/04/77
TEST # 002232-5254
CODE #
TAPE NO 72431

STUDENT PROFILE

First CRT — OBJECTIVE: (LEARNER WILL(IDENTIFY)...)

OBJ CATALOG NO / DIA PROBE NOS	OBJ MST	ITEM	RIGHT
1 KNOW HOW TO MAKE CHANGE — MM1	Y	1 + 2 +	3 +
2 FIND TOTAL INCOME FROM AVG WEEKLY INCOME — MM2	Y	4 + 5 +	6 +
3 CALCULATE WAGES FROM HOURLY RATE AND HOURS — MM3	Y	7 + 8 +	9 +
4 DETERMINE AND COMPARE UNIT COSTS — MM4	N	10 + 11 +	12 +
5 FIND TAKE HOME PAY FROM SALARY AND DEDUCTION — MM5	Y	13 + 14 +	15 +
6 FIGURE DAILY AMOUNTS FROM WEEKLY BUDGET — MM6	Y	16 + 17 +	18 +
7 FIND MULTIPLES OF ITEMIZED WEEKLY EXPENSES — MM7	Y	19 + 20 +	21 +
8 COMPUTE A SALES SLIP, INCLUDING TAX — MM8	Y	22 + 23 +	24 +
9 ESTIMATE WEEKLY SAVINGS TO BUY AN ITEM — MM9	Y	25 + 26 +	27 +
10 CALCULATE WEEKLY WAGES FROM PIECEWORK RATE — MM10	Y	28 + 29 +	30 +
11 COMPUTE MONTHLY RATE TO REPAY DEBT IN A YEAR — MM11	Y	31 + 32 +	33 +
12 COMPUTE TOTAL AND AVERAGE SCORES IN SPORTS — MM12	Y	34 + 35 +	36 +
13 FIND TOTAL MATERIALS COST FROM UNIT COSTS — MM13	N	37 - 38 +	39 +
14 DETERMINE RECIPE AMOUNTS FOR DIFF SIZE GROUP — MM14	Y	40 + 41 +	42 +
15 CALCULATE DISTANCE FROM TIME AND RATE — MM15	Y	43 + 44 +	45 +
16 COMPUTE UTILITIES COST AND COMPARE WITH BILL — MM16	N	46 + 47 +	48 +
17 FIND AMOUNT OF FLOOR COVERING NEEDED FOR ROOM — MM17	Y	49 + 50 +	51 +
18 FIGURE DISTANCE, TIME, AND GAS COST FOR A TRIP — MM18	N	52 + 53 +	54 -
19 COMPUTE COST OF PET CARE OVER NUMBER OF YEARS — MM19	Y	55 + 56 +	57 +
20 FIND AMOUNT OF MATERIAL NEEDED TO MAKE AN ITEM — MM20	N	58 + 59 -	60 +

© 1974, Science Research Associates, Inc. All rights reserved.

% OF OBJ MASTERED 75   NO OBJ MASTERED 15   NO OBJ DID NOT MASTER OBJ

Y = YES, MASTERED OBJ   N = NO, DID NOT MASTER OBJ   + = RIGHT ANSWER   - = WRONG ANSWER   0 = OMISSION

Second CRT — OBJECTIVE: (LEARNER WILL (IDENTIFY)...)

OBJ CATALOG NO / DIA PROBE NOS	OBJ MST	ITEM	RIGHT
1 UNDERSTAND MEDICAL TERMS AND INSTRUCTIONS — MR1	Y	1 + 2 +	3 +
2 UNDERSTAND CAUTION LABELS ON BOTTLES, ETC. — MR2	Y	4 + 5 +	6 +
3 SELECT USE OF ITEMS BASED ON CONSUMER TERMS — MR3	Y	7 + 8 +	9 +
4 RESPOND PROPERLY TO ROAD SIGNS — MR4	N	10 + 11 +	12 +
5 FOLLOW SIMPLE DIRECTIONS — MR5	Y	13 + 14 +	15 +
6 UNDERSTAND COMMON INFORMATION SIGNS — MR6	Y	16 + 17 +	18 +
7 USE BUILDING FLOOR PLAN AND SCHEDULE — MR7	Y	19 + 20 +	21 +
8 RECALL FACTS FROM HANDBOOK ON SAFETY — MR8	Y	22 + 23 +	24 +
9 KNOW HOW TO USE A STREET GUIDE AND ITS MAP — MR9	Y	25 + 26 +	27 +
10 BE ABLE TO FILL IN BLANKS ON A FORM — MR10	Y	28 + 29 +	30 +
11 SELECT USE OF PRODUCT BASED ON INGREDIENTS — MR11	Y	31 + 32 +	33 +
12 KNOW HOW TO USE TELEPHONE DIRECTORY — MR12	Y	34 + 35 +	36 +
13 KNOW HOW TO USE A BUILDING DIRECTORY — MR13	N	37 - 38 +	39 +
14 IDENTIFY ITEMS FROM A BUSINESS STATEMENT — MR14	Y	40 + 41 +	42 +
15 KNOW HOW TO USE AN ENTERTAINMENT GUIDE — MR15	Y	43 + 44 +	45 +
16 ORDER A MEAL FROM A MENU AND FIGURE THE BILL — MR16	N	46 - 47 +	48 +
17 IDENTIFY FACTS IN AD AND JUDGE ITS SINCERITY — MR17	Y	49 + 50 +	51 +
18 USE A PLANE SCHEDULE TO DEVELOP A TRAVEL PLAN — MR18	Y	52 + 53 +	54 +
19 IDENTIFY CONDITIONS OF A CONTRACT — MR19	Y	55 + 56 +	57 +
20 FOLLOW AND IDENTIFY PARTS OF A CONCERT PROGRAM — MR20	Y	58 + 59 +	60 +

© 1974, Science Research Associates, Inc. All rights reserved.   PRINTED IN THE UNITED STATES OF AMERICA

% OF OBJ MASTERED 75   NO OBJ MASTERED 17   % OF OBJ MASTERED 85   NO OBJ MASTERED 17

Ⓐ LIST OF OBJECTIVES FOR FIRST CRT   Ⓒ LIST OF OBJECTIVES FOR SECOND CRT
Ⓑ STUDENT PERFORMANCE ON ITEMS AND OBJECTIVES FOR FIRST CRT   Ⓓ STUDENT PERFORMANCE ON ITEMS AND OBJECTIVES ON BOTH CRT's
Ⓔ OVERALL STUDENT PERFORMANCE

FIGURE 5-2.
SST individual student profile.
From Mastery: *Survival Skills Test,* Science Research Associates Staff. Copyright © 1974, Science Research Associates. Reprinted by permission.

be administered in one hour or less. The two editions of the test are designed for grades 6–12 (school edition) and for grades 11–adult (adult edition). The test can be locally scored or computer scored. Several options of computer scoring are available.

Interpreting the SST

Figure 5-2 is an individual student profile. The profile contains the following information: a list of objectives for each test, performance on individual items and objectives for each test, and overall performance on each test. There are 20 specific objectives for each test with three items for each objective. The profile gives scores for each item so that test results can be evaluated in detail. In addition, a review of the specific objectives reveals information that can be used in career planning. For example, mastery of the objective of making change can be directly related to requirements for certain jobs. Tests such as this one, which are designed to measure mastery of specific skills, provide information of inestimable value for counseling students in middle grades through high school on planning future instruction and for adults on skills needed in daily living.

Case of a Counselee with Limited Educational and Vocational Experience

Rita was referred to the career counselor by a local social service agency. She had been deserted by her husband after ten years of marriage and left with three children. She had little work experience. Her school grades were poor, and she had dropped out of school while in the seventh grade to get married. One of her immediate problems was managing personal expenditures because her husband had paid the bills and handled the money. The counselor decided to administer a skills test that would provide information for making a decision about prevocational training by identifying Rita's specific deficiencies in managing money—for example, problems in developing a budget, computing bills, and doing comparative shopping.

The results of the test chosen, the SST, indicated that Rita had not mastered the following objectives: estimating the weekly savings needed to buy an item; computing the monthly payment necessary to repay a debt in a year; determining recipe amounts for different size groups; computing the cost of utilities and comparing the cost with the bill; figuring distance, time, and cost of gas for a trip; finding the amount of material needed to make an item; understanding caution labels on bottles; and selecting items based on consumer information.

The first step for Rita was placement in a prevocational training program designed to help her overcome the problems identified by the SST. Specifically, instruction included information on financial planning, budgeting, comparative shopping, food preparation, and other home-related tasks.

The results of the test also revealed that Rita had the math skills necessary for making change correctly. She had been given responsibility for handling money by her parents, who sent her to stores to make purchases, and she expressed confidence in her abilities in this area. When the counselor asked her to relate this skill to a job opportunity, she replied "Check-out clerk or store clerk." The counselor realized that this source of immediate employment could help Rita supplement her income while considering other employment opportunities.

In this case the SST not only provided information that could be used to identify personal needs for home management but also provided clues for employment, both now and in the future. The counselor was aware that problems in the home, if not resolved, would eventually affect Rita's ability to function on a job.

A WRITERS SKILLS TEST

The Basic Skills Assessment Program, consisting of tests of reading, mathematics, and writing skills, was developed by Educational Testing Service (ETS) with a national consortium of school districts. The tests may be administered as a battery, or individual tests may be selected as needed. Each test can be administered in approximately 45 minutes. They can be machine or hand scored. One of these tests, A Writers Skills Test, illustrates the use of a single-subject achievement test.

A Writers Skills Test consists of 75 multiple-choice items covering spelling, punctuation, capitalization, logic, and evaluation. In addition the test uses four exercises to measure an individual's writing ability: writing a job application letter, completing a form, conveying information or directions, and writing creatively. A well-prepared manual is provided for evaluating the writing sample by an analytical or holistic scoring procedure.

Reliability estimates computed by KR-20 for total scores on A Writers Skills Test are high (.95). Subtest reliabilities range from .73 to .89. Content validity appears well established from the description of the development of specifications for the test. Concurrent validity was established by reporting the relationship of teachers' judgments of a student's need for remedial work to scores on the test. See reviews by Plake (1985) and Ravitch (1985) for more information on the validity.

Interpreting A Writers Skills Test

A scaled score (mean = 150, S.D. = 25) and the percentage of scores below a given score for grades 8, 9, and 12 are provided for interpretation. In addition, means and standard deviations for each grade are reported. A list of individual item responses is optional.

A Writers Skills Test is unique in that it provides an evaluation of actual writing proficiency. The writing exercise portion scored by an analytical system provides results as yes/no (pass/fail) for each exercise. The criteria used to determine a yes score are established by the user based on local standards. For example, the user decides the relative emphasis to be put on spelling, punctuation, and legibility. Results from the holistic scoring method are reported in numbers; 4 (superior), 3 (meets minimal local standards), 2 (does not meet minimal local standards), and 1 (is extremely weak).

There may be some argument about the validity of the scoring procedures for the writing exercises. But the manual carefully explains the standardized scoring procedures adopted. In addition, ETS offers consultant/workshop packages for helping users improve their scoring skills. As these procedures are refined and validated, an increasingly accurate appraisal of an individual's writing ability will be available.

Case of a Counselee Aspiring to a Specific Job

For ten years Jacob took care of his parents. After their deaths, Jacob, now 28, needed to find a job to support himself. He told the counselor that he made average grades in high school but dropped out during his junior year to care for his parents. He had never seriously considered a career. Reading had been his primary pastime, and he had developed an interest in newspaper work. Specifically, he expressed a desire to write or edit for the hometown newspaper. The counselor recalled a recent conversation with the owner of the paper inquiring about qualified individuals in the community. However, he did not know whether Jacob had the skills necessary, although he observed that Jacob expressed himself well verbally. The counselor and Jacob decided that a writing and grammar test would help them decide whether an interview with the newspaper owner was warranted at this time.

The counselor wanted a test that would provide an index of Jacob's basic skills in capitalization, punctuation, logic, and spelling as well as a writing sample. A Writers Skills Test from the Basic Skills Assessment Program was selected. The counselor obtained the assistance of the high school English department in scoring the writing sample by the analytical method. He asked the scorers to score the writing sample on the basis of 12th grade norms.

The results indicated that Jacob's primary weakness was in punctuation, but he received pass scores on all other criteria. The scorers recommended a remedial program for upgrading his punctuation skills. The counselor and Jacob decided that he would complete the recommended program and then apply for a job with the local newspaper. In this case, the results of the test and particularly the writing sample were used to identify both weaknesses and strengths related to the requirements of the job under consideration.

SUGGESTIONS FOR CAREER DEVELOPMENT

Many of the following suggestions for fostering the career development of students and adults can be modified and used interchangeably to meet the needs of both groups. These suggestions should not be considered exhaustive of all possibilities of using assessment results to enhance career development but rather as examples from which exercises can be developed to meet local needs and needs of other groups.

For Schools:
- Ask students to identify personal strengths and weaknesses as measured by achievement test results. Using this information, identify related work tasks for selected occupations or career clusters.
- Ask students to identify relationships between ability and achievement.
- Ask students to develop a plan for improving their academic skills.
- Form discussion groups for the purpose of linking basic skills to occupations.
- Ask students to identify and compare levels of achievement to selected occupations.
- Ask students to discuss the relationships between student roles and work roles.
- Ask students to relate academic skills to interests and values.
- Ask students to identify basic skills used in selected occupations in the community and compare them with their own.
- Ask students to discuss the relationship of academic achievement and self-concept development.

For Adults:
- Form groups and ask adults to discuss and identify the relationships of obsolescence to achievement results.
- Ask adults to identify the changes in training requirements for selected occupations. Match their achievement results with some new and/or different occupations.
- Ask adults to identify the necessity of acquiring basic skills for many occupations. Make a list of occupations with matching basic skills. Compare achievement test results with requirements of selected occupations.
- Ask adults to identify and discuss the limitations of advancement in many occupations because of poor basic skill achievement. Using assessment results, have them develop plans for improving basic skills.
- Ask adults to discuss the necessity of training for making career transitions. Relate achievement to training requirements.
- Using achievement test results, have them develop educational plans to meet requirements of selected jobs.
- Ask adults to develop a positive view of self by assessing strengths, and potentials, from achievement test results.
- Ask students to compare self-rated achievement results with the results of a standardized test. Share conclusions.

OTHER ACHIEVEMENT TESTS

Because many published achievement tests are currently available, the following list is far from complete. The first three examples given are survey batteries; the next two are diagnostic tests; and the last four are separate subject tests.

Comprehensive Test of Basic Skills. This survey battery is designed primarily to measure basic skills in reading, language, mathematics, reference, science, and social studies. The reading, language, and mathematics subtests are further divided into parts.

Iowa Test of Basic Skills. Five major areas are tested by this survey battery: vocabulary, reading comprehension, language skills, work study skills (reading graphs and maps and using reference material), and mathematics. Some item overlap exists across grades. Scores are provided as grade equivalents and grade percentile norms.

Metropolitan Achievement Test High School Battery. Skills in language, reading, arithmetic, science, social studies, and study techniques are measured by this survey battery. Three or four forms are available for each level—primer through advanced. Four scores are reported for each subtest: standard score, grade equivalent, stanine, and percentile rank.

Diagnostic Reading Scales. This test is designed to measure reading disabilities. It contains reading passages, word recognition lists, and phonetics tests.

Stanford Diagnostic Arithmetic Test. This test has two levels. Level 1 (grades 2.5–4.5) covers concepts of numbers, computation, and number factors. Level 2 (grades 4.5–8.5) covers concepts of numbers, number factors, computation with whole numbers, with common fractions, with decimal fractions, and with percents.

Cooperative Mathematics Test. This series of nine tests measures performance in arithmetic, structure of number systems, algebra I, algebra II, algebra III, geometry, trigonometry, analytic geometry, and calculus.

Cooperative English Test. This test provides measures of reading comprehension and English expression.

Cooperative Social Studies Test. This test measures achievement in American history (Grades 7–12), American government (grades 10–12), modern European history (grades 10–12), and world history (grades 10–12).

Cooperative Science Test. This test measures achievement in general science (grades 7–9), advanced general science (grades 8–9), and high school biology, chemistry, and physics.

SUMMARY

Academic achievement is a primary consideration in educational and vocational planning. For educational planning there is a direct relationship, and almost all jobs are linked to achievement of basic skills. Compared with aptitude tests, achievement tests measure much narrower content areas and more limited learning experiences. Aptitude tests measure broader areas of abilities and experiences. There are two types of achievement tests: general survey batteries and single-subject tests. Achievement test results are reported as norm-referenced scores, criterion-referenced scores, or both.

QUESTIONS AND EXERCISES

1. Explain the difference between achievement and aptitude tests. Illustrate your explanation with an example of a case in which you would use one or the other kind of test.
2. What is the difference between a norm-referenced and a criterion-referenced test? What circumstances would indicate when to use one or the other?
3. Describe cases in which you would use a general survey battery, a single-subject test, and a diagnostic test.
4. Give an example of how you would interpret a scaled score to an individual and then illustrate how you would interpret a scaled score to a high school class.
5. Would you choose a norm-referenced or a criterion-referenced achievement test for a 54-year-old, Black mother of four who has never worked outside the home? Why?

Chapter Six

Using Interest Inventories

In one way or another almost everyone has been involved in the exploration of interests to decide which activities to pursue in leisure, in a career, or both. To help in this exploration, interest inventories have long been associated with career guidance.

Strong (1943) pioneered the development of interest inventories by introducing innovative principles for the measurement of interests. He gathered data concerning the likes and dislikes of individuals for a variety of activities, objects, and types of persons commonly encountered. He found that individuals in different occupations have common patterns of interests that differentiated them from individuals in other occupations. In this way the results of interest inventories provide the opportunity for individuals to compare their interests with those of individuals in specific occupational groups. More recently, Holland's (1985) typology provides a system for matching interests with one or more of six types that have been discussed in the preceding chapters and will be more fully discussed in this chapter.

Because sex bias in interest assessment has received considerable attention, I present a summary of this issue at the beginning of the chapter. This summary is followed by a discussion of two widely used interest inventories: the Strong Interest Inventory and the Kuder Occupational Interest Survey. Other inventories reviewed are the Self-Directed Search (Holland, 1987b), the Harrington/O'Shea Systems for Career Decision-Making (Harrington & O'Shea, 1992), and the Non-Sexist Vocational Card Sort (Dewey, 1974). Several examples of the use of interest inventories are provided.

SEX BIAS AND SEX FAIRNESS IN INTEREST ASSESSMENT

In the past a considerable body of literature has concerned sex bias and unfairness in career interest measurement. A number of the most relevant articles have been compiled by Diamond (1975) under the sponsorship of the National Institute of Education (NIE). The NIE publishes guidelines that identify sex bias as "any factor that might influence a person to limit—or might cause others to limit—his or her consideration of a career solely on the basis of gender" (Diamond, 1975, p. xxiii).

According to Diamond, the guidelines have led to some progress in reducing sex bias in interest inventories by calling for fairness in the construction of item pools ("Items such as statements, questions, and names of occupations used in the inventory should be designed so as not to limit the consideration of a career solely on the basis of gender"), fairness in the presentation of technical information ("Technical information should include evidence that the inventory provides career options for both males and females"), and fairness in interpretive procedures ("Interpretive procedures should provide methods of equal treatment of results for both sexes"). Generally, the guidelines are aimed at encouraging both sexes to consider all career and educational opportunities and at eliminating sex-role stereotyping by those using interest inventory results in the career counseling process.

Harmon (1975) suggests that sex bias is prevalent in most currently used interest inventories primarily because they assume that work is dichotomized into man's work and woman's work. This argument raises the issue of the kind of norms that should be used for interest measurement—that is, should there be separate or combined sex norms?

One answer to this question is given by Prediger and Johnson (1979). According to them, a method of reducing sex bias in interest inventories is the use of sex-balanced scales such as those provided in the unisex edition of the American College Test Interest Inventory. In this inventory, which uses combined sex norms, items are sex balanced because "they capture the essence of a work-related activity preference while minimizing sex-role connotations" (Prediger & Johnson, 1979, p. 11). The rationale is that combined sex norms can be used because sex-balance items elicit similar responses from men and women. The authors argue that different sets of occupational scales for men and women perpetuate sex-role stereotyping in that such items suggest the typical kinds of work performed by members of each sex.

Johansson (1975), however, believes separate norms should be used because, according to him, sex bias in interest inventories is a result of our socialization process—that is, male/female stereotypes are an integral part of our society. Therefore, he recommends the use of separate sex norms for interpretive purposes until further research on sex bias in our society can be done. He points out that both the Strong-Campbell Interest Inventory and the Kuder Occupational Interest Survey employ separate sex norms.

Along the same lines, Holland (1975) suggests that vocational aspirations of men and women differ because of their histories. As women's lives are changed in a society free of sex-role stereotyping or by counseling programs designed to minimize the effects of sex-role stereotyping, different patterns of interest will emerge. Holland argues that attention should be directed toward achieving an androgynous society rather than toward attacking interest inventories, which reflect early socialization and conditioning.

Conversely, Cole and Hansen (1975) suggest that we do not have to wait for a society free of sex-role stereotyping to evolve in order to broaden the interest patterns of women. They contend that presenting expanded career options for women in interest inventories will encourage exploration of a wide range of careers and thus provide increased opportunities. Within this frame of reference interest inventories should indeed be criticized if they do not provide equal options for men and women.

Birk (1975) suggests that the problem lies in the interpretation of interest inventory results. She believes that the lack of instructions for interpreting interest inventories to women perpetuates sex bias in career counseling programs. Because counselors may have to rely heavily on information contained in the test manual, she recommends that interest inventory manuals discuss problems of occupational stereotyping and other issues of sex bias and sex fairness. For example, the counselor should be informed that all jobs are available to any individual regardless of sex, that the purpose of interest inventories is to generate career options for both males and females, and that false notions concerning sex-role stereotyping among women need to be discussed and clarified. Furthermore, a summary of Title IX of the 1972 Educational Amendments of Higher Education should be provided. In essence, Birk suggests that revising the interest inventory manuals is the way to overcome the limitations of inventories caused by sex-role stereotyping.

In addition, Birk (1975) suggests that interpretation formats and materials should include guidelines for using score results to counsel women. Case studies of women in a variety of occupations would provide the counselor with representative examples of both sexes in the work force. Also, the same interpretation format should be used for both sexes. Interpretive materials should thus clearly establish that both men and women are to be encouraged to consider all occupations and college majors.

As Diamond (1975) points out, changes in interest inventory approaches may be slow. In the meantime, the career counselor has to rely heavily on manuals and research reports that describe limitations in the use of interest inventory scores for women. As more research becomes available, better guidelines for sex-fair interest inventories will be developed.

EXAMPLES OF INTERESTS BY HOLLAND'S TYPES

In this section Holland's types will be further elaborated with emphasis on occupations associated with each type. In earlier discussions general areas of interests were covered with some examples of specific occupations. More information about matching occupations with combinations of codes is given in the *Dictionary of Holland Occupational Codes* (Gottfredson & Holland, 1989). Other helpful references are Hansen (1985), Levin (1991), and Brew (1987).

Following are the six Holland's types as they relate to interests:

1. *Realistic:* Realistic people are interested in action-type occupations such as building, mechanics, machine operator, and repair. They tend to like the outdoors and prefer to work in rural areas. Typical hobbies are fishing, camping, and working on cars. Some realistic occupations include carpenter, rancher, engineer, forester, veterinarian, and welder.

2. *Investigative:* People with high scores in investigative abilities have a strong interest in science. They like abstract tasks and solving problems while working independently. Such activities as collecting data, conducting research, and organizing material for analysis appeal to investigative people. Some investigative occupations include biologist, mathematician, psychologist, pharmacist, and dental hygienist.

3. *Artistic:* The artistic person values the aesthetics in life and is dedicated to self-expression. Typical work activities are writing, composing, and designing while working independently. Work environments include museums, theaters, galleries, and concert halls. Examples of artistic occupations include artist, music teacher, librarian, photographer, and interior designer.

4. *Social:* Social people enjoy working with people and are concerned for the welfare of others. Typical activities are informing, teaching, coaching, and leading discussions. Work environments include social service agencies, religious establishments, mental-health clinics, personnel offices, and medical facilities. Examples of social occupations include teacher, guidance counselor, playground director, social worker, and juvenile probation officer.

5. *Enterprising:* Enterprising people tend to be ambitious and competitive and to seek leadership positions. Typical activities include selling, managing, giving speeches, and leading groups of people. Work environments include marketing agencies, investment banking firms, retail and wholesale firms, and small, independently owned businesses. Examples of occupations include corporation executive, sales manager, elected public official, computer salesperson, and stockbroker.

6. *Conventional:* Being precise and accurate while attending to detail in well-defined activities are typical traits of conventional people. Activities included in this type are keeping records, scheduling, and maintaining adopted procedures of an organization. Preferred work environments include large corporations, business offices, and accounting firms. Examples of occupations include bookkeeper, accountant, secretary, key-punch operator, cashier, and banker.

INTERPRETING FLAT AND ELEVATED PROFILES

One problem that causes confusion for client and counselor are flat or elevated profiles. Flat, or depressed, profiles consist of scores around the average range with little differences among scores. In contrast, elevated profiles have a large number of scores that are considered to be high in interest levels. These types of profiles can be used productively as discussed by Hansen (1985).

Flat or depressed profiles may indicate one of the following:

1. A narrow interest range and an individual with highly defined interests. A profile with a narrow interest range will more than likely show high scores in one or two interest areas.

Such an individual may be completely satisfied with an occupation and may have achieved significant positive feedback.

2. A client with very little knowledge about the world of work and the workplace. Such an individual may be reluctant to respond aggressively to questions about the work world.

3. Mood swings. An individual may be unwilling to differentiate among offered choices just because he or she is having a "bad" day.

4. Indecisiveness. An individual who is unwilling to make a commitment or a change may indicate a lack of readiness to respond to an interest inventory.

5. An unwillingness to work.

Elevated profiles may indicate:

1. Individuals who are reluctant to say "dislike" or "indifferent" to items. Some may feel such responses would type them as negative individuals, and so their results show a high percentage of "like" items.

2. A wide diversity of interests. Focusing on only a few interests may be difficult for these individuals.

Knowledge of some of the reasons and causes for flat or elevated interest profiles prepares the counselor for suggesting intervention strategies. Although profiles of this type may seem to provide little in the way of counseling opportunities, this information can be of significant assistance in career planning.

STRONG INTEREST INVENTORY (SII)

The SII replaced the well-known Strong-Campbell Interest Inventory. The development of the SII was based on research by Strong (1943) that has covered several decades of compiling empirical information. He made no proper assumptions concerning the specific interest patterns of workers in the occupational groups he researched. Strong postulated that an individual who has interests that are similar to those of persons working in a given occupation is more likely to find satisfaction in that particular occupation than is a person who does not have common interests with those workers.

The SII contains 325 items that measure a respondent's interests in a wide range of occupations, occupational activities, hobbies, leisure activities, school subjects, and types of people. It typically takes about 30 minutes to take the SII; the reading level is sixth grade. The appropriate age range is 13 years through adulthood. The SII has been translated for administration into Spanish, French-Canadian, and Hebrew.

The SII has been as well researched as other inventories that have been authored by Strong. The stability of the SII is well documented and reliability and validity studies suggest that the SII is well suited for career development counseling. The following reviews have been made of the previously published Strong-Campbell Interest Inventory: Crites (1978), Dolliver (1978), Johnson (1978), Lunneborg (1978), Anastasi (1988), and Aiken (1988).

The strength of the SII is the variety of data generated on the interpretive report. These data are useful in counseling and provide information that is usually not found on interest inventory profiles. In addition, the SII has a well-documented history, which increases confidence in using this instrument.

Interpreting the SII

The interpretation process proceeds from a review of the general occupational theme scores, which provide a general overview of interest patterns, to the increasingly specific basic interest scores, and finally to measures of interest for specific occupations. The SII profiles are structured around Holland's (1985) six occupational-modal-personal styles—realistic, investigative, artistic, social, enterprising, and conventional. Each of the six themes is reported by a standard score (mean = 50, S.D. = 10), indicating whether the interest level is considered very low, low, average, high, or very high.

The basic interest scales focus on subdivisions of the general occupation themes, subdivisions from which career groups or clusters of occupations can be derived. For example, the R-theme focuses on agriculture, nature, adventure, military activities, and mechanical activities. A standard score and norms are given for each scale.

Specific occupational scales are also grouped according to Holland's six themes. Standard scores and male and female norms are reported, indicating whether the subject's interests are very dissimilar, dissimilar, moderately dissimilar, mid-range, moderately similar, similar, or very similar, for each of the occupations.

Ten administrative indices are reported on the SII profile. Among these is an infrequent response index, which indicates whether the individual has marked a significant number of rare or uncommon responses. In this event, a negative score is reported and responses should be carefully checked. In some cases individuals may have become confused when filling out the answer sheet and answered the items in the wrong order. Other individuals may have purposely marked false choices. Still others may have unique interests.

The academic comfort scale indicates the degree to which the individual likes academic work, such as reading, writing, and doing research. This scale should be checked for individuals considering higher education as follows: B.A. students should have a mean score of 50, M.A. students 55, and Ph.D. students 60 on this scale. A comprehensive list of these scores for male and female occupations is in the manual.

The introversion–extroversion (IE) index is an indicator of the individual's preference for working with things or with people. This scale provides an index to preferences for people-oriented occupations or non–people-oriented occupations.

Another index reports the percentages of like (LP), indifferent (IP), and dislike (DP) responses for each section of the inventory. Unusual responses can be determined by comparing these percentages with those in the table provided in the test manual. These percentages provide important information for the counselor. For example, high percentages on dislike indicate that an individual may be strongly committed to a specific interest area; in other words, the individual has narrowed interests or likes to one or a few occupational areas. An individual with few like responses to occupational choices may also have intensely focused interests or that individual's interests may not have crystallized yet. The counselor will want to explore these possibilities by further analysis of responses to various items on the SII.

To make maximum use of the information on the SII profile, a systematic evaluation is recommended. For this purpose a SII summary evaluation form such as Table 6-1 can be devised. The counselor begins by checking the number of total responses. If there are fewer than 310, the results of the inventory should be considered questionable. Steps 2–5 concern the administrative indices and should be completed as outlined.

TABLE 6-1.
SII Summary Evaluation Form

Steps	
1	Responses—if less than 310, stop for checking
2	Infrequent responses (minus number)—check manual
3	ACS—B.A. mean score of 50, M.A. mean score of 55, Ph.D. mean score of 60
4	IE—considered extroverted if 40 or under, introverted if 60 or over

(continued)

TABLE 6-1. *(continued)*

Steps

5   LP, IP, DP (boundary 5–60)

Record section that is outside of limits and refer to page 90 of manual.

_____   _____   _____

6   Summary code for three highest General Occupational Themes and two examples of variation of theme.

_____   _____   _____

_____   _____   _____

_____   _____   _____

7   Record Basic Interest Scales shown as high and very high.

_____

_____

_____

8   Record Occupational Scales with scores from 45–55.

_____

_____

_____

_____

9   Record Occupational Scales with scores of 55 or higher.

_____

_____

_____

_____

The pattern, or the general occupational themes, should be reviewed next. This pattern is a reflection of the counselee's general occupational preferences or modal personal styles. An individual whose highest standard scores are 61 for C theme, 50 for I theme, and 45 for E theme has a summary code of CIE. This person's primary modal personal style (C) is conventional, which indicates a practical, rather conservative individual according to Holland's (1985) typology. The occupation associated with this style is general office work, such as that done by an accountant or credit manager. Information on the secondary modal personal style (I) and information on the overall pattern (CIE) also provide clues for the career counseling process.

The highest scores on the basic interest scales should also be carefully reviewed. Particular attention should be given to the career groups reported as high or very high. An interest in a career group or cluster may be the key to further exploration if a specific occupation cannot be identified.

The occupational scales provide specific information for a career search. A score of 45 or higher on an occupational scale indicates interests that are similar to those of individuals in that occupation. A score of 55 or higher indicates a very similar interest pattern. Scores of 45 and higher should be carefully reviewed as possible career choices.

Case of a College Freshman Undecided about a Career

Al, a second-semester freshman in college, told the career counselor that he needed help in determining his interests. He added that none of the college courses he had taken so far had stimulated him to consider a specific career. As a result he felt as though he were drifting. His father, successful in business, was putting pressure on Al to make up his mind. Al appeared to be serious about wanting to determine his interests for career considerations.

Counselor:	We will gladly administer and interpret an interest inventory for you. However, I want you to understand that the results of the inventory may not pinpoint a career for you to consider.
Al:	Oh! I thought it would tell me what I should do for the rest of my life.
Counselor:	Many students share your belief. They have high expectations of interest inventories and are disappointed when they get their results. Realistically, we can expect to find some occupations for you to explore further or an occupational group you may wish to investigate. I should add that we also often find that a student will simply have his or her interests confirmed by a test.
Al:	Okay, that's fair enough. I need some information to help me get started toward making a career decision.

The counselor continued with an explanation of the career decision-making process. After he was satisfied that Al understood that interest inventory results are to be used with other factors in career exploration, the counselor discussed the selection of an interest inventory. "The SII provides a comparison of your responses to responses of individuals in a number of career fields. With these results you can determine how similar your interests are to those of individuals who have made a commitment to a specific career. You will also be able to identify some of your general occupational interests and some of your basic interests." The counselor and Al selected the SII because it includes many careers that require a college degree and suggests many occupational groups for further exploration. Al's results from the SII were compiled as shown in Figure 6-1.

The counselor began the interpretation session with a review of the career decision process. He then presented Al with the profile of the results. He explained the occupational themes designated by certain letters: "The first is the R theme, which stands for realistic. Individuals who have high scores on this theme generally prefer to work with objects, machines, or tools. Examples are those in the skilled trades such as plumbers, electricians, and machine operators. Other examples are photographers and draftsmen. You have a low score for this theme." The counselor continued to explain each theme in a similar manner.

The counselor directed Al's attention to the summary code of his three highest general occupational themes. He emphasized the importance of considering combinations of interests as opposed to considering just one high interest area. In Al's case the AES summary code suggested an interest in occupations that involve art, writing, sales, and management and that are service oriented. The counselor suggested that consideration be given to different combinations of the summary code: EAS, SAE, and so on.

The counselor then went to the next part of the report and explained that the basic interest scales are also grouped according to one of the six themes. Al's highest scores were noted, and specific occupational scales were discussed. Finally, the counselor pointed out occupational scales with scores from 45 to 55. Several of the occupations seemed to interest Al.

The counselor suggested that they review the results of the SII by having Al summarize what he learned about himself: "I seem to be interested in artistic kinds of work. At least this was my highest general occupational theme. I also have an interest in enterprising activities

Steps

1   Responses - less than 310 - (stop for checking) **325**

2   Infrequent responses - (minus number) check manual *none*

3   ACS - (BA mean score of 50, MA mean score of 55, Ph.D. mean score of 60) **52**

4   IE - (considered extroverted if 40 or under, introverted if 60 or over) **31**

5   LP, IP, DP (boundary 5-60) *none*

Record section which is outside of limits and refer to Page 90 of manual.

_____   _____   _____

6   Summary code for three highest General Occupational Themes and two examples of variation of theme.

A	E	S
E	A	S
S	A	E

7   Record Basic Interest Scales as shown as high and very high.
- A - *art and writing*
- E - *merchandising, sales, business management*
- S - *social service*

8   Record Occupational Scales with scores from 45-55.
art teacher, photographer, interior decorator, life insurance agent

_____

9   Record Occupational Scales with scores of 55 and higher.
advertising executive, artist, sales manager

_____
_____
_____

FIGURE 6-1.
SII summary evaluation form for Al.

and socially related activities. I guess I like working with people to some extent, particularly influencing or persuading them. Specific occupations that interest me are advertising and sales work. I would like to explore the advertising and public relations occupations."

The counselor was satisfied with this summary, as Al was able to link the inventory results with potential career fields. The counselor encouraged Al to refer to the interest inventory results for other options if he was not satisfied with his career search.

KUDER OCCUPATIONAL INTEREST SURVEY (KOIS)

Kuder (1963) identified clusters of interest by administering questionnaires listing various activities to individuals employed in different occupational areas. Items that were highly correlated with one another were grouped together in descriptive scales. Groups of items that had lower correlations with one another were formed into nine clusters and designated as broad areas of interest. In this system a specific occupational interest is determined by common factors or traits found within a broad area.

Kuder developed four inventories as shown in Table 6-2. The most recent inventory, the KOIS, is illustrated here to provide an example of the use of the inventories for career counseling. The format of the inventories requires the individual to respond to triads of items by indicating the most liked and least liked activity. The following scales are used in the Kuder surveys: outdoor, mechanical, computation, scientific, persuasive, artistic, literary, musical, social service, and clerical. A list of specific occupations correlated with each scale is provided. None of the inventories has a time limit, but each can usually be taken in 30 to 40 minutes. The KOIS requires computer scoring.

TABLE 6-2.
Four Kuder Inventories

Preference Schedule or Interest Survey	Form	Target Population	Scoring
Kuder Preference Record—Vocational	CP and CM	High school students and adults	CP—Hand scored CM—Machine scored
Kuder Preference Record—Personal	AH	High school students and adults	Hand scored
Kuder General Interest Survey	E	Junior and senior high school students	Hand scored
Kuder Occupational Interest Survey	DD	Students in grades 9–12, college students, and adults	Computer scored

From the *Kuder Occupational Interest Survey*, Form DD, Interpretive Leaflet 1979, 1974, 1970, 1966, G. Frederic Kuder. Reprinted by permission of the publisher, CTB Macmillan/McGraw-Hill.

The KOIS DD/PC counselor's report form for females is shown in Figure 6-2. The first two columns report vocational interest estimates in percentiles with scores compared to females and males in rank order. Likewise, the second group of scores report occupational groups that are most similar and next most similar to the survey taker's interests. Comparisons of scores with other occupational groups are also presented. This is followed by correlations with the survey taker's interests and college major groups by male and female. Finally, a group of experimental scales are presented, which offer only tentative information and should be reviewed in the test manual.

On the first page of the report form, the verification (V) scale is used to determine whether the individual is sincere or capable of responding to the survey. A V score of 44 or less calls into question the validity of the scale scores. Questionable survey results may be caused by carelessness, faking, or poor reading ability. If the V score is below 44, the counselor should make a determination of the cause before continuing the interpretation. (Specific instructions for determining the cause of low scores are provided in the manual.)

```
                                              Counselor's Report


Kuder DD/PC Counselor's Report                        LARSEN

K U D E R    O C C U P A T I O N A L    I N T E R E S T    S U R V E Y

Survey-Taker  CAROLYN HOGGAN        Sex  FEMALE   Date  10/12/92
ID Number                          Numerical Data  4084223231


Building       TRIDENT NORTH       City            MONTEREY, CA


        Caution!  The survey-taker's interest patterns are very
                  unusual.  The profile may not be accurate.

        V-Score =  41

VOCATIONAL INTEREST ESTIMATES (Percentiles)

Compared to Females                Compared to Males

HIGH                               HIGH
    Literary             94            Literary              95
    Scientific           82            Artistic              87
AVERAGE                                Social Service        86
    Artistic             71            Scientific            76
    Mechanical           70         AVERAGE
    Social Service       61            Mechanical            27
    Persuasive           27         LOW
LOW                                    Persuasive            19
    Computational        18            Clerical              15
    Clerical             12            Computational         11
    Musical               3            Musical                3
    Outdoor               1            Outdoor                1


OCCUPATIONAL GROUPS (Correlations with Survey-Taker's interests)

These are the most similar:        Nutritionists, F          .42
                                   Physicians, F             .42
Lawyers, F               .52       Dentists, F               .41
Journalists, F           .50       Film/TV Prodrs/Directrs ,F .41
Audiologists/Spch Paths, F  .47    Ministers, M              .40
                                   Personnel Managers, F     .40
These are the next most similar:   Psychologists, M          .40


Insurance Agents, F      .45       The rest are listed in order of
Lawyers, M               .45       similarity:
Podiatrists, M           .45
Audiologists/Spch Paths, M  .44    Counselors, High School, F  .39
Psychologists, F         .44       Film/TV Prodrs/Directrs ,M  .39
Social Workers, F        .44       Optometrists, M           .39
Coll Sdt Personnel Wkrs, F  .43    Personnel Managers, M     .39
Journalists, M           .43       Police Officers, F        .39
Social Workers, M        .43       Real Estate Agents, F     .38
Librarians, M            .42       Bookstore Managers, F     .37
Ministers, F             .42       Counselors, High School, M  .37
```

FIGURE 6-2.
KOIS DD/PC counselor's report.
From the *Kuder Occupational Interest Survey*, Form DD, copyright 1993, 1979, 1974, 1970, 1966, G. Frederic Kuder. Reprinted by permission of the publisher, CTB Macmillan/McGraw-Hill.

Counselor's Report

Kuder DD/PC Counselor's Report   Page 2

Survey-Taker   CAROLYN HOGGAN   Sex FEMALE   Date 10/12/92
ID Number   Numerical Data 4084223231

Building   TRIDENT NORTH   City   MONTEREY, CA

OCCUPATIONAL GROUPS (cont.)

Interior Decorators, F	.37	Pharmacists, M	.26
Physical Therapists, F	.37	Science Teachers, HS, M	.25
Physicians, M	.37	Engineers, M	.24
Statisticians, M	.37	Auto Salespersons, M	.23
Interior Decorators, M	.36	Beauticians, F	.23
Librarians, F	.36	Insurance Agents, M	.23
Religious Educ Directrs, F	.36	Math Teachers, High Sch, F	.23
Architects, M	.35	Meteorologists, M	.23
Dental Assistants, F	.35	Bookkeepers, F	.22
Dietitians, F	.35	Buyers, M	.22
Occupational Therapists, F	.35	Plant Nursery Workers, M	.22
Physical Therapists, M	.35	Bank Clerks, F	.21
Accountants/CPAs, F	.34	Florists, M	.21
Computer Programmers, F	.34	Office Clerks, F	.20
Nurses, M	.34	TV Repairers, M	.20
Travel Agents, M	.34	Police Officers, M	.19
Architects, F	.33	Extension Agents, M	.18
Bankers, F	.33	Math Teachers, High Sch, M	.18
Bookstore Managers, M	.33	Veterinarians, M	.18
Engineers, F	.33	Bankers, M	.16
Pharmaceutical Sales, M	.33	Dept Store Salespersons, F	.16
Pharmacists, F	.33	Foresters, M	.15
Photographers, M	.33	Postal Clerks, M	.14
Radio Station Managers, M	.33	Bookkeepers, M	.13
X-ray Technicians, F	.33	Supervisors, Industrial, M	.13
Accountants/CPAs, M	.32	Farmers, M	.12
Mathematicians, M	.32	Plumbing Contractors, M	.11
Nurses, F	.32	Building Contractors, M	.10
Chemists, M	.31	Painters, House, M	.08
Elementary Sch Teachers, F	.31	Bricklayers, M	.07
Elementary Sch Teachers, M	.31	Electricians, M	.07
Extension Agents, F	.31	Plumbers, M	.07
School Superintendents, M	.31	Truck Drivers, M	.07
Science Teachers, HS, F	.31	Welders, M	.05
Florists, F	.30	Machinists, M	.04
Secretaries, F	.30	Auto Mechanics, M	.03
Computer Programmers, M	.29	Carpenters, M	.03
Dentists, M	.29		
Real Estate Agents, M	.28		
Veterinarians, F	.28		
X-ray Technicians, M	.28		
Clothiers, Retail, M	.27		
Printers, M	.27		

FIGURE 6-2. *(continued)*

Kuder DD/PC Counselor's Report   Page   3

Survey-Taker   CAROLYN HOGGAN   Sex FEMALE   Date 10/12/92
ID Number   Numerical Data 4084223231

Building   TRIDENT NORTH   City   MONTEREY, CA

COLLEGE MAJOR GROUPS (Correlations with Survey-Taker's interests)

These are the most similar: Art and Art Education, M   .31
                                     Physical Education, F   .31
Political Science, F   .48   Mathematics, F   .30
Political Science, M   .47   Service Academy Cadet, M   .30
English, F   .46   Engineering, F   .29
English, M   .46   Music and Music Educ, M   .29
History, M   .46   Physical Education, M   .29
History, F   .45   Architecture, M   .27
Psychology, F   .42   Physical Science, M   .27
Psychology, M   .42   Business Administration, F   .26
                                     Business Administration, M   .26
These are the next most similar: Mathematics, M   .26
                                     Engineering, M   .20
Elementary Education, F   .41   Forestry, M   .16
Foreign Language, M   .41   Animal Science, M   .13
Drama, F   .40   Agriculture, M   .12
Foreign Language, F   .40
Sociology, M   .40
Sociology, F   .39
Nursing, F   .38
Elementary Education, M   .36
Health Professions, F   .36
Home Econonics Educ, F   .36
Premed/Pharmacy/Dentist, M   .36

The rest are listed in order of
similarity:

Biological Sciences, F   .35
Biological Sciences, M   .34
Economics, M   .34
Art and Art Education, F   .33
Music and Music Educ, F   .32

Experimental Scales:

Women   .35   Men   .23
Women (best impression)   .53   Men (best impression)   .51

Sons   .22   Daughters   .39
Fathers of Sons   .28   Mothers of Daughters   .34

FIGURE 6-2. (continued)

The relationship of the individual's responses to the response patterns of a given occupational group is determined by a special correlation technique. Over three-fourths of the individuals in the 30 occupational groups compiled by Kuder scored .45 or over on the items for their groups. Thus, a score of .45 or more indicates an occupational scale that should be considered in a career search. A word of caution: Some high school students may score low on the occupational scales because of their lack of experience in and awareness of the world of work. Conversely, because of their current academic experiences, some high school students may score high on college major scales.

Occasionally, most coefficients on a profile are below .31. These low scores may be a consequence of immaturity and a lack of experience and may thus indicate interests have not been crystallized. Low scorers may also have misunderstood the directions or may simply have marked responses in a careless, random manner. At any rate, if only a few coefficients reach .32–.39, caution should be used in the interpretation of the scores (Kuder, 1979).

Scores on opposite-sex scales should be given consideration especially by females when female norm scales are not available. Significantly high scores reported for females on male norms indicate possible areas to consider in the career search. Broad patterns should also be considered, as many individuals have not crystallized their interests.

A survey taker's report, primarily in narrative form, presents an explanation of interest areas with a profile showing ten interest scales by percentiles and by low, average, or high as shown in Figure 6-3.

Next, occupational groups that are most similar and next most similar to the individual's interest patterns are presented with a narrative explanation of how the individual may use the results. Such a report is shown in Figure 6-4.

Finally, college major scales are presented with an explanation of options to follow in the career decision-making process. In the final part of the report several sources of more information on careers and specific occupations are provided.

Two types of reliability are reported in the KOIS manual. Test-retest reliabilities (two-week interval) for students in grade 12 and in college had stable coefficients in that the median coefficient was .90. Other test-retest studies involving male high school seniors and female college seniors yielded coefficients in the .90s. One long-term study (approximately three years) of engineering students yielded a test-retest coefficient of .89. Concurrent validity was established by studying errors of classification of six validation groups. The findings suggested that the KOIS is able to discriminate between various criterion groups (W. B. Walsh, 1972). There is a need for more data on the predictive validity of this instrument.

The KOIS interpretive material is straightforward and easily used. The separation of occupational scales and college major scales adds to the flexibility and usefulness of this inventory. The KOIS has been reviewed by Brown (1982), Anastasi (1988), Aiken (1988), Herr (1989), and Tenopyr (1989).

Case of a High School Senior Rebelling against Parental Expectations

Ann, a high school senior, had been the topic of conversation during many coffee breaks in the teachers' lounge at City High School. The major concern of the teachers was her complete lack of interest in academic courses. Yet Ann's parents were well educated and were prominent members of the art and music groups in the city. Ann's grades reflected her lack of interest, and she had successfully resisted receiving any counseling assistance. Her parents finally convinced her to see the school counselor. As expected, Ann approached the counselor in a casual manner and quickly admitted that the visit was her parents' idea. The counselor spent several sessions with Ann attempting to get her to respond positively. Ann responded with enthusiasm only when the counselor brought up the subject of future plans.

The counselor decided that she might be able to win Ann's confidence through career exploration. Ann had taken the KOIS during her junior year. A review of the results revealed that only a few of the coefficients reached .36 and .39. The counselor remembered that the manual mentioned that such scores should be used with caution. However, she decided to discuss the results with Ann. Ann said, "I didn't care about that test. What's the use of taking an interest inventory when you don't have many choices in the first place?"

Kuder DD/PC Survey-Taker's Report   Page   2

Survey-Taker   CAROLYN HOGGAN   Sex FEMALE   Date 10/12/92
ID Number   Numerical Data 4084223231

Building   TRIDENT NORTH   City   MONTEREY, CA

INTEREST AREAS

Vocational interests can be divided into different types.
The Survey analyzes your attraction to each of ten types of
interests. It also arranges them in rank order to reflect
your personal priorities. Your interest areas are useful in
identifying general groups of occupations or groups of
hobbies and leisure activities that might be attractive to
you.

You may feel that you already know your interests. But you
probably do not know how strong they are compared with other
people's interests in the same activities.

As you look over your report, remember that your results are
estimates based on your current interests. New experiences
can sometimes change how important an interest is to you.
If, after such experiences, you took the Survey again, it
could show your interests in a somewhat different order.

Percentiles for Female Survey-Takers

Interest Area		Low	Average	High
Literary	94	XXXXXXXXXXXXX	XXXXXXXXXXX	XXXXXXX
Scientific	82	XXXXXXXXXXXXX	XXXXXXXXXXX	XX
Artistic	71	XXXXXXXXXXXXX	XXXXXXXXXX	
Mechanical	70	XXXXXXXXXXXXX	XXXXXXXXXX	
Social Service	61	XXXXXXXXXXXXX	XXXXXXXX	
Persuasive	27	XXXXXXXXXXXXXX		
Computational	18	XXXXXXXXXXX		
Clerical	12	XXXXXXXXXX		
Musical	3	XXXX		
Outdoor	1	X		

Here is what each of the ten types of interests means.

Literary--Reading and writing
Scientific--Solving problems and discovering facts
Artistic--Visually creative work involving design, color,
          form, and materials
Mechanical--Using machines and tools
Social Service--Helping people
Persuasive--Meeting and dealing with people, promoting
          projects, selling things and ideas
Computational--Working with numbers
Clerical--Working with precision and accuracy

FIGURE 6-3.
KOIS DD/PC survey taker's report.
From the *Kuder Occupational Interest Survey,* Form DD, copyright 1993, 1979, 1974, 1970, 1966, G. Frederic Kuder.
Reprinted by permission of the publisher, CTB Macmillan/McGraw-Hill.

```
Kuder DD/PC Survey-Taker's Report                    Page    3

Survey-Taker  CAROLYN HOGGAN       Sex  FEMALE   Date  10/12/92
ID Number                          Numerical Data  4084223231

Building      TRIDENT NORTH        City           MONTEREY, CA


    Musical--Making or listening to music
    Outdoor--Being outside, working with plants or animals

    Here is how your interests compare with Males

    Percentiles for Male Survey-Takers
    Interest Area       |   Low      | Average    |  High
                        |            |            |
    ----------------------------------------------------------
    Literary         95 |XXXXXXXXXXXXX|XXXXXXXXXXX|XXXXXXXX
    Artistic         87 |XXXXXXXXXXXXX|XXXXXXXXXXX|XXXX
    Social Service   86 |XXXXXXXXXXXXX|XXXXXXXXXXX|XXX
    Scientific       76 |XXXXXXXXXXXXXXXXXXXXXXXXXXX
    Mechanical       27 |XXXXXXXXXXXXXX
    Persuasive       19 |XXXXXXXXXXXXX
    Clerical         15 |XXXXXXXXXXX
    Computational    11 |XXXXXXXXXX
    Musical           3 |XXXX
    Outdoor           1 |X
```

FIGURE 6-3. (continued)

```
OCCUPATIONS

The KOIS has been given to groups of people in many different
occupations.  These people are experienced in and satisfied
with their work.  Their typical patterns of preferences have
been compared with yours.  In your report, the comparisons
are shown in the order of their similarity to your
interests--from the most similar to the least similar.


If you have interests that are compatible with those of
people in certain occupations, you may be satisfied working
in one of those occupations or in a related one.

Some occupations have a high proportion of men or women in
them.  For instance, there are more women in the occupation
of secretary or dietitian.  There are more men in the
occupation of carpenter or optometrist.  Your similarities
to groups of women and men in various occupational groups
are shown here.


Look over the occupations that this report shows are the
most similar to your activity preferences.  Can you see a
pattern in them?  For example, are they mostly in science or
medical work?  Maybe they focus on business occupations.  Are
```

FIGURE 6-4.
KOIS DD/PC survey taker's report by occupations.
From the *Kuder Occupational Interest Survey*, Form DD, copyright 1993, 1979, 1974, 1970, 1966, G. Frederic Kuder. Reprinted by permission of the publisher, CTB Macmillan/McGraw-Hill.

they concerned with helping others? Is art high on the list?
How much schooling do they require?

You might want to make up one or two phrases that describe
your highest similarities, like "technical sales" or "health
service careers."

You may find that you have more than one pattern among the
occupations in which interests most similar to yours are
found. This is because people usually have the potential to
be happy in more than one field of work. If you have more
than one pattern of most similar occupations, you may select
the one that uses abilities and skills you possess.

Conversely, you may find that you rank high on one of the
interests, but that you are not similar to people you know
who work in related occupations. For example, Science may be
your highest vocational interest. Yet you may rank
relatively low on the occupation of physician. How could
this happen? It could be that all your interests focus on
science, while physicians have more varied interests.

Whenever your interest patterns and most similar occupations
don't seem to agree, you need to know more about the
occupations.

The following occupational groups have interest patterns that
are most similar to yours:

Lawyers, F   Audiologists/Spch Paths, F
Journalists, F

These occupations are next most similar:

Insurance Agents, F	Librarians, M
Lawyers, M	Ministers, F
Podiatrists, M	Nutritionists, F
Audiologists/Spch Paths, M	Physicians, F
Psychologists, F	Dentists, F
Social Workers, F	Film/TV Prodrs/Directrs ,F
Coll Sdt Personnel Wkrs, F	Ministers, M
Journalists, M	Personnel Managers, F
Social Workers, M	Psychologists, M

FIGURE 6-4. *(continued)*

The counselor asked Ann to explain her remarks. Ann indicated that she had marked the
inventory haphazardly without even reading some of the options. When the counselor asked her
to explain her statements about not having many choices, Ann was rather hesitant. After a brief
pause she responded "Nobody cares or understands, so why bother?" Ann eventually revealed
that she felt hemmed in and unable to identify with her parents' expectations. She expressed a
negative view of their lifestyle and emphasized that she wanted something different. She felt her
parents were unaccepting of her needs and interests. Ann summed up her feelings: "So what's
the use of saying what I want?"

In the sessions that followed the counselor encouraged Ann to express her interests and individuality. Nevertheless, Ann remained confused about a career. Ann agreed to retake the KOIS but with a changed attitude and a different approach to responding to the choices.

When the counselor received the results of the KOIS, she began by observing the V score. Because that score was well above .44, the scores were considered valid. Next, she reviewed Ann's high scores.

Ann seemed eager to discuss the results when she arrived for the next counseling session. The counselor cautioned Ann that these scores would not solve all her problems but would provide vital information that could be used for career exploration. The counselor then explained the scores, and Ann pointed out those above .45. Although Ann seemed interested in the results of the KOIS, this was the first time she had given serious thought to exploring a career on her own, and she needed reinforcement by the counselor. She expressed an interest in working with people in some capacity but also recognized that her knowledge of careers and working environments was extremely limited. She agreed to become a part of a career decision-making group, which she entered armed with several occupational considerations provided by the KOIS. The counselor was pleased with Ann's progress, particularly in expressing her individual needs and interests.

SELF-DIRECTED SEARCH (SDS)

The SDS is based on Holland's (1985) theory of career development. It can be self-administered, self-scored, and self-interpreted. Individuals begin by making a list of occupational aspirations, then indicate likes or dislikes for certain activities. Next they indicate activities that they can perform well or competently and identify occupations that appeal to or interest them. Finally, they evaluate themselves on 12 different traits based on previous experience. Individuals calculate their scores according to easily understood directions and subsequently record the three highest scores in order. The three highest scores are determined by adding scores of responses to most liked activities, activities done most competently, interest in occupations, and self-estimates of traits. These scores are organized to reveal a summary code of three letters representing the personality styles in Holland's typology—realistic, investigative, artistic, social, enterprising, and conventional.

The following information can be obtained for each summary code: primary modal personal style, primary occupational environment, specific occupations, and DOT numbers of specific occupations (from Viernstein, 1972) for cross-reference. Individuals are then able to compare their occupational codes to occupational aspirations and to codes for 495 occupations provided in *The Occupations Finder* (Holland, 1987a). A portion of the information found in *The Occupations Finder* is shown in Figure 6-5.

If, for example, an individual's summary code is RSC, the occupations listed under this code are primary occupations for further exploration. In the Holland system the more dominant the primary modal personal style, the greater the likelihood of satisfaction in the corresponding work environment (Holland, 1985). In order to investigate other career possibilities, the individual is required to list related summary codes. In the above example, different combinations of the summary code RSC should be explored: SRC, SCR, CRS, CSR, and RCS.

Internal consistency was calculated by KR-20 and yielded coefficients ranging from .67 to .94 from samples of 2000 to 6000 college freshmen. Of that group, coefficients for men ranged from .63 to .88 and for women from .53 to .85. Test-retest reliabilities (3–4 week intervals) for high school students yielded a median coefficient of .81 for boys and a median coefficient of .83 for girls. A sample of 65 college freshmen yielded test-retest reliability coefficients ranging from .60 to .84 over a seven- to ten-month interval. There appears to be sufficient evidence of content validity from item content. A number of studies supporting the predictive validity of the SDS have been compiled and are reported in the SDS manual (Holland, 1987b).

REALISTIC OCCUPATIONS (CONTINUED)

CODE: RSE (cont.)	ED	CODE: RCI (cont.)	ED
Waiter/Waitress (311.677-010)	3	Instrument Mechanic (710.281-026)	4
Parking-Lot Attendant (915.473-010)	2	Motion-Picture Projectionist	
Soda Clerk (319.474-010)	2	(960.362-010)	4
Warehouse Worker (922.687-058)	1	Office-Machine Servicer (633.281-018)	4
		Signal-Tower Operator (Railroad Trans)	
CODE: RSC	**ED**	(910.362-010)	4
Exterminator (389.684-010)	3	Supervisor, Painting (840.131-010)	3
Elevator Operator (388.663-010)	2	Surveyor Helper (869.567-010)	3
Stock Clerk (222.387-058)	2		
Kitchen Helper (318.687-010)	1	**CODE: RCS**	**ED**
		Furrier (783.261-010)	4
CODE: RSI	**ED**	Tailor (785.261-010)	4
Vocational Agriculture Teacher		Telephone Repairer (822.281-022)	4
(091.227-010)	5	Bus Driver (913.463-010)	3
Appliance Repairer (637.261-018)	4	Sewage-Plant Operator (955.362-010)	3
Weaver (683.682-038)	3	Blaster (859.261-010)	3
Knitter (685.665-014)	2	Bricklayer (861.381-018)	3
		Cement Mason (844.364-010)	3
CODE: REC	**ED**	Dressmaker (785.361-010)	3
Supervisor, Natural-Gas Plant		Furnace Installer (862.361-010)	3
(542.130-010)	4	Garment Cutter (781.584-014)	3
		Mail Carrier (230.367-010)	3
CODE: REI	**ED**	Meter Reader (209.567-010)	3
Ship Pilot (197.133-026)	4	Miner (939.281-010)	3
Shop Supervisor (638.131-026)	4	Paperhanger (841.381-010)	3
Supervisor, Paper Machine		Plasterer (842.361-018)	3
(539.132-010)	4	Sailor (911.687-030)	3
		Tile Setter (861.381-054)	3
CODE: RES	**ED**	Industrial-Truck Operator	
Fish and Game Warden (379.167-010)	5	(921.683-050)	2
Cattle Rancher (410.161-018)	4	Spinner (682.685-010)	2
Locomotive Engineer (910.363-014)	4		
Crater (920.484-010)	3	**CODE: RCE**	**ED**
Braker, Passenger Train		Crane Operator (921.663-010)	3
(910.364-010)	3	Lumber Inspector (669.587-010)	3
Construction Worker (869.664-014)	3	Tractor Operator (929.683-014)	3
Fisher (442.684-010)	2	Tractor-Trailer-Truck Driver	
Track Layer (s869.687-026)	2	(904.383-010)	3
		Truck Driver, Light (906.683-022)	3
CODE: RCI	**ED**	Fork-Lift Truck Operator	
Surveyor, Geodetic (018.167-038)	5	(921.683-050)	2
Carpenter (860.381-022)	4		

FIGURE 6-5.

Portion of *The Occupations Finder.*

From *The Occupations Finder* for use with *The Self-Directed Search* by John L. Holland, copyright © 1978. Consulting Psychologists Press, Inc. Reprinted by permission.

The SDS is designed to furnish the individual with a model of systematic career exploration. Although the SDS can be self-interpreted, the individual should be stimulated to seek further career guidance. Many individuals will want to clarify their interests with a counselor who can provide additional information for career decision making. The SDS provides results that can be easily incorporated into group and individual career counseling programs.

One of the major criticisms of the SDS centers around a need for monitoring the self-scoring of the instrument. Also, individuals often need assistance in using *The Occupations Finder.* Finally, more data are needed and should be reported in the manual on the use of the SDS for women, minority groups, and adults. Extensive reviews of the SDS include those by Crites (1982), Anastasi (1988), and Aiken (1988).

Holland is to be commended for encouraging people to consider their careers by using a straightforward format. The popularity of the SDS demonstrates the need for this type of format. His theoretical approach to personality development as a primary consideration in career decision making has greatly influenced methods for presenting results on a number of widely used interest inventories.

Case of a Group Program in a Community College

A community college counseling center regularly offered seminars in career exploration. A major component of the program involved interest identification. In one all-male group, the SDS was administered with the counselor monitoring the scoring.

After each student had recorded his SDS code, the counselor explained Holland's six modal personal styles and their corresponding codes, then grouped students according to their personal styles. Using *The Occupations Finder,* each group was assigned the responsibility of writing and presenting at the next session a description of its primary modal personal style and of one or more specific occupations that matched this style.

In the next counseling session, the counselor explained how to use *The Occupations Finder* for locating specific occupations by summary codes. The counselor noted that DOT codes as well as educational levels were listed for each of the summary codes. When the counselor was sure that everyone understood how to use the booklet, he made this assignment: "Each of you is to use the career resource center library and write a description of two more occupations under your summary code using our career planning notes to record your comments. Bring these completed forms with you to our next session." Figure 6-6 gives examples for draftsman (RIE) and pharmacist (IES).

During the next group meeting the counselor encouraged members to relate problems encountered with locating careers according to their summary codes and to ask questions concerning their career exploration. Each member was encouraged to investigate other combinations of his SDS code. For example, the counselor suggested that the individual who made the report on drafting, RIE, investigate occupations under IRE, IER, and other combinations. Each member was requested to share his career planning notes with other members in his group. All group members were invited for individual counseling sessions and were encouraged to evaluate other occupations they were considering, including an evaluation of the educational/training requirements and potential for employment.

HARRINGTON/O'SHEA SYSTEMS FOR CAREER DECISION MAKING—REVISED (CDM-R)

The CDM-R (Harrington & O'Shea, 1992) can also be self-administered and self-interpreted. Holland's (1985) theory of career development is the framework on which the system has been constructed. Five of Holland's six occupational types have been given different names: realistic has been changed to crafts, investigative has been changed to scientific, artistic has been changed to the arts, social remains as is, enterprising has been changed to business, and conventional has been changed to clerical (Harrington & O'Shea, 1992). Care was taken to make all items in the system applicable to both men and women. The results are reported independently of sex.

The format requires the individual to list occupational preferences, choose favorite school subjects, indicate future educational plans, choose four job values from a list, estimate four strongest abilities, and indicate interests and activities by responding with "like," "can't make up my mind," or "dislike." See Figure 6-7 on pages 75–77.

Coefficients of internal consistency for the six interest scales for high school and college males ranged from .86 to .90 and for females from .84 to .90. Test-retest reliability coefficients (30-day interval) for high school students ranged from .75 to .88 for males and from .78 to .90 for females. Test-retest reliability coefficients (30-day interval) for graduate students in social science ranged from .76 to .94 for males and from .78 to .88 for females. These measures of reliability appear to be sufficient, although the number of cases (24–75) was small.

The authors have accumulated impressive evidence of construct and concurrent validity primarily by comparing the CDM-R scales with corresponding SCII and SDS scales. Predictive validity is not attempted because the authors suggest that the CDM-R is designed for self-exploration, not for predicting the occupation an individual will enter. For further evaluation of this instrument refer to the reviews by Willis (1982) and Droege (1984).

1. Occupation _Draftsman_
2. Source of Information _Encyclopedia of Career and Vocational Guidance, Vol II_
3. Educational Requirements _Some college and technical training_
4. Personal Requirements _Good hand-eye, visual-motor coordination. Be able to work with detailed plans and lay-out sketches. Be able to visualize objects in three-dimensional form._
5. Salary Range _$10,000 to $15,000_
6. Outlook _Favorable although employment is affected by general business year._
7. Other Notes _Conditions of work are good, that is, usually work is well-lighted, air-conditioned buildings._

1. Occupation _Pharmacist_
2. Source of Information _Opportunities in Pharmacy Careers_
3. Educational Requirements _5 years of college, 4 years of college and 1 year in pharmacy._
4. Personal Requirements _Be good in sciences, particularly in chemistry. Be willing to keep precise records and work with precise measures._
5. Salary Range _$12,000 to $20,000 and up_
6. Outlook _Good work available with firms, drug chains, or on your own._
7. Other Notes _Pharmacists usually work long hours and are respected in the community._

FIGURE 6.6.
Career planning notes completed by community college students.

The CDM-R provides a comprehensive model for career decision-making. It can best be used for those in junior high school and older subjects (including adults). Minority group norms are available, and the authors claim the test has no sex bias. Although scores can be self-interpreted, the authors recommend seeing a professional for continuation of career planning. Again, the major purpose of the CDM-R is to provide data that will encourage self-exploration in the career decision process.

Learning About the Career Areas

Each job on the following pages is listed with number and letter codes.
This page tells you what the numbers and letters mean.

EXAMPLE

JOB GROUP	TYPICAL JOBS
	Plants and Animals
	Training: APP/OJT
Manual	Animal Caretaker E - 410
	Farm Hand P - 421
	Fisher F - 441

Training

This tells you the *minimum* training usually required for the job.

APP/OJT
You learn by an apprenticeship or on-the-job training.

V/T
You are trained in a vocational or technical school or junior college.

C
You need a four-year college degree or more.

Job Opportunities

Each job listed on the following pages has a letter beside it. This letter tells you about the opportunities for that job. For example E (Excellent) means many jobs should be available.

E – means Excellent

G – means Good

F – means Fair

P – means Poor

NA – means Information Not Available

Dictionary of Occupational Titles

The 3-digit number after each job is from the *Dictionary of Occupational Titles.*

You can add to your job list by using these numbers to find similar jobs in the *Dictionary.*

FIGURE 6-7.
The Harrington/O'Shea Systems for Career Decision Making—Revised.
From the *Career Decision-Making System Revised,* 1992, by T. G. Harrington and A. J. O'Shea. Published by American Guidance Service, Circle Pines, Minn., Level 1 Hand-Scored Booklet, p. 9, 12–13, 18–19. Reprinted by permission.

NON-SEXIST VOCATIONAL CARD SORT (NSVCS)

One promising method of exploring women's interests is the NSVCS, developed by Dewey (1974). This instrument was derived from a version of the Tyler vocational card sort method (Tyler, 1961), modified by Dolliver (1967). The NSVCS is described as a nonsexist method in that

Medical-Dental

Medical-Dental Training: C for all Medical-Dental		Health Specialties	
		Audiologist	E-076
		Chiropractor	F-079
		Optometrist	G-079
Dentistry		Physical Therapist	E-076
Dentist	F-072	Speech Pathologist	E-076
Orthodontist	F-072		

Medicine		**Veterinary Medicine**		SCHOOL SUBJECTS	JOB VALUES	ABILITIES
Anesthesiologist	G-070	Veterinarian	G-073	Agriculture	Creativity	Language
Cardiologist	G-070			English	Good salary	Leadership
General Practitioner	E-070			Math	High achievement	Manual
Obstetrician	G-070			Science	Independence	Math
Pathologist	F-070				Job security	Mechanical
Pediatrician	G-070				Leadership	Scientific
Podiatrist	E-079				Respect	Social
Psychiatrist	G-070				Variety	Space Relations
Radiologist	F-070				Work with mind	
					Work with people	

FIGURE 6-7. (continued)

the same occupational options are presented to both sexes, occupational titles have been neutralized (salesperson rather than salesman), and sex-role biases are confronted and discussed. The NSVCS consists of 76 3×5 cards containing occupational titles derived from male and female forms of the SVIB and KOIS. Each occupation is coded according to Holland's classification system as discussed earlier.

Administration of the NSVCS has four steps. First, the individual sorts the cards into three piles: "would not choose," "in question," and "might choose." Second, the individual then cites reasons for placing occupations in the other two categories. Third, the individual selects and rank orders ten occupations based on their personal appeal, fantasy of associated lifestyle, and perceptions of associates on the job. The counselor encourages the individual to also consider such factors as values and abilities. Fourth, the individual and the counselor discuss the remarks recorded in earlier sessions, and the individual describes perceptions of certain occupations. During this time women are encouraged to discuss sex-role biases associated with occupations and to clarify their own positions in regard to sex-role stereotyping.

Dewey suggests that the NSVCS encourages women to form new self-perceptions and attitudes about themselves and to confront the issue of sex-role stereotyping in career decision making. Although she does not claim that these procedures and techniques will completely solve the problem of sex-role stereotyping, they do provide women with the opportunity to enhance their career potential.

The NSVCS and other card-sort programs are viable alternatives to standardized interest inventories for women. After comparing the impact of the SCII and the NCVCS, Cooper (1976) concludes that the NSVCS is more effective than the SCII for encouraging career exploration

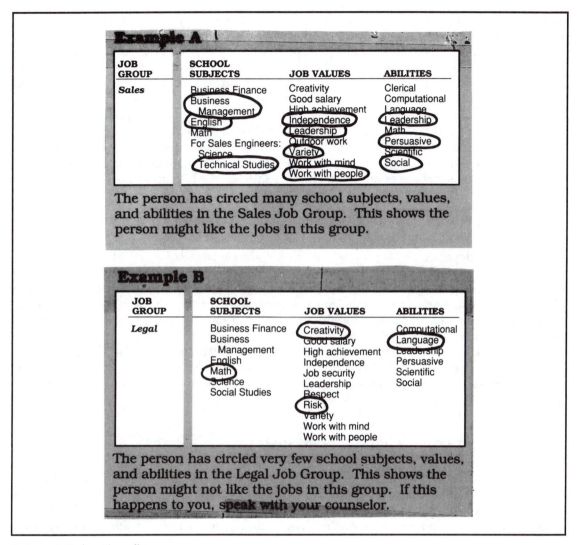

FIGURE 6-7. (*continued*)

among women. Dolliver (1982) suggests that a major advantage of the card sort is that client attitudes and self-perception are elicited during the sorting process. This process encourages women to confront the issues of sex-bias and sex-role stereotyping in the career decision-making process.

Case of a Woman Dissatisfied with Secretarial Work

Jackie, a 23-year old woman, was employed as a secretary even though she had a B.A. in psychology. She was considering enrolling in graduate school as a way of escaping the monotony of her low-paying job. After administering the NSVCS, the counselor noted several themes: "I am depressed; I feel wasted and angry. I want to be involved in a kind of work which is socially relevant but do not want to work directly with people. I want to be able to express my creativity and to have the freedom to choose the directions I develop toward. While I want autonomy, I am really afraid of being in a leadership position with a lot of responsibility."

Because the counselor was familiar with this last fear—having a lot of responsibility—she pointed out to Jackie that many women lower their vocational aspirations as a result of this fear. The session that followed dealt with how easy it was for Jackie to accept the limits that she had internalized as a result of the female socialization process without ever testing them out for herself. She told of an experience in adolescence that fit this theme. She had wanted to run for student government president in her high school but had been encouraged by her advisor, her mother, and female friends to seek the vice-presidency instead. She recalled other times when she had set goals for herself that others had sabotaged by redirecting her to a different goal. The counselor acknowledged Jackie's anger and resentment and pointed out that women are taught in many subtle ways that they function best in supportive, nurturing, or secondary roles.

One field Jackie chose to explore further was parapsychology, a field that both challenged and excited her. She had given up her interest in it before in response to her parents' notion that it was weird. Through the NSVCS experience, Jackie began to get some notion of how she could separate her own feelings, values, and experiences from those of her family and friends. She was thus able to begin the process of redirecting her energy toward fulfilling her own needs.[1]

OCC-U-SORT

The Occ-U-Sort developed by Jones (1981) is another good example of a currently used card sort. This instrument is designed to encourage career exploration by stimulating thinking about motives for making occupational choices. The reasons for not choosing certain occupations are discussed as well as the reasons for making selections. The cards may be used by eighth graders through adults. On the front side of each card is printed the occupational title, DOT number, General Educational Level, and a two-letter Holland occupational code. On the back side the occupational description is given along with card identification material. A self-guided booklet may be used, encouraging the individual to write reasons for choosing and not choosing occupations. One of the distinct advantages suggested by the author is the sex-fairness of this approach in career decision making.

SUGGESTIONS FOR CAREER DEVELOPMENT

Many of the following suggestions for fostering the career development of students and adults can be modified and used interchangeably to meet the needs of both groups. These suggestions should not be considered exhaustive of all possibilities of using assessment results to enhance career development but rather as examples from which exercises can be developed to meet local needs and needs of other groups.

For Schools:
- Ask students to identify interests as components of personal uniqueness. Share the results with others.
- Ask students to use interest results to match their personal goals and needs. Summarize in a paragraph or verbally.
- Ask students to identify and compare interest results with selected occupations. Share in groups.
- Ask students to compare interest results with achievement scores. Discuss results.
- Ask students to compare interest results with aptitude scores. Write about findings.
- Ask students to link interests to a variety of occupations. Share in group discussions.
- Ask students to develop a list of on-site community visits from their interest inventory results. Share their findings.
- Ask students to relate how different interests among individuals must be respected to maintain positive peer relationships.
- Ask students to discuss how interests influence career behavior patterns.
- Ask students to link occupational interests to academic interests.

[1]Adapted from the *Non-Sexist Vocational Card Sort*, by C. R. Dewey. Copyright © 1976 by Cindy Rice Dewey. Reprinted by permission.

For Adults:

- Ask adults to give examples of how interest inventory results can verify and reinforce self-concepts.
- Ask adults to give examples of how interests can influence adjustments, adaptations, and socialization in work environments.
- Ask adults to discuss how interests influence career and life goals.
- Ask adults to discuss how interests are related to learning and leisure.
- Ask adults to discuss how some interests have remained the same over the life span and others have changed.
- Ask adults to discuss how interests influence relationships with peer affiliates in the work place.
- Ask adults to discuss how interests have influenced career decision making. Use current inventory results as an example.

OTHER INTEREST INVENTORIES

The following are examples of other interest inventories currently being used. This list is far from complete, as a considerable number of interest inventories are published today. Some measure general interests, whereas others measure interests in specific occupational fields.

Ohio Vocational Interest Survey. This survey is for students in grades 8–12. Testing time is between 60 and 90 minutes. The 24 interest scales are related to people, data, and things. This survey is designed primarily to measure general interests.

Brainard Occupational Preference Inventory. This inventory is designed for use in grades 8–12. Testing time is approximately 30 minutes. Scores are expressed in percentiles for men and women. Scores yield individual preference for six broad fields: commercial, mechanical, professional, aesthetic, scientific, agriculture (men only), and personal service (women only). These measured preferences provide guidelines for career exploration.

Occupational Aptitude Survey and Interest Schedule (OASIS)—Interest Schedule. This instrument is designed to measure 12 interests areas: Artistic, Scientific, Nature, Protective, Mechanical, Industrial, Business Detail, Selling, Accommodating, Humanitarian, Leading-Influencing, and Physical Performing. It is untimed but most students finish the inventory in 30 minutes. Norms for junior and senior high school students are available by male and female and combined sex. Scores expressed in percentiles and stanines are to be used for vocational exploration and career development.

California Occupational Preference System. The target population for this inventory is middle school, high school, college, and adults. Reported scores are raw scores and percentiles for science, consumer economics, outdoor, business, clerical communications, arts, service, and technology. Scoring can be done on site or by computer.

Jackson Vocational Interest Inventory. This inventory is designed to assist high school and college students and adults with educational and career planning. Scores are reported by raw score, standard scores, and percentiles by 34 basic interest scales and 10 general occupational themes. It also compares the individual's score to college and university student groups by 13 major areas such as engineering, education, and liberal arts. It can be hand or machine scored, and a computerized extended report is available.

Career Assessment Inventory. This computer-scored inventory can be administered in 45 minutes. It is for individuals 15 years and older. There are three types of scales provided. One is a general occupational theme scale providing a measure of an individual's orientation to work. Basic attitude scales provide measures of interest and their relationship to specific careers. This inventory is designed to be used primarily with individuals who are not planning on going to college.

Minnesota Vocational Interest Inventory. This inventory is designed for men 15 years and older. There are 21 occupational scales and 9 general interest scales. Standard T scores (mean = 50, S.D. = 10) are reported. This inventory is useful for measuring interest in non-professional occupations.

The Campbell Interest and Skill Survey (CISS). This instrument is a part of a new integrated battery of psychological surveys that currently includes the CISS, an attitude-satisfaction survey, and a measure of leadership characteristics. Two other instruments being developed will complete this integrated battery—a team development survey and a community survey. The CISS was built for individuals 15 years and older, has a reading level of sixth grade, has 200 interest and 120 skill items on a six-point response scale. The results yield parallel interest and skill scores: Orientation Scales (Influencing, Organizing, Helping, Creating, Analyzing, Producing, and Adventuring), Basic Scales (29 basic scales such as leadership, supervision, counseling, and international activities); Occupational Scales (58 of them, such as financial planner, translator/interpreter, and landscape architect). Special scales include an academic comfort and extraversion measure.

SUMMARY

Interest inventories have a long association with career counseling. Strong and Kuder were pioneers in the interest measurement field. More recently Holland's theory of careers greatly influenced the presentation of interest inventory results. The NIE guidelines on sex bias (Diamond, 1975) have led to some reduction in sex biases on interest inventories. However, we need to reevaluate our entire approach to interest measurement.

QUESTIONS AND EXERCISES

1. In what instances would you choose the SII over the KOIS? Give reasons for your choice.
2. How would you explain to a high school senior that measurements of interests do not necessarily indicate how successful one would be in an occupation?
3. A college student states that he knows what his interests are but can't decide on a major. How would you justify suggesting that he take an interest inventory?
4. How would you interpret an interest inventory profile that has no scores in the above-average category? What would you recommend to the individual who took the inventory?
5. Defend or criticize the following statements: Interests are permanent over the life span. An individual will have the same interests in 1995 as in 1940.

Chapter Seven

Using Personality Inventories

The term *personality* can cover a multitude of perceptions. For example, the statement "She has the personality to be a good sales representative" suggests that the individual has such traits as gregariousness, friendliness, aggression, strong drive, and is well adjusted. All of these are the kinds of characteristics and traits a career counselor is interested in measuring to some degree. Counselors turn to personality inventories to measure individual differences in social traits, motivational drives and needs, attitudes, and adjustment—vital information in the career exploration process.

A number of career theorists have stressed the importance of considering personality factors and characteristics in career guidance. Super (1990) emphasizes the importance of self-concept in career counseling. Holland (1985) relates modal personal style to work environments. Roe (1956) stressed the influence of early personality development on vocational direction. Tiedeman and O'Hara (1963) emphasized the role of total cognitive development in decision making.

More recently, Lowman (1991) has provided an excellent review on the use of personality inventories for the clinical practice of career assessment. Although there appears to be an increased interest in the use of personality inventories for career counseling, they have not been extensively used for several reasons.

Because personality inventories were primarily developed to measure psychopathology, their use for career assessment has been limited. Although efforts were made to relate personality measures to career fit projections, the results have not been impressive (Lowman, 1991). More personality measures are needed that are specifically designed to evaluate those personality traits that are relevant to success in certain careers. Specifically, more research is needed to establish relationships between occupational fit and personality variables, and between abilities and interests and personality variables.

In the meantime, personality measures should be used as a means of evaluating support for or opposition to a career under consideration. For example, an individual may find support for a sales career from a high score on a personality trait that is related to interpersonal skills. Nevertheless, the score alone should not be viewed as a predictor of success or failure in a sales career but should be compared with other data, including abilities and interests.

Perhaps Cronbach's (1984) suggestion is very significant in this context. He recommends that personality measures be used like interest measures—that is, "as a mirror to help the individual examine his or her view of self." Like interest inventories, personality measures provide topics for stimulating dialogue. Through discussion the individual confirms or disagrees with the results and comes to understand the relationship of personality characteristics to career decisions.

Four computer-scored measures of personality are presented in this chapter along with one non–computer-scored inventory. In addition, examples are provided that illustrate the use of personality inventories in career counseling.

EDWARDS PERSONAL PREFERENCE SCHEDULE (EPPS)

The EPPS measures 15 personality variables based on Murray's (1938) manifest needs. The instrument was designed to measure "normal" personality variables for research and counseling purposes. The inventory is untimed, can be taken in approximately 40 minutes, and is hand or computer scored. These 15 personality variables are measured by the EPPS (Edwards, 1959): achievement—a need to accomplish tasks well; deference—a need to conform to customs and defer to others; order—a need to plan well and be organized; exhibition—a need to be the center of attention in a group; autonomy—a need to be free of responsibilities and obligations; affiliation—a need to form strong friendships and attachments; intraception—a need to analyze behaviors and feelings of others; succorance—a need to receive support and attention from others; dominance—a need to be a leader and influence others; abasement—a need to accept blame for problems and confess errors to others; nurturance—a need to be of assistance to others; change—a need for variety and novel experiences; endurance—a need to follow through on tasks and complete assignments; heterosexuality—a need to be associated with and attractive to members of the opposite sex; and aggression—a need to express one's opinion and be critical of others.

The inventory consists of pairs of statements that are related to needs associated with each variable. Individuals are required to choose the statement more characteristic of them. Some of the paired statements require the individual to indicate likes and dislikes, as shown by this example:

A. I like to talk about myself to others.
B. I like to work toward some goal that I have set for myself.

Other paired statements require the individual to describe feelings, as shown by this example:

A. I feel depressed when I fail at something.
B. I feel nervous when giving a talk before a group.[1]

As individuals select these statements, they are indicating needs as measured by this instrument. Thus, someone choosing statements associated with the achievement variable may have a strong need to be successful, to be a recognized authority, to solve difficult problems. Likewise, someone choosing statements associated with the succorance variable may have a strong need to have others provide help and to seek encouragement from others.

Interpreting the EPPS

Results are reported as percentiles (Figure 7-1). Percentile tables are provided for college students and general adult groups with separate sex norms. A consistency variable is used to determine whether the answering pattern is consistent enough to be considered valid.

---

[1]From *Edwards Personal Preference Schedule*, by A. L. Edwards. Copyright 1954, © 1959 by The Psychological Corporation. Reprinted by permission.

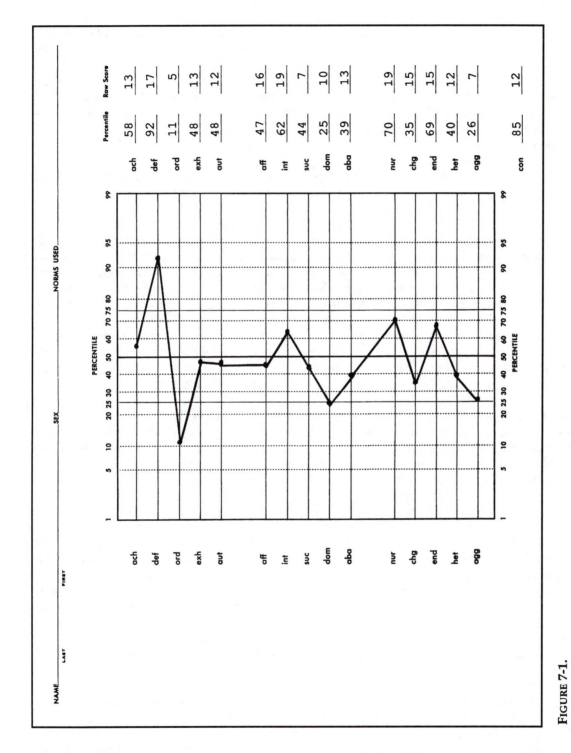

FIGURE 7-1.
Profile for EPPS.
From *Edwards Personal Preference Schedule*, by A. L. Edwards. Copyright 1954, © 1959 by The Psychological Corporation. Reprinted by permission.

Although the EPPS is not widely used at the present time, it can provide useful information for career counseling. For example, a significantly high score on the deference scale indicates that the individual prefers to let others make decisions and does not have a strong need to be placed in a leadership role. By the same token, an individual with a significantly low score on the order scale would probably not enjoy a job requiring neatness and organization. This individual should probably not be directed to office work that has highly structured procedures and strict rules and regulations.

Combinations of needs can also be explored for their relationship to careers. A combination of achievement and dominance, for example, indicates that an individual needs to be recognized as an authority and prefers to direct the actions of others. Such an individual may be task oriented, may strive to become a recognized authority, and may tend to dominate others. These personality traits are desirable in many managerial and sales positions.

A word of caution: An individual's needs do not always have the same priority—that is, an individual's preferences may change over the life span. EPPS results indicate current preferences, needs, and personal orientation and should be considered as only one factor in career decision making.

Split-half reliabilities for the 15 scales of this inventory range from .60 to .87; test-retest reliabilities (one-week interval) range from .74 to .88. Few validity data are reported in the manual. Independent validation studies have yielded inconclusive results (Anastasi, 1988). According to Anastasi (1988) the EPPS is in need of "(a) revision to eliminate certain technical weaknesses particularly with regard to item form and score interpretation, and (b) properly conducted validation studies." For further evaluation of this instrument see reviews by Cronbach (1984), Anastasi (1988), Cooper (1990), and Kapland and Saccuzzo (1993).

Although the EPPS has questionable validity, the needs measured by this instrument are a viable consideration in career counseling. The results can be used effectively to explore an individual client's currently dominant needs in relation to less dominant ones. Thus, this instrument is recommended for promoting discussion of personal needs and their relationship to careers.

Case of a College Sophomore Undecided about a Specific Career Area

Marie, a college sophomore, was interested in a business career but could not decide on the area of business that would be best for her. Past academic performance and previous achievement test data indicated that Marie was a capable college student. Following the counselor's suggestions she collected information on a variety of careers through conferences with faculty members from the school of business and in the career resource center.

In the next conference with the counselor she reported that she was able to eliminate some careers through her research but remained interested in several possibilities, including accounting, insurance, marketing, and management. The counselor asked Marie whether she had ever considered need fulfillment in relation to a career. The idea of meeting personal needs in the business field intrigued Marie, and she became interested in learning more about her needs. The EPPS was selected and administered primarily because it measures manifest needs. The counselor's strategy was to have Marie identify her needs and relate them to the work environments of the occupations she was considering.

Marie's three highest scores were on the change, exhibition, and dominance scales. Her lowest scores were on the deference and abasement scales. The counselor asked Marie to read the explanation of the manifest needs associated with her three highest scores and two lowest scores in the manual.

Marie summarized the results: "I like variety and change in daily routine. I also have a need to live in different places. I like to experiment and experience the excitement that goes with it. This I agree with wholeheartedly! I can't see myself sitting in an office every day, month after month. I also cannot see myself doing the same thing over and over again. Yes, I have a need for change and variety.

"The exhibition scale worried me at first. But I have to agree. I do have a need to be considered witty by others, and I like being clever and the center of attention. I guess I've always wanted to be popular and be around people.

"I definitely agree with the dominance scale. I have a strong need to be a leader. In fact, I have always striven for a leadership position. To be a leader is important to me. This seems to verify my low-order needs as measured by this inventory—deference (deferring to others) and abasement (feeling inferior to others). I'm just the opposite."

The counselor praised Marie for her summary and asked her how these identified needs could be translated into a career choice. The counselor suggested that Marie review the information she had compiled from researching occupations and relate this information to need satisfaction. Marie responded that she could probably satisfy her need to be a leader in almost all the careers she had considered in business. However, after some thought, she came to the conclusion that management and marketing would provide greater opportunities for variety and change than would accounting and insurance.

Marie and the counselor continued their discussion of management and marketing. They concluded this session with an agreement on the next step in the career exploration process: Marie was to gather additional information on the current and projected job market for the two careers before making a final decision.

SIXTEEN PERSONALITY FACTOR QUESTIONNAIRE (16PF)

The first form of the 16PF was published in 1949 (Cattell, Eber, & Tatsuoka, 1970). There are now several forms for measuring the same 16 personality dimensions in individuals 16 years and older. Four forms (A, B, C, D) have an adult vocabulary level; two forms (E, F) are for low-literacy groups.

The 16 personality characteristics, or factors, measured are shown in Figure 7-2. These 16 primary factors are source traits or combinations of traits considered to be components of an individual's personality. Items in the test were selected because they correlated highly with a particular factor, but a given item may also correlate with other factors (Cattell et al., 1970). Thus a combination of items measures each distinct factor, but parts of that factor may be correlated with parts of other distinct factors. Understanding this principle aids in the interpretation of this instrument.

The first 12 traits in the 16PF are designated by letters A–M, used for identifying these personality factors within a universal standard system. This alphabetical identification system is widely used by professional psychologists when referring to personality factors. In communicating the meaning of the personality factors to the general public, more descriptive terms are used. The factors Q1 through Q4 have been given these labels because they are unique to the 16PF (Cattell et al., 1970).

Attention should be directed to factor B, which is considered an intelligence scale. This scale has been designed to give equal weight to fluid and crystallized ability factors (Cattell, 1963) and to provide a dimension of general ability. It is suggested that this scale be supplemented with other intelligence tests when providing career counseling for occupations requiring high ability levels.

Interpreting the 16PF

The 16PF personality factors shown in Figure 7-2 make up the profile and are reported by the use of stens. A bipolar description is provided for each source trait to make the interpretation of scores meaningful.

A major part of the research on the 16PF has been devoted to identifying vocational personality patterns and occupational fitness projections. In the handbook (Cattell et al., 1970) over 70 occupational patterns are reported by sten units. Specific occupations are arranged in 24 occupational groups. For example, the group air industry personnel contains reports on airline hostesses, pilots, engineers, and apprentices. Table 7-1 provides a description of two occupations as an example of the information the career counselor will find useful.

```
            N A R R A T I V E    S C O R E    R E P O R T
            for The Sixteen Personality Factor Questionnaire--16 PF
```

This report is intended to be used in conjunction with professional
judgment. The statements it contains should be viewed as hypotheses
to be validated against other sources of data.   All information in
this report should be treated confidentially and responsibly.

NAME-John Sample   February 9, 1989
ID NUMBER-   AGE-29; SEX-M

VALIDITY SCALES

SCORES		1 2 3 4 5 6 7 8 9 10	
Raw	Sten		
1	2		Faking good is very low.
5	8		Faking bad is high.

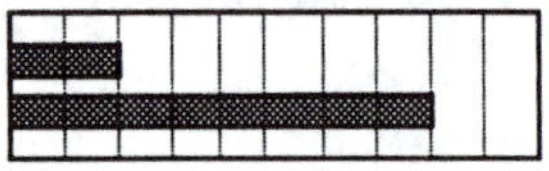

SCORES					16 PF PROFILE			
Raw	Sten U C		LEFT MEANING	1 2 3 4 5 6 7 8 9 10		RIGHT MEANING	%
8	4	4	A	Cool, Reserved			Warm, Easygoing	23
10	8	8	B	Concrete Thinking			Abstract Thinking	89
10	2	3	C	Easily Upset			Calm, Stable	11
22	10	10	E	Not Assertive			Dominant	99
21	9	9	F	Sober, Serious			Enthusiastic	96
11	4	4	G	Expedient			Conscientious	23
19	7	7	H	Shy, Timid			Venturesome	77
9	6	6	I	Tough-Minded			Sensitive	60
11	8	8	L	Trusting			Suspicious	89
16	7	7	M	Practical			Imaginative	77
4	2	2	N	Forthright			Shrewd	4
15	8	7	O	Self-Assured			Self-Doubting	77
15	9	9	Q1	Conservative			Experimenting	96
14	8	8	Q2	Group-Oriented			Self-Sufficient	89
12	5	5	Q3	Undisciplined			Self-Disciplined	40
14	7	6	Q4	Relaxed			Tense, Driven	60

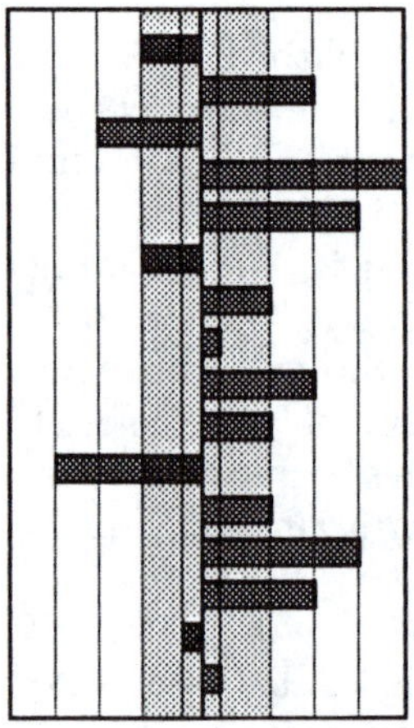

                                  average

Note: "U" indicates uncorrected sten scores. "C" indicates sten scores corrected for distortion (if appropriate). The interpretation will pro-
ceed on the basis of corrected scores. This report was processed using
male adult (GP) norms for Form A.

FIGURE 7-2.
The 16PF report.

The 16PF can be hand scored or computer scored. The hand-scored forms report scores for 15
personality factors and an intelligence measure as shown in Figure 7-2. The computer-scored narrative interpretation form provides an abundance of information in addition to the personality
profile. An example of a narrative report form is shown in Figure 7-3.

TABLE 7-1.
Two 16PF Occupation Descriptions

Group	Specific Occupations	Significant Characteristics
Air industry personnel	Aircraft engineering apprentice	High ego strength and high self-discipline, preference for technical, realistic orientation, low sophistication.
Executive and industrial supervisors	Supermarket personnel	Interpersonal warmth, raised level of anxiety, paying attention to detail, mediocre general ability.

Adapted from 16PF Manual by IPAT Staff, 1972, 1979, Institute for Personality and Ability Testing, Inc. Reproduced by permission of the copyright owner.

Name: John Sample   February 9, 1989

PERSONAL COUNSELING OBSERVATIONS

Adequacy of adjustment is above average (6.5).[1]
Effectiveness of behavior controls is below average (4.2).

INTERVENTION CONSIDERATIONS

The influence of a controlled environment may help. Suggestions include:

A graded series of success experiences to improve self-confidence.
A structured active program to reduce anxiety.

PRIMARY PERSONALITY CHARACTERISTICS OF SPECIAL INTEREST

Capacity for abstract skills is high.

Involvement in problems may evoke some emotional upset and instability.

In interpersonal relationships he leads, dominates, or is stubborn.

His style of expression is often lively, optimistic, and enthusiastic.

He tends to project inner tension by blaming others, and becomes jealous or suspicious easily.

In his dealings with others, he is emotionally natural and unpretentious, though somewhat naive.

He is experimenting, has an inquiring mind, likes new ideas, and tends to disparage traditional solutions to problems.

Being self-sufficient, he prefers tackling things resourcefully, alone.

BROAD INFLUENCE PATTERNS

His attention is directed about equally toward the outer environment and toward inner thoughts and feelings. Extraversion is average (5.9).

At the present time he sees himself as somewhat more anxious than most people. His anxiety score is above average (7.1).

In comparison with those who tend to approach problems coolly and dispassionately or those who emphasize the emotional relationships involved, he is average (4.9).

---

[1]Sten scores.

FIGURE 7-3.
A narrative report of the 16PF.

His life style is independent and self-directed, leading to active attempts to achieve control of the environment. In this respect, he is extremely high (10.0).

He tends to be very expedient and to pursue his own wishes rather than the expectations of others. Thus, he may lack restraint and may fail at times to meet his responsibilities. This tendency is above average (6.8).

VOCATIONAL OBSERVATIONS

At client's own level of abilities, potential for creative functioning is very high (9.0).

Potential for benefit from formal academic training at client's own level of abilities is high (7.6).

In a group of peers, potential for leadership is average (5.6). Conditions of interpersonal contact or isolation are irrelevant, but extremes should be avoided.

Need for work that tolerates some undependability and inconsistent habits is very high (9.0).

Potential for growth to meet increasing job demands is below average (4.1).

The extent to which the client is accident prone is high (8.0).

Occupational fitness projections provide a comparison of the individual's profile with a sample of occupational profiles as shown below.

OCCUPATIONAL PROFILE COMPARISONS

In this segment of the report his personality profile is compared with various occupational profiles. Roughly, high scores (stens above 7) mean that his profile is quite similar to the occupational profile, stens between 4 and 7 indicate an average degree of similarity, and stens below 4 indicate that his profile is not very similar to the occupational profile. All comparisons should be considered with respect to other relevant vocational information about him, particularly his interests and abilities.

1.   **ARTISTIC PROFESSIONS**

     Artist ....very high (9.2)
     Musician ....extremely high (9.8)
     Writer ....extremely high (10.0)

2.   **COMMUNITY AND SOCIAL SERVICE**

     Anesthesiologist ....high (7.8)
     Athletic Training..very high (8.9)
     Corrections Officer...above average (7.1)
     Employment Counselor ....above average (7.2)
     Firefighter...above average (7.1)
     Group Therapist...extremely high (10.0)
     Judges...average (6.0)
     Lutheran Clergy ....very low (2.1)
     Nurse..high (7.8)
     Pharmacist...high (8.4)
     Physician..high (8.0)
     Police Officer...average (5.4)
     Politician..extremely high (9.5)
     Priest (R.C.) ....low (3.3)
     Psychiatrist..high (8.2)
     Service Station Dealer....................................very low (2.4)
     Social Worker...below average (4.4)

3.   **SCIENTIFIC PROFESSIONS**

     Biologist...above average (6.9)
     Chemist...above average (6.8)

FIGURE 7-3. *(continued)*

Engineer..above average (7.0)
Geologist..high (7.9)
Physicist..average (6.3)
Psychologist ....very high (8.5)
Scientist...high (7.6)

4. TECHNICAL PERSONNEL

Accountant ....average (6.3)
Airline Flight Attendant............................above average (7.0)
Airline Pilot...very high (8.7)
Carpenter...high (7.7)
Computer Programmer ....very high (8.6)
Dental Assistant...average (5.2)
Editorial Worker ....average (6.0)
Electrician ....average (5.5)
Mechanic..below average (3.7)
Psychiatric Technician ....average (5.1)
Time/Motion Study Analyst ....average (6.4)

5. INDUSTRIAL/CLERICAL PERSONNEL

Janitor..low (2.9)
Kitchen Worker...extremely low (1.2)
Machine Operator ....low (2.9)
School Bus Driver.......................................below average (3.7)
Secretary/Clerk ....high (7.8)
Truck Driver ....above average (6.5)

6. SALES PERSONNEL

Life Insurance Sales...................................high (7.9)
Real Estate Agent ....above average (7.2)
Retail Counter Clerk ....extremely high (10.0)
Sales Representative ....average (5.8)

7. ADMINISTRATIVE AND SUPERVISORY PERSONNEL

Business Executive ....average (6.0)
Business Manager ....extremely high (10.0)
Finance Manager ....very high (8.7)
Middle-Level Manager................................average (4.8)
Nursing Administrator................................above average (7.4)
Plant Foreman..average (4.6)
Store Manager..average (6.4)
Technical Manager ....very high (8.8)

8. ACADEMIC PROFESSIONS

Education Administrator ....above average (7.0)
Teacher-Elementary Level...........................high (8.2)
Teacher-Junior High Level ....very high (8.8)
Teacher-Senior High Level..........................very high (9.2)
Teacher-Special Education ....average (5.1)
University Professor ....average (6.0)
School Counselor..average (5.9)
School Superintendent ....average (5.1)
University Administrator ....average (6.1)

FIGURE 7-3. (*continued*)

The computer interpretation not only provides much more information about the individual than does the profile alone but also saves the counselor considerable time in the interpretation process. Continued research with the 16PF occupational fitness projections should make them even more valuable to the career counselor in the future.

The publication of the 16PF generated considerable controversy, especially over Cattell's claim that the instrument measures source traits of normal personality functioning (Bloxom, 1978). Specifically, Cattell's use of factor analysis as a method of discovering the casual traits that lead to comprehensive descriptions of personality has been challenged (J. A. Walsh, 1978). According to Anastasi (1988), factor analysis should be used for grouping test items and then matching these against empirical criteria in validity studies. Cronbach (1984) complains that there is no consistency in classifying and defining psychological traits. Cattell provides 16 personality factors, but other theorists have combined or have extended the list of these personality dimensions. Furthermore, Cattell suggests that personality inventories like the 16PF are not built around a definite theory. It appears that we can best use the 16PF results for promoting discussion in career counseling. Extensive reviews of this instrument are provided by Harrell (1992), Aiken (1988), and Kaplan and Saccuzzo (1993).

Test-retest reliabilities (2–7 day intervals) indicate that most scales of the 16PF are satisfactory. However, some of the scales fall below .70 and should be used with caution. For forms A and B the correlation range for the scales is .45 to .93; scales B, L, M, N, and Q1 are less than .70. The range for forms C and D is .67 to .86; scales M, N, and Q2 are less than .72. Bloxom (1978) suggests that form E should not be used until its equivalent form has been developed and the combined forms provide acceptable reliability and validity coefficients.

As illustrated earlier, the 16PF does provide information that can be most useful in career exploration. One should be cautious when using the terms associated with the various scales because they can be confusing and misleading to some individuals. They need to be qualified and explained thoroughly.

Case of a High School Senior Undecided about His Future

Mark, a high school senior, told the counselor that he was completely undecided about what to do after graduation from high school. He had considered going to college but was also thinking of looking for a job. Mark's grades in high school were above average. Mark stated that, because his parents wanted him to go to college as his brothers and sisters had done, he had taken the ACT for college admission. His composite score was well above average with his highest subtest score in natural sciences. His scores on the interest inventory section of the ACT indicated an interest in the sciences.

The counselor asked Mark to clarify his reasons for going to college and for going to work. Mark made it clear that he preferred going to college, but because he was undecided about a major he was considering working until he could make a decision. The counselor informed Mark that many students in his class who planned to attend college were undecided about a major. Besides, the counselor explained, "Most courses you take during your freshman year are required of most majors." The counselor then discussed with Mark the pros and cons of going to college directly after graduation from high school. Eventually, Mark decided that he would feel better about attending college now if he could come to a tentative decision about a major.

The counselor had Mark take a battery of inventories including the 16PF. The 16PF was selected primarily because of its occupational fitness projections. The counselor reasoned that these measures might stimulate Mark to explore several possible majors. Mark's profile closely resembled profiles in the scientific professions as described in the handbook. As the counselor and Mark reviewed his profile, the following exchange took place.

Counselor: Your scores on this personality inventory suggest that you have personality characteristics that are similar to those of individuals in the sciences. Within the scientific group your profile closely resembles that of a biologist.

Mark: Does this mean that I would be an outstanding scientist?

Counselor: No, this does not guarantee that you are going to be an outstanding scientist. It simply indicates that your personality is similar to those of people who work in this field, and there is a good chance that you would feel comfortable in and like this kind of work. However, it does not guarantee that you will be successful.

Mark: Oh, I see. These scores verify that I'm like the people in this field, but they don't mean that I'll be successful unless I'm smart enough or apply myself.

Counselor: Yes, that's exactly right, Mark. You would have to commit yourself to going to college and studying very hard to achieve in one of the scientific professions.

The discussion of personality characteristics as related to occupational environment ignited Mark's interest in career exploration. He decided to investigate several scientific professions in detail. As a result of taking the 16PF, Mark was able to approach the career decision-making process with an understanding of how to relate himself to working conditions. Projecting his personality characteristics into occupational environments was difficult for Mark but not counterproductive. Armed with information about his individual characteristics, Mark could consider careers in a sophisticated way that was interesting for him.

PERSONAL CAREER DEVELOPMENT PROFILE (PCD PROFILE)

The PCD Profile, developed by Walter (1984), is a computer interpretation of the 16PF designed specifically for career guidance. The format is narrative in style and nontechnical in nature. The PCD Profile includes the following: problem-solving patterns, patterns for coping with stressful conditions, patterns of interpersonal interaction, and personal career considerations. The 16PF profile is reported along with clinical observations for the qualified professional; these observations can be easily detached from the nontechnical PCD Profile.

The PCD Profile report is comprehensive; up to 50 specific occupations are compared with each individual's 16PF scores. In addition, profile similarities are provided for occupational groups. The report is designed to be easily interpreted by professionals and by most individuals who complete the questionnaire.

Case of an Older Man Changing Careers

Mr. Sample reported to a community college counseling center for pre-enrollment counseling concerning a major and a career choice. He was 34 years old, was married, had two children, and had spent ten years in the Navy as a yeoman. His duties as a yeoman included doing clerical work and handling payroll. Mr. Sample said that he did not reenlist in the Navy because he wanted to spend time with his family. He was now seeking training for a job that would provide his family with a comfortable living. He expressed interest in a variety of business careers such as clerical work, banking, and computer programming. He had saved money to see him through a couple of years of training.

Mr. Sample graduated from high school with average grades. His extracurricular activities included collecting stamps and building boat models. Mr. Sample's interests were fairly well determined, and the skills he had developed in the Navy could be applied to the careers under consideration. The counselor decided that an informal skills identification survey and a personality inventory would be used to stimulate further career exploration. The 16PF and the PCD Profile were chosen because of their nontechnical format and the career profiles they yield.

Mr. Sample's profile is shown in Figure 7-4. The counselor asked Mr. Sample to read the profile carefully before discussing it.

Problem-Solving Patterns

Mr. Sample functions quite comfortably with problems that involve abstract reasoning and conceptual thinking. He is quite able to integrate detail and specifics into meaningful, logical wholes. He is very alert mentally. He sees quickly how ideas fit together and is likely to be a fast learner. If Mr. Sample feels like doing it, he shows above-average potential to achieve well in the kind of controlled learning experiences that formal university training offers.

Mr. Sample's approach to tasks is usually balanced between getting things done efficiently and having an awareness of the often hidden steps and outcomes that are part of the process of getting things done.

Patterns for Coping with Stressful Conditions

For the most part, Mr. Sample seems to be well adjusted. He does not usually show signs of tension and worry, even when he is under a lot of pressure. Nevertheless, Mr. Sample is likely to show his emotions, feelings, and worries in situations that he finds upsetting to him. However, he may have various ways of showing his emotions or concerns, and as a result, others may find him hard to understand or predict. He tries to be calm and even-tempered most of the time. He rarely allows his emotional needs to get in the way of what he does or tries to do in situations or relationships. He seems to be quite casual in the way he reacts to most circumstances and situations. He usually follows his own urges and feelings. He seldom gives much attention to controlling his behavior and sometimes finds it hard to consciously discipline himself. Generally, when Mr. Sample is faced with conflict or disagreement with others, he likes to challenge those who differ with him and to clearly state his views on the subject. However, if pushed far enough, he is likely to either give in or to break off the conversation—whichever seems to be best for him.

Patterns of Interpersonal Interaction

On the whole, Mr. Sample tends to be able to give about equal amounts of attention to the concerns of others and his own concerns and problems. He likes to put forth a feeling of warmth and easygoingness when interacting with others. He is a good-natured person and one who generally prefers participation in group activities. He is generally very forward and bold when meeting and talking with others. Mr. Sample may sometimes want to get others to do something so much that he may try too hard and, as a result, he could run the risk of coming across as overly pushy and demanding in such instances. Nevertheless, he appears to relate to most people with ease and comfort.

Mr. Sample is normally inclined to state his desires and needs clearly and quite forceful-ly. He likes to have things his way most of the time and prefers freedom from other people's influence. Although Mr. Sample usually likes to be free from other people's influence, he can easily adjust his manner and he can be thoughtful of other people and their concerns or needs when it is important to do so. He normally feels closest to people who are competitive and who understand the importance of being in firm control of their lives and what they do to reach their goals. Sometimes, Mr. Sample may be in such a hurry to get things done that he tends to forget how others may be affected by his actions and how others may feel about matters that are important to them. Mr. Sample seems to have a sharp sense of what is socially necessary, and he is usually aware of the right thing to say and do when relating to

FIGURE 7-4.
The PCD Profile report for Mr. Sample.
Copyright ©1977, 1982, 1984 by Verne Walter & Affiliates, Escondido, CA and The Institute for Personality and Ability Testing, Inc., Champaign, IL. "16PF" is a trademark of IPAT, Inc.

others. For the most part, he tries to be accepting of people since he tends to be trusting and accepting of himself and what he does in life. Mr. Sample tends to gain his greatest satisfaction in life from being involved in activities that have chances for personal achievement while competing with others. When things are going well between himself and others, he likes to have influence over other people as he faces and meets difficult challenges.

Organizational Role and Work-Setting Patterns

Mr. Sample may prefer a role of leadership in most organizational settings, and he is likely to accept such a role with a group of friends or co-workers if provided the opportunity. Mr. Sample generally attempts to influence others by directing, persuading, and challenging them to get things done. He seems to truly enjoy talking and interacting with people to get them to agree with his points of view when it's important to him. Mr. Sample generally prefers to build feelings of mutual respect and interdependence among people. He usually likes to share with others whatever power may be necessary to accomplish assignments. He appears to value objective working relationships between superiors and subordinates.

Mr. Sample is likely to feel most at home when working in relaxed and flexible settings that are not boring or routine in nature. If some structure would be necessary, he likes to design it himself rather than having someone else impose it on him. He is basically quite flexible. He does not usually feel the need to follow rigid or long-established practices. He should enjoy and do a good job on trouble-shooting-type assignments in which he has chances to tackle and solve difficult problems.

Patterns for Career Activity Interests

Mr. Sample's profile suggests that he is likely to enjoy career-oriented and/or avocational activities that entail:

■ Convincing, directing, or persuading others to attain organizational goals and/or economic gain—activity characteristic of persons who find satisfaction working in the sales, marketing, and management aspects of business, or in the professions of consulting, law, and politics. They usually enjoy having the opportunity to exercise control over matters important to them, like to have some degree of influence over people and to work in situations where they can make decisions in efforts to get things accomplished—the Venturous-Influential Interest Pattern.

■ Solving problems through discussions with others, and encouraging relationships between people so as to enlighten, serve, or train them—activity characteristic of persons who find satisfaction working in the counseling, education, health care, religious, social service or training professions. They usually enjoy opportunities whereby they can show a genuine concern for people, especially if people may require some sort of assistance, training, or education—the Nurturing-Altruistic Interest Pattern.

■ Organizing information according to prescribed plans and well-established procedures through the use of verbal and numerical skills—activity characteristic of that performed by people who enjoy working in well-defined work roles such as in the fields of accounting, banking, data processing, finance, methods and systems, personnel, and office administration. They usually like being involved in the details of day-to-day administrative or operational activities so as to keep things running smoothly—the Procedural-Systematic Interest Pattern.

FIGURE 7-4. *(continued)*

Mr. Sample's predominant career activity patterns are like those of people typically employed in the occupations that are listed below. In reviewing this list, he may find support for past or present career choices. However, the list of occupations is not exhaustive, nor is it meant to suggest only career or occupational choices for which he may already have proven abilities, skills, interests, or experience and training. Rather, he may find it helpful to also review his interests, skills, and experience with respect to occupations he may not have considered before.

In addition, if Mr. Sample reviews this list in terms of how people work in these roles, and the types of conditions in which they work, he could possibly learn more about the kinds of work-related activities and settings in which he would feel most comfortable. As a result of such analysis, Mr. Sample should find it easier to seek out and identify work situations that enable him to share important aspects in common with people who work in some of the following occupations: administrative services director, branch manager, general manager, chamber of commerce executive, city manager, community service director, compensation-benefits director, consultant, customer service director, education and training director, hospital administrator, hotel manager, industrial relations director, insurance agency manager, marketing director, public relations director, retail store manager, wholesaler.

Additional occupations Mr. Sample may wish to explore include: administrative director, bank executive, certified public accountant, credit manager, human resource director, insurance claim manager, insurance underwriting manager, personnel placement director, procurement services manager, purchasing manager, realtor, salary and wage administrator, appraiser, and account executive, advertising manager, art center director, attorney, buyer, radio/television director.

The occupational information given here is based on analysis of Mr. Sample's general personality orientation. Again, as mentioned before, the occupational listings should not be treated as specific job suggestions. Some may not appeal to him. Others may not relate well to his training and experience. However, each represents an option for Mr. Sample to consider in his efforts to achieve personal growth and meaningful career planning at this point in time. A careful review on his part, nonetheless, may bring to mind other alternatives that represent even more appealing career paths.

FIGURE 7-4. (*continued*)

Each of the profile patterns was discussed, and the counselor asked Mr. Sample to summarize what he learned about himself.

Counselor: Do you feel that your past working experience has helped you in dealing with stressful conditions?

Mr. Sample: Well, yes, I believe that had I taken this test sometime earlier, like in my early twenties, it probably would have different results. I think that the experiences I've had have certainly helped me to put things in perspective.

Counselor: You have had to make some important decisions in the past, and you seem to be well satisfied with those decisions. You seem to have decided now that you want to be with your family, and that decision has prompted you to consider a career that keeps you at home. The patterns of interpersonal interaction suggest that you are focusing your thoughts primarily on inner feelings and your own personal situations and have made your decisions based primarily on them.

Mr. Sample: Well, yes, I think that I have always felt confident in myself, and I have usually made decisions based on that confidence. In other words, I have felt fairly self-reliant and like to control working situations by doing the work myself.

Counselor:	Well, how would these feelings affect your performance in managerial or leadership position?
Mr. Sample:	Yes, I've thought about that. I may have some problems in expecting too much of others; I sort of experienced that in the Navy. However, my superior in the Navy was able to depend on me, and I feel that I followed through on most assignments fairly well. But not being able to delegate work could be a problem for me as a manager.

The counselor and Mr. Sample continued their discussions concerning interpersonal relationships and problem-solving patterns. Whenever it was plausible, the counselor related work environments to personality characteristics. In the final phase of the counseling session, career development was discussed.

Mr. Sample:	I see they have recommended a number of career considerations. However, I think I can eliminate some of those right off. For example, I don't believe I am interested in hospital administration or in industrial relations or a retail store career. I think I lean more toward working with people in some capacity.
Counselor:	Good! You've been able to eliminate some of the possibilities, and I noticed that in your patterns for career activity interests you are a people person and prefer to be involved with people with some sort of relationship like solving problems with them or encouraging relationships between people.
Mr. Sample:	I understand that personnel work is a very good field and I believe that I may be interested in pursuing this as a possible career. I'm not quite sure what area of personnel work I would like to get into, but I would definitely like to look into this as a possible career field.
Counselor:	Very well. We have some information in our career resource center on this topic, and I can also recommend some people for you to see. What about other considerations? Perhaps you should look at two or three fields at this time.
Mr. Sample:	I agree. I want to take a look at what might be available in different branches of personnel work, but I'm not sure as to what kind of industry I would like to work in.

The counselor and Mr. Sample continued to discuss possible career considerations using the list of careers provided on the computer printout as a stimulus. Mr. Sample was able to expand this list and thus consider a number of different options.

TEMPERAMENT AND VALUES INVENTORY (TVI)

The TVI measures two variables: temperament dimensions of personality as related to career choice and values as related to work rewards (pleasant work environments). A rational-empirical approach was used to select and refine the items. Specifically, rational judgments were used in determining the personality aspects of temperament and the values to include in the inventory, and the scales were pretested and subsequently statistically analyzed. The reading level is eighth grade, and the inventory is not recommended for use below the ninth grade. The inventory is untimed and computer scored. Two parts of the inventory require the individual to respond on a Likert-type scale (very similar to very dissimilar values). The third part is a true/false questionnaire.

Interpreting the TVI

The temperament scales are referred to as personal characteristics on the score report profile as shown in Figure 7-5. Standard scores are reported on a bipolar scale ranging from 20 to 80 with a mean of 50 and standard deviation of 10. The advantage of the bipolar scale is that scores are not as likely to be looked on as outstanding or poor, but simply as describing dimensions of an individual's personality.

Differences in scales are regarded as significant if they are three standard scores or greater. Also as shown in Figure 7-5, the reward value scales are reported by standard scores ranging

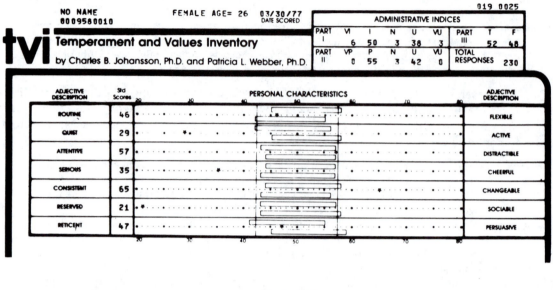

FIGURE 7-5.
Top: TVI personal characteristics profile. *Bottom:* TVI reward value profile.
From *Temperament and Values Inventory,* by C. B. Johansson and P. L. Webber. Copyright 1977 by NCS/Interpretive Scoring Systems. Reprinted by permission.

from 20 to 80, with a mean of 50 and a standard deviation of 10. The manual (Johansson, 1977) reports mean scores for various occupational groups for additional interpretation.

There are two computer-generated report formats. One is composed of a profile as shown in Figure 7-5, reporting standard scores with an asterisk. On the back of this report form is a narrative description of each scale. Administrative indices discussed in the manual are also reported.

The other report format is a comprehensive narrative description of the individual. This report begins with a discussion of the usefulness of the results and a brief description of how to interpret the results. The remainder of the report is divided into three parts: personal characteristics, reward values, and response data. A narrative interpretation of the individual's score is reported in detail for the seven personal characteristics scales and the seven reward value scales. An example for quite-active, one of the personal characteristics scales, follows:

> Compared to females and males in a general population your score is in the average range, although slightly more toward the quiet end. Low scores are related to preferences for quiet types of activities, such as reading, building models, watching sports rather than actively participating, or sitting and talking with friends on a free weekend. In contrast, very high scores on this scale indicate more of a liking for being on-the-go, moving around rather than sitting still, and being a participant in active sports rather than a spectator. Sometimes you may feel that you are constantly

on-the-go, while at other times you enjoy just sitting and relaxing. Generally, high school students tend to have higher scores on this scale than do adults, but there is a wide range of individual differences for each age group. Compared to just your sex and age group, your score is in the average range.[2]

An example for social recognition, one of the reward value scales, follows:

Compared to females and males in a general population, your score is in the range of scores for people who feel that social recognition is not as important to them as it is to most people. This indicates that even though you may like other people to be seeking your advice, to be friendly to you, or to depend upon you, other things may be as important or even more important to you, such as depending upon your own sense of worth. Scores similar to yours tend to be related to interest in scientific activities and skilled trades, where social recognition is not of major importance. In contrast, individuals who have high scores on this scale tend to have interests associated with working in business-enterprising careers, such as sales, public administrator, or school superintendent. Compared to just your sex and age group your score is below the average range of scores.[3]

The TVI thus provides the counselor with information on the individual's work-related temperament and desired work environments—information that can be compared to information on interests and abilities. This information is most useful in the overall career counseling sequence and can be matched with an individual's career aspirations. The counseling information generated by the TVI can be used in career seminars, group career counseling programs, work reentry counseling, and career education programs.

The TVI should be the subject of further research. The instrument appears to have fairly good face validity in that the items for each section appear to measure what they attempt to measure. In general, more data are needed to establish construct and concurrent validity and reliability. To determine construct validity the TVI was compared with scales on the SCII, the Career Assessment Inventory, and the Self Description Inventory. Although there is evidence of validity, the sample was relatively small for the SCII (123) and Career Assessment Inventory (197). The authors should be commended for the detailed comparisons of each TVI scale with those of other instruments. However, in some instances moderate relationships (correlations of .27 to .32) are not explained, and the reader is left to draw his or her own conclusions. Although the authors present an impressive discussion of concurrent validity, the number of cases from which differentiation among the various groups studied was determined was small. This number should be increased in the future. Test-retest reliabilities (1- and 2-week intervals) range from .82 to .93 for the personal characteristics scales and from .79 to .93 for the reward value scales. Median internal consistency estimates by age group and sex for each scale are in the low .80s. Schrank (1984) has suggested that future editions should include reliability and validity studies from a broader population and finer tuning of items designed to reduce ambiguity and redundancy.

Case of a High School Junior Considering Dropping Out of School

Jamal, a high school junior, had lost interest in school and was considering quitting and going to work. He was referred to the the counseling center for assistance. The counselor obtained the following information from Jamal's cumulative folder. Jamal's father was employed in a local factory, and his mother did odd jobs such as housekeeping and baby sitting. His academic record was below average, but aptitude and ability tests indicated that he was at least of average intelligence and had good mechanical aptitudes.

---

[2]From *Temperament and Values Inventory,* by C. B. Johansson and P. L. Webber. Copyright 1977 by NCS/Interpretive Scoring Systems. Reprinted by permission.

[3]From *Temperament and Values Inventory,* by C. B. Johansson and P. L. Webber. Copyright 1977 by NCS/Interpretive Scoring Systems. Reprinted by permission.

It was clear that Jamal was undecided about his future and had not established career goals. As the conversation progressed, the counselor asked Jamal to specify a job choice. Jamal stated that he wasn't sure what was required for various jobs but agreed that if he had the opportunity to be trained to do a specific job he would like that much better than just going out and seeking a job.

The counselor then suggested several inventories to help clarify Jamal's career goals. One was the TVI, which was chosen to stimulate discussion of work environments as related to personality characteristics and of temperament dimensions as related to career choice. The counselor used the TVI results to encourage Jamal to consider an occupational environment as opposed to seeking just any job: "This test is divided into two parts. The first part of the test measures personality characteristics. The second part of the test measures what you consider important in a career or find rewarding in a career. You have high scores on the routine, active, and attentive scales. Specifically, the first score indicates that you prefer rather routine kinds of schedules and set routines in working. The second score shows that you prefer active participation. The third high score suggests that you are not easily distracted when you are doing a task and are able to concentrate even when there is not complete silence."

Jamal agreed with the results in general. He especially agreed to preferring routine and vigorous activities. He also reported that he had had to learn to concentrate despite noise in a home with six siblings. Other scores from this part of the test were similarly discussed.

The counselor then said: "Now, let's take a look at the second part of the test. All but two of your scores were near average. Your high score on task specificity suggests that you prefer to work on jobs where the tasks are highly structured and that you like to be able to check out your work in detail rather than hurrying through it. Your high score on work independence suggests that you prefer being your own boss and establishing your own schedule for work."

At this point Jamal seemed confused as to what the results meant in relation to a job. The counselor decided to summarize the results in an attempt to link the scores to job duties.

Counselor: Let's remember that you like rather routine type jobs, that you prefer vigorous activities, and that you are not easily distracted. Also, you like to work on tasks where you know exactly what is expected. You like to be able to check your work in detail. You like to set your own schedules and work at your own pace. Now, there are probably a lot of jobs that might fit into this area. Can you think of a job that is routine and requires tasks that are detailed and have to be checked?

Jamal: Well, I guess it fits pretty well with television repair. Television repair people tackle specific problems, and you've got to check out your work in detail.

The counselor and Jamal discussed other possible occupations such as auto mechanic, electrician, and small engine repairer. They selected several of the occupations for further exploration. Jamal and the counselor also explored the benefits of completing high school and the possibility of entering a vocational training program.

The discussion of the TVI results directed Jamal to specific consideration of work tasks and work environments. Considering occupations from this perspective was a realistic approach to searching for a job. Not only was Jamal prepared to consider the requirements of a job, but he was able to relate tasks and the work environment to his own values and temperament.

MYERS-BRIGGS TYPE INDICATOR (MBTI)

The MBTI is a measure of psychological types described by C. G. Jung (1921/1971), who suggested that the basic differences in behavior are the way individuals prefer to use their perception and judgment. According to Jung, people differ in interests, values, motivation, and skills through individualized judgments that have been formed by numerous perceptions of events and experiences. This instrument is designed to measure perception, judgments, and attitudes used by different types of people. The two-choice format requires individuals to choose between items that measure:

EXTROVERSION	E	vs.	I	INTROVERSION
SENSING	S	vs.	N	INTUITION
THINKING	T	vs.	F	FEELING
JUDGING	J	vs.	P	PERCEIVING

Responses to items are rated according to a prediction ratio and the total rated scores provide an index to the respondent's preferences. For example, higher total points for E than for I would translate into classifying a person as an extrovert and suggests that person spends more time extroverting than introverting. Numbers are also assigned to preferences to indicate the strengths of the preference. A low score can indicate that there is no or little difference between preferences.

According to Jungian theory of psychological types, each type has gifts and strengths as well as potential for vulnerability. The differences between types provide clues for developmental activities as well as indicators of preferences for career direction. The manual recommends that counselors should become familiar with Jung's theory before using this instrument.

The MBTI is more appropriate for high school students and adults. The reading level is estimated to be at seventh to eighth grade level. Form F contains 166 items, form G contains 126 items, and form AV, the abbreviated version, contains 50 items. There are no time limits and scoring can be done by stencil or by computer.

Interpreting the MBTI

The manual contains a description of 16 possible psychological types the counselor may use for interpretive purposes. The profile presents brief descriptions of psychological types and combinations of types according to four hierarchical preferences. Hierarchical preferences are classified as very clear, clear, moderate, and light. An appendix in the manual contains tables of occupations empirically attractive to psychological types.

According to Carlson (1989) the MBTI has yielded satisfactory split-half and test-retest reliabilities and favorable validity coefficients. In general, Carlson suggests the use of the MBTI for career counseling. Healy (1989), however, suggests that at least two of the four scales depart from Jung's definition. Healy also points out that there is limited evidence that the recognition of one's mode of sensing and judging will improve career decision making. Other criticisms of the MBTI include a lack of male and female norms and a failure to provide demographic information about occupational groups that are reported to be attractive to different psychological types. Because the user has no information about occupational norms, scores could perpetuate discrimination of different ethnic, racial, and socioeconomic groups. Healy has suggested that the MBTI be considered as experimental and should not be routinely used in career counseling.

McCaulley (1990) has suggested that the MBTI is a measure of preferences and not of abilities and accomplishments; therefore, counselors should consider it as a hypothesis-testing attitude. More specifically, it provides a measure for understanding perceptual and cognitive styles. Sharf (1992) points out that combined norms of men and women are used whereas separate norms by sex would be more helpful.

Before using the MBTI, counselors are encouraged to read both pro (Carlson, 1989) and con (Healy, 1989) articles. Counselors are also encouraged to recognize the complex nature of interpretating the MBTI.

Case of a Confused Adult Concerning a Future Work Role
Chuck had considered going for counseling for several months before making an appointment. "Why is it that I'm having difficulty holding on to a job," he mused "I can't seem to be satisfied with anything anymore—my whole life seems to be a waste of time. Maybe, just maybe, a counselor can help me." With much ambivalence Chuck reported for his first counseling session.

After appropriate introductions and small talk the counselor stated:

Counselor: Chuck I noticed on your request form that you want to discuss your future. Could you be more specific?

Chuck: Huh—well—yes—I've had problems settling down and finding something I like to do.

Counselor: You've not been able to find a satisfactory job.

Chuck: Yes— but it's more than that— I don't know how to say it, but I feel different than other people I've worked with. I don't seem to fit in and I'm not sure what I do that irritates others.

As the conversation continued, Chuck stated that he had had numerous jobs but soon became bored with them and either was fired or quit. He made reference to a lack of interest in work.

Chuck: It's more than just identifying interests—I don't understand myself and how and why I think the way I do. I seem to be out of sync with other people.

The counselor made note of Chuck's desire for identifying interests and later in the conversation made the following comment.

Counselor: Chuck, earlier you mentioned identifying interests—would you like to take an interest inventory questionnaire?

Chuck: Not now, but maybe later. I'm more interested in knowing what kind of person I am—like maybe my personality.

As the conversation continued, it became apparent that Chuck would benefit from an inventory that would provide insights into his perception of the world around him. The counselor suggested an inventory that might help clarify perceptions of self and to provide him with a better understanding of his judgments concerning the behavior and actions of peer affiliates in the work place. For this purpose the counselor chose the MBTI.

The results of the MBTI indicated that Chuck's preference scores were INTJ as described here:

Usually have original minds and a great drive for their own ideas and purposes, in fields that appeal to them, they have a fine power to organize a job and carry it through with or without help. Skeptical, critical, independent, determined, sometimes stubborn. Must learn to yield less important points in order to win the most important. Live their outer life more with thinking, inner more with intuition (Myers & McCaulley, 1985, p.21).

After the counselor explained how to interpret the report form, Chuck read the description of his reported type.

Chuck: One thing is for sure—I'm introverted and I like to think things over a long time—sometimes too much because I never get anywhere.

Counselor: Do you agree with the description of your identified type?

Chuck: Some of it, I guess, but one point is really true, I'm stubborn and I like to come out on top.

Chuck continued to reflect on the results of the inventory, and the counselor encouraged him to express his thoughts fully concerning his self-evaluations. This instrument helped establish rapport between Chuck and the counselor, and after several more counseling sessions a career decision-making model was introduced to Chuck to provide direction for career exploration.

The results of the MBTI reinforced Chuck's strengths and pointed out some areas for improvement. Chuck was now better prepared to further evaluate his interests, experiences, and other factors in pursuit of the career decision.

The list of occupations attractive to his preference scores provided in the MBTI manual were discussed and put aside for future reference. Chuck and the counselor decided that he was now ready to explore interests, values, and aptitudes in more depth before developing a lists of specific occupations to explore.

In this case the MBTI was used to provide a basis for discussing perceptions and judgments of peer affiliates in the workplace. The classification of how one perceives and judges others may need to be clarified before appropriate and adequate judgments can be made about work environments.

SUGGESTIONS FOR CAREER DEVELOPMENT

Many of the following suggestions for fostering the career development of students and adults can be modified and used interchangeably to meet the needs of both groups. These suggestions should not be considered exhaustive of all possibilities of using assessment results to enhance career development but rather as examples from which exercises can be developed to meet local needs and needs of other groups.

For Schools:
- Using identified personality traits, ask students to write a composition describing themselves.
- Ask students to develop an ideal work environment that matches their personality characteristics and traits.
- Ask students to develop a list of occupations that match their personal characteristics and traits.
- Ask students to identify and discuss personal uniqueness by comparing personality characteristics and traits with abilities, achievement, and interests.
- Ask students to share, describe, and discuss how differences among people can influence lifestyle and work-related goals.
- Ask students to form groups according to personal characteristics and traits and to share future goals.
- Ask students to write a short paragraph identifying what they consider to be personal characteristics and traits of someone in a chosen occupation. Compare and contrast with their personal traits and characteristics.
- Have students role play "Who Am I?" based on personal characteristics and traits.
- Using personality results, ask students to project their future lifestyle in 5 or 10 years.

For Adults:
- Ask adults to describe how their personal characteristics and traits influenced their career development.
- Ask adults to describe how their personal characteristics and traits influenced perceptions of their work role.
- Ask adults to share how their personal characteristics and traits influenced lifestyle preferences.
- Ask adults to describe the match or lack of match between their personal characteristics and traits and past work environments and peer affiliates.
- Ask adults to describe how their and their spouse's personality characteristics and traits influenced perceptions of dual career roles.
- Ask adults to share and discuss how their personal characteristics and traits can influence one's interaction with supervisors and peer affiliates in the workplace.
- Ask adults to identify personal characteristics and traits that have contributed to their desire for a career change.
- Ask adults to discuss and identify how their personal characteristics and traits could influence choices in the career decision making process.

OTHER PERSONALITY INVENTORIES

In addition to the personality inventories discussed in this chapter, the reader may find the following inventories useful in career counseling. The evaluation of the normative sample and the description of the scales will help determine their usefulness.

California Test of Personality. There are five levels of this inventory, including one for grades 7–10, one for grades 9–college, and one for adults. The inventory is divided into two parts: Part I (six subtests) provides a measure of personal adjustment. Part II (six subtests) is a measure of social adjustment. A combination of the two parts provides a total adjustment score. Scores are expressed as standard scores.

Omnibus Personality Inventory. This instrument is to be used with adolescents and adults. The normative samples for standardization were derived from college students. There are 16 scales—for example, autonomy, altruism, anxiety level, and practical outlook—and one intellectual disposition scale. The manual presents case studies as examples for using this instrument.

Guilford-Zimmerman Temperament Survey. This survey is a measure of the following traits: general activity, restraint, ascendance, sociability, emotional stability, objectivity, friendliness, thoughtfulness, personal relations, and masculinity. Norms were derived from college samples. Single scores and total profiles may be used to determine personality traits to be considered in career decision making.

Minnesota Counseling Inventory. This inventory was designed to measure adjustment of boys and girls in grades 9–12. Scores yield criterion-related scales as follows: family relationships, social relationships, emotional stability, conformity, adjustment to reality, mood, and leadership. Scales are normed separately for boys and girls. The scores provide indices to important relational and personal characteristics to be considered in career counseling.

Thorndike's Dimensions of Temperament. This instrument has ten scales: sociable–solitary, ascendant–withdrawing, cheerful–gloomy, placid–irritable, accepting–critical, tough-minded–tender-minded, reflective–practical, impulsive–planful, active–lethargic, and responsible–casual. Percentile norms are based on males and females in grades 11 and 12 and in their freshman year of college.

Jenkins Activity Sequence. This instrument was designed as an aid for detecting Type A behavior patterns of adults ages 25–65. It can be hand scored or machine scored. Four scales are given. Type A scale assesses coronary prone behavior and three independent components of Type A behavior: speed and impatience, job involvement, and hard driving and competitive.

Early School Personality Questionnaire. This instrument is designed to measure personality characteristics of children ages six to eight. Questions are read aloud to students by teachers or can be administered by an audio cassette tape. It is untimed and scores are presented in 13 primary personality dimensions similar to the 16PF. Separate and combined-sex tables are available.

Children's Personality Questionnaire. This instrument is designed to measure 14 primary traits of children. Broad trait patterns are determined by combinations of primary scales. Scores are presented by percentile and standard scores. Separate and combined sex tables are available.

Gordon Personal Profile. This inventory measures four aspects of personality: ascendancy, responsibility, emotional stability, and sociability. These four traits also yield a measure of self-esteem. This inventory contains a forced-choice format in which the respondent reacts to alternatives by indicating being most like themselves and being least like themselves. Percentile ranks for high school, college, and certain occupational groups are provided.

Self-Description Questionnaire. This instrument seems to have a promising future for measuring self-concepts in grades two to six. At the present time norms are based on responses from students in New South Wales, Australia. Items require responses to simple declarative sentences on a five-point scale in which the individual indicates false, mostly false, sometimes false/sometimes true, true, or mostly true. Results present nonacademic self-concepts (physical abilities, physical appearance, peer relations, and parent relations), and academic concepts are derived from responses to such simple declarative sentences as "I'm good at mathematics." "I make friends easily." Finally, a general self-concept is derived from a combination of the nonacademic and academic scores.

Coopersmith Self-Esteem Inventory. This inventory is designed to measure attitudes toward self and social, academic, and personal contexts. The scales are reported to be significantly related to academic achievement and personal satisfaction in school and adult life. One form is designed for children ages 8–15, and the adult form is designed for ages 16 and above.

SUMMARY

The consideration of individual characteristics and traits in career exploration has been stressed by a number of career theorists. Personality measures provide individuals with the opportunity to examine their views of themselves. Computer-generated narrative reports may provide the impetus needed for improving the quality and increasing the quantity of personality measures used in career counseling. The computer-generated interpretive reports described in this chapter provide examples of the potential use of personality inventories.

QUESTIONS AND EXERCISES

1. How would you explain the suggestion that personality measures act as mirrors to help individuals examine their views of themselves? What are the implications for career counseling?
2. Give an example of a counseling case in which you would recommend using a personality inventory.
3. A faculty member has recommended using a personality inventory as a predictive instrument for academic success. What would you reply?
4. Explain how you would establish the need for a personality inventory during a counseling interview.
5. What would your strategy be for interpreting personality inventory results that conflict with an individual's career goals?

Chapter Eight

Using
Value Inventories

Increasing awareness of the relationship between individual values and career selection and satisfaction has focused attention on the measurement of values in general and of work values specifically. Clarification of values has come to be identified as one of the relevant components of career decision making (Brown, 1990). The usefulness of value assessment in career counseling is underscored by Gordon (1975), who suggests that values tend to remain fairly stable and to endure over the life span. Thus, the identification of individual values can help in the career decision-making process.

Value assessment overlaps the measures of interest and personality. The choice among these types of inventories in career counseling depends on the purpose for using the results. For example, confusion and conflicts in values concerning religion, work, politics, and friends may best be resolved by discussing the results of a value inventory; the results are directly related to the purpose of testing. A counselor may choose a value inventory because he or she plans an exercise in value clarification. Another counselor may determine that value preferences are more easily related to considerations of career exploration than measured traits from personality and interest inventories. Thus, the choice between a value, personality, or interest inventory should be primarily determined by the needs of the counselee and the objectives of counseling.

Defining values is a complex task. Because value judgments are an integral part of an individual's priorities and world views, most definitions are general in nature. For example, Kluckhorn (1961, p. 18) states that values are "a selective orientation toward experience, implying deep commitment or repudiation, which influences the ordering of choices between possible alternatives and action." Fitzpatrick (1961, p. 93) defines values as "those ideals, norms which guide man's behavior, according to which he judges whether his behavior is right or wrong." Gordon (1975, p. 2) provides another general definition of values: "Values are constructs representing generalized behaviors or states of affairs that are considered by the individual to be important." A most useful explanation of values for career counseling is simply "the importance you attach to stimuli, events, people, and activities" (Zimbardo, 1979, p. 491). In career counseling we are most interested in those values that affect career decisions. Our major goal is to assist individuals in clarifying these values from a self-report.

In this chapter a work values inventory and an inventory that measures needs and values are discussed. In addition, inventories that measure general values are reviewed and their use in career counseling is illustrated. Examples from both group and individual career counseling programs are presented.

WORK VALUES INVENTORY (WVI)

The WVI is designed to assess the forms of satisfaction men and women seek in their work. It is used for academic and career counseling of high school and college students and for personnel selection and development. The individual is required to rate the importance of each of 45 work values on a five-point scale. Testing time is approximately 15 minutes.

Reliability data are based on 99 tenth graders. Test-retest reliabilities (two-week interval) range from .74 to .83. The manual reports evidence for construct, content, and concurrent validity. The author reports that data for predictive validity are being collected (Super, 1970).

The WVI measures 15 work values (Super, 1970, pp. 8–10): achievement—values a feeling of accomplishment; altruism—values service to others; aesthetics—values beauty and artistic endeavors; creativity—values inventiveness; intellectual stimulation—values independent thinking; independence—values independent actions; prestige—values status and power; management—values planning and organizing tasks for others to do; economic returns—values ample financial rewards; security—values running little risk of losing a job; surroundings—values a pleasant environment; supervisory relations—values work under a supervisor who is fair and easy to get along with; associates—values working with likable and desirable people; way of life—values a desirable lifestyle; and variety—values doing a variety of tasks.

Interpreting the WVI

Score results are presented in percentile equivalents for each scale. Norms are available for males and females in grades 7–12. Means and standard deviations are available for a limited number of adult male samples derived from older forms of the inventory.

The author suggests that the first step in the interpretation process is to evaluate the raw scores. The two or three values that have the highest rating are to be considered in the counseling process. Next, one should look at the normative data by sex and grade. The manual provides an extensive definition of each value with specific examples of how each value is related to suggested occupations. Interpretations of combinations of scores are provided by factor analytical studies that appear to be tentative and inconclusive. Although no examples of the use of the WVI for counseling are provided in the manual, the definition of each scale provides guidelines for using the results in career counseling. For example, someone who scores high on the altruism scale would probably be interested in jobs such as social worker, counselor, teacher, and religious leader.

This inventory appears to have considerable possibilities as a counseling tool for career exploration. Of serious concern, however, is the lack of data on the long-term stability of the inventory or at least on its stability beyond the two-week intervals used in establishing reliability. The small number of cases used to establish reliability needs to be increased, and, in fact, all data need updating from the 1970 and earlier editions. The use of the instrument is enhanced by the reported means and standard deviations of occupational samples, even though these samples are small. For in-depth reviews of this instrument, see Bolton (1985) and Anastasi (1988).

Case of a Group Counseling Program

Sue, Fred, Ruth, and Jim, first-semester freshmen undecided about careers, agreed to discuss their WVI results in a group led by their counselor. This excerpt illustrates how the counselor led the discussion and directed the group in relating work values to broad occupational areas.

After introducing the group members to one another and explaining the purpose of the inventory, the counselor provided members with profiles of their scores. The counselor explained the meaning of percentile equivalents and asked members to locate their three highest scores and their three lowest scores. The counselor then directed members to read the interpretations of their scores as recorded in the manual. After all members had ample time for review, the counselor asked them to discuss their scores.

Jim volunteered: "My surroundings score was the highest, being in the 95th percentile; economic returns was in the 80th percentile; and way of life was in the 75th percentile. My lowest scores were altruism, aesthetics, and creativity. It seems that I highly value a pleasant environment. The more I think about working, the more this seems to be true. I also like to be comfortable and would like to earn a lot of money. As far as my lowest scores are concerned, I don't value artistic endeavors or being creative or providing service to others."

The counselor recorded Jim's highest and lowest scores on the chalkboard. Next he had the members relate these work values to career options by asking them to record careers congruent with Jim's measured work values. In addition, they were to record occupations in which Jim would not find value congruence. After a brief time, the counselor called for their suggestions.

Sue was the first to speak: "I don't think Jim would want to be a mechanic or to work in a machine shop. He wants a cushy place to work. I'd suggest banker, real estate agent, or some kind of business career." The other members agreed with Sue's observation and offered further suggestions such as architect, dentist, and optometrist. The counselor then asked the members to specify how they arrived at their conclusions.

Fred:	Well, I think that people who value nice surroundings and economic returns would be happier in business careers or professions that provide opportunities for making a lot of money.
Ruth:	I agree, and in Jim's case he does not value art, creativity, and service to others. He would not want to be an art teacher, for example. They probably also don't make enough money to take care of Jim's needs. This makes it much clearer that you'd be happier in the occupations we mentioned.
Sue:	This is like a puzzle—you try to put all the parts together. Sometimes they fit, and other times they don't.
Counselor:	Very good! You have recognized that we have many considerations in choosing a career. Work values are one important factor.

A discussion of each group member's scores followed a similar pattern. The counselor made certain that each member left the session with a list of career considerations.

MINNESOTA IMPORTANCE QUESTIONNAIRE (MIQ)

This questionnaire is a measure of vocational needs and values that are considered to be important aspects of work personality. Currently there are two forms, one of which requires the individual to rank preferences concerning an ideal job; the other requires the individual to choose between paired statements. There are normative data for different age groups (18–70) and by sexes. Results present an individual's relative position on six values (achievement, comfort, status, altruism, safety, and autonomy) and component needs that define each value. In order to effectively use this instrument, counselors must be prepared to become familiar with work adjustment studies conducted at the University of Minnesota for several decades.

The MIQ has two forms—paired and ranked. The paired form requires the individual to choose between two statements whereas the ranked form requires the individual to rank-order statements. In both forms the MIQ assesses the importance of six values associated with 20 work needs, shown in Figure 8-1 as a part of a sample report form. For example, the value "achievement" has two associated work needs, ability utilization and achievement. Examples of statements found in the questionnaire are also presented. The sample report form also presents scores that range from 0.0 to –1 for values and work needs measured as unimportant, and form 0.0 to +3 for those measured as important.

Through factor analysis the need scales have been reduced to six underlying dimensions or values as follows: (1) *achievement* (ability utilization, achievement); (2) *comfort* (activity, independence, variety, compensation, security, working conditions); (3) *status* (advancement, recognition, authority, social status); (4) *altruism* (co-workers, social service, moral values); (5) *safety* (company policies and practices, supervision-human relations, supervision-technical); and (6) *autonomy* (creativity, responsibility) (Rounds et al., 1981).

Because of the emphasis placed upon these values for career counseling they are further clarified as follows:

1. *Achievement:* This value is associated with work environments that provide opportunities for individuals to use their abilities to the fullest and experience a sense of achievement. For example, a brick mason is able to build a wall using a design pattern he or she has mastered.
2. *Comfort:* The important reinforcers for this value include experiencing a variety of tasks associated with a job, having the opportunity to take independent actions in a pleasing work environment, receiving adequate compensation, and feeling secure.
3. *Status:* How one is perceived by others and preferably recognized as an authority are important components of this value. Social status and opportunities for advancement in the workplace are high priorities.
4. *Altruism:* The needs associated with this value are doing work that is considered morally correct and being identified with social service in a work environment that has compatible peer affiliates.
5. *Safety:* Orderliness, structure, and predictability in the workplace are needs associated with this value. Other factors are clear-cut company policies and practices, particularly those involving safety issues and lines of authority.
6. *Autonomy:* This value is associated with a work environment that provides ample opportunities for creative expression and assuming responsibility for one's actions.

Benson (1985) suggests that the technical aspects of the MIQ are acceptable but further research is needed to validate the benefits of the use of Occupational Reinforcer Patterns (ORP) in the interpretation process (ORPs will be discussed in the next section). Also, the technical manual should be updated with more thorough information concerning reliability and validity studies. More importantly, the MIQ should be clearly tied to a specific theoretical orientation.

Interpreting the MIQ

A sample MIQ report form is shown in Figure 8-2. The individual's responses on the MIQ are compared to Occupational Reinforcer Patterns (ORPs) for 90 representative occupations. A summary of the concept of Occupational Reinforcer Patterns is presented here. For more in-depth information, refer to Lofquist and Dawis (1984).

To achieve consonance or agreement between individual and work environment, the individual must successfully meet the requirements of the job, and the work environment must fulfill the requirements of the individual. Stability on the job, which can lead to tenure, is a function of correspondence between the individual and the work environment. The process of achieving and maintaining correspondence with a work environment is referred to as work adjustment.

Four key points of the theory of work adjustment can be summarized from Dawis and Lofquist (1984): (1) work personality and work environment should be amenable, (2) individual needs are most important in determining an individual's fit into the work environment, (3) individual needs and the reinforcer system that characterizes the work setting are important aspects of stability and tenure, and (4) job placement is best accomplished through a match of worker traits with the requirements of a work environment.

Dawis and Lofquist (1984) have identified occupational reinforcer patterns (ORPs) found in the work environment as being vital to an individual's work adjustment. They have evaluated work settings to derive potential reinforcers of individual behavior. In the career-counseling process, individual needs are matched with occupational reinforcers to determine an individual's fit into a work environment. Some examples of occupational reinforcers are achievement, advancement, authority, co-workers, activity, security, social service, social status, and variety. ORPs and occupational ability patterns are given for 1700 careers in the *Minnesota Occupational Classification System* (Rounds et al., 1981).

The strength or the importance of a need on the MIQ is indicated by a C index, as shown in Figure 8-2. If the C value is greater than .49, then that occupation is considered satisfying or of

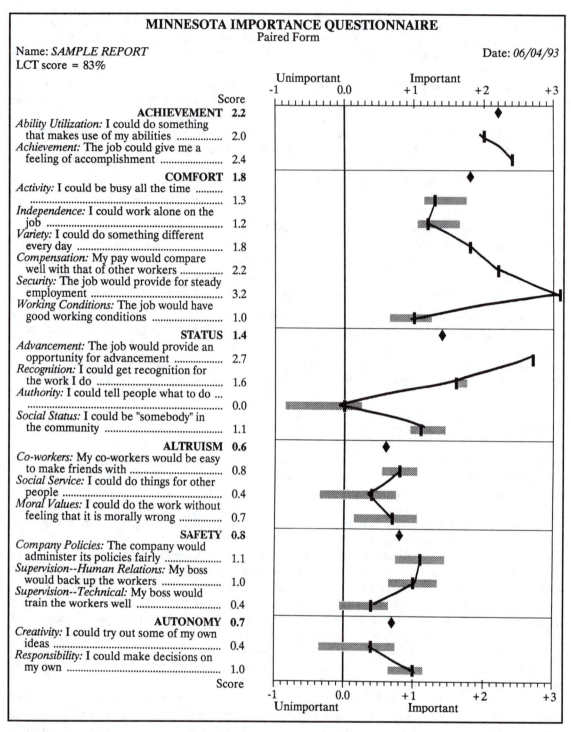

FIGURE 8-1.
Minnesota Importance Questionnaire.
Copyright © 1984 Vocational Psychology Research, Department of Psychology, University of Minnesota. Reprinted by permission.

value to the client. A C index between .10 and .49 indicates likely job satisfaction, and a C index less than .10 indicates no job satisfaction. The sample report form in Figure 8-2 indicates that the scores predict "Satisfied" for several of the representative occupations, including the following: electronics mechanic, elevator repairer, office-machine servicer, and statistical-machine servicer.

Minnesota Importance Questionnaire

Correspondence report for *SAMPLE REPORT*   06/04/93

The MIQ profile is compared with Occupational Reinforcer Patterns (ORPs) for 90 representative occupations. Correspondence is indicated by the C index. A prediction of *Satisfied (S)* results from C values greater than .49, *Likely Satisfied (L)* for C values between .10 and .49, and *Not Satisfied (N)* for C values less than .10. Occupations are clustered by similarity of Occupational Reinforcer Patterns.

	C Index	Pred. Sat.		C Index	Pred. Sat.
CLUSTER A (ACH-AUT-Alt)	.17	L	**CLUSTER B (ACH-Com)**	.36	L
Architect	.11	L	Bricklayer	.29	L
Dentist	.11	L	Carpenter	.44	L
Family Practitioner (M.D.)	.27	L	Cement Mason	-.03	N
Interior Designer/Decorator	.24	L	*Elevator Repairer*	.74	S
Lawyer	.27	L	Heavy Equipment Operator	.37	L
Minister	.11	L	Landscape Gardener	.07	N
Nurse, Occupational Health	.06	N	Lather	.11	L
Occupational Therapist	.15	L	Millwright	.29	L
Optometrist	.33	L	Painter/Paperhanger	.41	L
Psychologist, Counseling	.08	N	Patternmaker, Metal	.43	L
Recreation Leader	.02	N	*Pipefitter*	.58	S
Speech Pathologist	.11	L	Plasterer	.07	N
Teacher, Elementary School	.20	L	Plumber	.40	L
Teacher, Secondary School	.25	L	Roofer	.01	N
Vocational Evaluator	.06	N	*Salesperson, Automobile*	.51	S
CLUSTER C (ACH-Aut-Com)	.48	L	**CLUSTER D (ACH-STA-Com)**	.64	S
Alteration Tailor	.46	L	*Accountant, Certified Public*	.51	S
Automobile Mechanic	.43	L	*Airplane Co-Pilot, Commercial*	.60	S
Barber	.31	L	*Cook (Hotel-Restaurant)*	.57	S
Beauty Operator	.23	L	Department Head, Supermarket	.42	L
Caseworker	.31	L	Drafter, Architectural	.48	L
Claim Adjuster	.47	L	*Electrician*	.66	S
Commercial Artist, Illustrator	.51	S	Engineer, Civil	.35	L
Electronics Mechanic	.57	S	Engineer, Time Study	.29	L
Locksmith	.45	L	*Farm-Equipment Mechanic I*	.73	S
Maintenance Repairer, Factory	.49	L	*Line-Installer-Repairer (Telephone)*	.50	S
Mechanical-Engineering Technician	.28	L	*Machinist*	.67	S
Office-Machine Servicer	.69	S	*Programmer (Business, Engineering, Science)*	.55	S
Photoengraver (Stripper)	.54	S	*Sheet Metal Worker*	.63	S
Sales Agent, Real Estate	.18	L	*Statistical-Machine Servicer*	.72	S
Salesperson, General Hardware	.35	L	*Writer, Technical Publication*	.55	S
CLUSTER E (COM)	.47	L	**CLUSTER F (Alt-Com)**	.33	L
Assembler, Production	.35	L	Airplane-Flight Attendant	.09	N
Baker	.56	S	Clerk, General Office, Civil Service	.32	L
Bookbinder	.58	S	Dietitian	.21	L
Bookkeeper I	.55	S	Fire Fighter	.33	L
Bus Driver	.23	L	Librarian	.21	L
Key-Punch Operator	.49	L	Medical Technologist	.39	L
Meat Cutter	.49	L	Nurse, Professional	.13	L
Post-Office Clerk	.43	L	Orderly	-.01	N
Production Helper (Food)	.47	L	Physical Therapist	.24	L
Punch-Press Operator	.44	L	Police Officer	.23	L
Sales, General (Department Store)	.33	L	Receptionist, Civil Service	.27	L
Sewing-Machine Operator, Automatic	.29	L	Secretary (General Office)	.30	L
Solderer (Production Line)	.45	L	Taxi Driver	-.02	N
Telephone Operator	.42	L	Telephone Installer	.44	L
Teller (Banking)	.38	L	Waiter-Waitress	.26	L

FIGURE 8-2.
Minnesota Importance Questionnaire correspondence report.
Copyright © 1984 Vocational Psychology Research, Department of Psychology, University of Minnesota. Reprinted by permission.

When interpreting the results of the MIQ the counselor should remember that job satisfaction is an important predictor of job tenure and recognize the factors associated with job satisfaction. Individual needs and values are significant components of job satisfaction (Dawis & Lofquist, 1984). These factors should be delineated in career-counseling programs designed to enhance work adjustment.

Case of a Client Beginning a Career Search

The results of the MIQ are rich sources of information to stimulate dialogue in the career-counseling process. The results may be used with individuals or in groups discussing work adjustment patterns. For the individual who is beginning a career search, value systems can be the topic of interesting dialogue. For example:

Seth (client):   I have heard about values, but this is the first time I have discussed them with anyone. I agree they ought to be considered important.

Counselor: The results of the MIQ indicate that you place a high value on autonomy and achievement. Let's take a look at some of the occupations that match up with these values.

As the counselor and Seth discussed specific occupations, the counselor was also interested in having the client gain a thorough knowledge of the autonomy and achievement values.

Counselor: Let's return to the two values mentioned earlier. What do autonomy and achievement as values mean to you?

Seth: You said that achievement means that I like to experience the opportunity to do well on a job.

Counselor: Yes, that is an important part of that value. But how will you know if that is possible in some of the occupations we discussed?

Seth: Hey, man, that's right! Whew! That is a good question.

The counselor then explained ORPs and how they can be identified in some occupations. The salient psychological needs manifested in work environments are powerful counseling tools that can help individuals identify the potential for job satisfaction. In this case the MIQ is used with measures of aptitude in the matching process. In helping individuals delineate their need and value systems counselors can use instruments such as the MIQ. However, the ORPs may become more elusive with predicted changes in job requirements.

Case of a Client Considering a Career Change

Work adjustment counseling is another area where the MIQ can be of great assistance. For example:

Meg (client):   I told you that I don't know why I hate my work. Oh, I have some ideas and we discussed them but I can't put my finger on it.

Counselor: Well, let's take a look at the results of the MIQ you took the other day.

The counselor pointed out that one of the highest index scores related to the altruism value. The counselor gave a brief explanation of the value and asked Meg to respond to the results in terms of what this may have to do with her work problem.

Meg: You know that I don't have much education, and some of these terms are new to me. But as I figure it, I don't fit into this job I just took.

Counselor: That's good, Meg. Now tell me more about not "fitting in."

Meg went on to state that she felt uncomfortable around her co-workers and, in fact, felt rejected by them probably because she did not like their approach to the work. She felt strongly that her co-workers made little effort to do a good job.

Although Meg had recognized her displeasure with the work environment, she was not quite able to specify problems with any feeling of certainty and may have continued indefinitely in an unhappy situation. The dialogue between counselor and client about the results of the MIQ helped Meg verbalize her problems and clarify, to some extent, her needs in a work situation. Meg decided to consider jobs that would provide reinforcers for her needs and match her level of skills.

In these two counseling cases values became the central point of discussion that led to better understanding of values taken from the MIQ and of how these values affect job satisfaction and adjustment. Job satisfaction is a significant variable in determining productivity, job involvement, and career tenure. Career counselors should use occupational information to assist clients in matching needs, interests, and abilities with patterns and levels of different reinforcers in the work environment. For example, the reinforcer of achievement is related to experiences of accomplishment in the workplace. Social service is related to the opportunities that a work situation offers for performing tasks that will help others. The developer of the MIQ will continue to develop ORPs, especially as work environments change in nature and content.

Survey of Interpersonal Values (SIV)

The SIV measures six ways in which an individual may want to relate to other people. These interpersonal values are broadly associated with an individual's personal, social, marital, and occupational adjustment. Gordon (1975, p. 1) defines the values measured by this instrument as follows: support—being treated with understanding; conformity—doing what is socially correct; recognition—being looked up to and admired; independence—having the right to do whatever one wants to do; benevolence—doing things for other people; leadership—being in charge of other people.

The inventory can be administered in 15 minutes. It consists of sets of three statements from which the individual must choose the most important and the least important. Three different value dimensions are represented in each triad. For example:

> To have a meal at noon.
> To get a good night's sleep
> To get plenty of fresh air.[1]

KR-20 reliability estimates range from .71 to .86. Test-retest correlations for an interval of 15 weeks range from .65 to .76. Black (1978) considers these reliabilities adequate, while LaVoie (1978) believes they are not high enough for individual interpretations. Predictive validity is based primarily on studies demonstrating significant differences between groups of workers such as managers and subordinates in a variety of settings. Validity is also demonstrated by correlations between the SIV and other inventories such as the Study of Values and the EPPS. This instrument has been reviewed by Mueller (1985).

Interpreting the SIV

The SIV scores are interpreted by percentile equivalents with norms available for both male and female groups. The following groups constituted the normative samples: ninth-grade vocational students, high school students, vocational junior-college students, college students, and adults. Minority groups are included in all norm groups. Percentile equivalents are grouped into five levels: very high—94th to 99th percentile; high—70th to 93rd percentile; average—32nd to 69th percentile; low—8th to 31st percentile; very low—1st to 7th percentile. In addition to percentile equivalents, means and standard deviation by sex are provided for each of the six values for the normative groups and for additional samples including foreign students.

The SIV is recommended for use in vocational guidance, where values can be related to occupations under consideration, and in personal counseling, where identified values can provide stimulus for discussion.

Despite these recommendations, relatively little information is available concerning the use of SIV results in career counseling. In a separate publication, Gordon (1975) presents profiles for various classes of occupations with recommendations for individual counseling. These profiles

---

[1]From *Survey of Interpersonal Values, Revised Examiner's Manual,* by Leonard V. Gordon. Copyright © 1976, 1960, Science Research Associates, Inc. Reprinted by permission of the publisher.

are based on seven typological clusters developed by Gordon from factor analysis: bureaucratic managerial (values controlling others in structured and regulated ways), influential indifferent (values controlling and influencing others with little concern for them), independent assertive (values personal freedom), bureaucratic subordinate (values conformity), welfare of others (values helping others), reciprocal support (values having warm, reciprocal relationships with others), and institutional service (values being of service to others).

Using these clusters, Gordon provides a series of profiles for a variety of occupations. For example, managerial and supervisory personnel generally value bureaucratic management and devalue reciprocal support. Retail clerks are generally service oriented and concerned with the welfare of others. Other occupations are reported in a similar fashion. One hopes that additional occupational groups will be described in the SIV manual in the future.

The use of the SIV would be greatly enhanced if the author would provide illustrations of its use in the manual. A detailed explanation of the interpretation of the scales would also increase the utility of this inventory. In addition, a clarification of the meaning and significance of high and low scores is lacking.

The career counselor should be cautious in using the inventory results. As Black (1978) points out, we cannot assume that choice of work accurately reflects what individuals value in relationships. Some individuals ignore the lack of certain values in an occupational environment.

The SIV seems appropriate for use with individuals and groups. It is particularly appropriate for helping individuals toward self-discovery in the career decision-making process. The results can also be used for improving interpersonal relationships generally and specifically within the work environment.

Case of an Older Woman Searching for a Career for the First Time

Ms. Lunt was considering a career for the first time in her life. She had recently been granted a divorce after a bitter legal battle with her husband. She told the counselor that her divorce presented her with the challenge of reevaluating her total lifestyle. She emphasized that a part of this reevaluation involved clarifying her values and establishing goals. The counselor suggested a values inventory, and the SIV was selected because of its indication of interpersonal values.

The SIV results suggested that Ms. Lunt highly valued support, conformity, and benevolence. The counselor asked to express the meaning of these values in relation to her recently receiving a divorce and having to rely on herself for support. Ms. Lunt immediately recognized that her strong need for support might be overemphasized at this point in her life. However, Ms. Lunt concluded that this value was probably longstanding and should be considered in her career plans.

The counselor suggested that Ms. Lunt consider a work environment that would be congruent with her value system—environments where she would be treated with understanding and kindness, where social conformity would be valued, and where she would be able to help others. Ms. Lunt decided that even though support was her highest measured value, she was more interested in a career that would provide her with the opportunity to help others. Ms. Lunt then evaluated careers in social service.

The SIV results provided the stimulus for relating Ms. Lunt's interpersonal values to a variety of occupations. Ms. Lunt was able to find several occupations in the social service group that would allow her to help others and to conform to social norms.

SURVEY OF PERSONAL VALUES (SPV)

The SPV was developed as a companion instrument to the SIV to measure another segment of the value domain—ways in which individuals may want to be in their daily lives. Gordon (1967) identifies six values this instrument measures: practical mindedness—values doing things that will pay off; achievement—values striving to accomplish something significant; variety—values doing things that are new and different; decisiveness—values having strong and firm convictions; orderliness—values having well-organized work habits; and goal orientation—values directing efforts toward clear-cut objectives.

The SPV can be self-administered and is untimed. Administration time is approximately 15 minutes. The individual is forced to choose the most important and least important from sets of three statements, as in the SIV.

Interpreting the SPV

Scores for the SPV, as for the SIV, are reported in percentile equivalents and are interpreted according to the five levels employed in the SIV. Regional high school norms by sex are based on representative examples of urban California students. The author strongly recommends that high schools develop local norms. National separate-sex norms are available for college students. The author suggests that the SPV may be used also with industrial and other adult groups. Apparently, the author feels that local norms would best serve the needs of these other groups.

Reliability studies include a test-retest (7–10 day intervals) of 97 college students and an application of the KR-20 formula to responses of 167 college students. The test-retest reliabilities range from .80 to .92, while the KR-20 reliabilities range from .72 to .92. The author claims validity through the use of factor analysis in that the scales maintained internal consistency through repeated item analysis. Validity was also assessed by comparing correlations of the scales and those of other instruments such as the SIV and the Study of Values. Most of the scales were found to be statistically significant, supporting the author's claim that different sets of values are measured by this instrument. However, these conclusions must be considered tentative as more data and more research are needed. A review by Erchul (1989) provides additional information on the development of this instrument.

The criticisms of this instrument for use as a career-counseling tool are similar to those for the SIV. Currently lacking is information on the use of the results and the meaning of the scale scores. In the meantime, the SPV items may be used as the basis for discussions concerning personal values and their relationship to careers.

Case of a High School Senior Needing to Link Values to Careers in a Concrete Way

Matteo, a high school senior, had spent considerable time in the counselor's office discussing his future. He was persistent in his efforts to discover the ideal career. Matteo requested and was administered an extensive battery of tests, including the SIV. He was stimulated by the results of most of the battery but was especially intrigued with the measures of his interpersonal values. However, he wanted to know more about his values, and specifically he wanted information about values that influenced his everyday living. Both Matteo and the counselor agreed that the SPV might serve this purpose. The SPV yielded very high percentile equivalents in achievement and variety. Matteo read the descriptions of these scales but was unable to link the results with a career.

Counselor:	Let's review some factors we have discussed in previous counseling sessions. Your test data indicate an interest and ability in mathematics and the sciences. You also have an outstanding academic record in these two courses. When reviewing occupations, you indicated an interest in becoming a college mathematics teacher. Now let's return to the high scores in achievement and variety on the SPV. I would like for you to project into the future for a few minutes and visualize how these values could influence your career as a mathematician.
Matteo:	(after a brief pause) Oh, I see! I probably want to be the best.
Counselor:	Go on.
Matteo:	I'd want a Ph.D. . . . I see what you mean. I could achieve in this field.
Counselor:	What about the other value—variety?
Matteo:	Well, if I did do well, I might be able to call the shots. A strong drive for achievement could lead to opportunities for variety.

After a lengthy discussion the counselor suggested that Matteo still needed to be able to link values to career options in specific ways because Matteo continued to make only superficial connections. Matteo was given the following assignment: Research at least two careers in mathematics and two in science in the career resource center. Write a paragraph on how each career might be congruent with your highest measured values. Examples of Matteo's completed assignment follow:

> Chemist—I've found that chemists with a master's degree may find work in government agencies and private industry. But better opportunities are available to those who have a Ph.D. There are all kinds of chemists—organic, inorganic, physical, analytical, and biochemists. Chemists are involved in research and development of new products. I would like this kind of work because I would like to accomplish something significant—my achievement value. In regard to my variety value, I would be working on challenging and difficult tasks that would provide me with a variety of experiences.
>
> Mathematician—Mathematicians are employed in government agencies and private industry as teachers, actuaries, computer specialists, and so on. The higher the degree, the greater the opportunities for entry and advancement. I believe that I would be most interested in conducting research to develop better techniques and equipment for computers. This career would provide me with a challenging work environment in which accomplishment of goals would be possible. I would have a variety of experiences while accomplishing new and different tasks. Both my achievement and my variety values would be covered with this career.

Both Matteo and the counselor agreed that consideration of a career should involve other data such as aptitudes, interests, and past academic performance. However, they also agreed that the discussion about values gave Matteo insight into additional considerations that are important in career exploration.

STUDY OF VALUES

The Study of Values was developed from Spranger's (1928/1966) six types of personality: theoretical, economic, aesthetic, social, political, and religious. According to Spranger, measuring an individual's values and attitudes is the best means of determining personality. Thus, the authors of this test (Allport, Vernon, & Lindzey, 1970) developed questions to measure the underlying values inherent in Spranger's types of personality. The following explanations of these six types are paraphrased from Allport et al. (1970, pp. 4–5): theoretical—values systematizing knowledge and the search for truth; economic—values practical and applied knowledge; aesthetic—values events on the basis of their artistic nature; social—values caring for and loving people; political—values influence and personal power over others; and religious—values unity in the world and values religious experiences as an affirmation of the purpose of life.

This inventory is untimed and can be self-administered and self-scored. In the first part individuals are required to indicate disagreement with, or slight preference for, controversial statements or questions. In the second part individuals respond to multiple-choice questions designed to reflect attitudes.

Interpreting the Study of Values

Individuals total their scores for each of the six categories and plot them on a profile as shown in Figure 8-3. Below the profile are instructions for interpreting the scores.

Although the test was developed primarily for college students and adults, high school norms by sex are available. Also included are norms for certain occupations. Means and standard deviations by sex are reported for a number of broad occupational fields such as business, medicine, and religion. The authors caution the career counselor not to become overreliant on the results of this inventory in that the values measured are much broader than occupational inter-

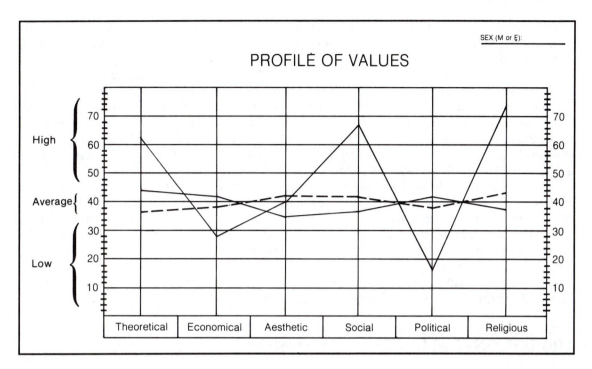

FIGURE 8-3.
Study of Values profile.
From *Study of Values* by G. W. Allport, P. E. Vernon, and G. Lindzey, © 1960 by Houghton Mifflin Company. Reprinted by permission of the publisher, The Riverside Publishing Company.

ests. Thus, the norms reported may be considered as illustrating differences in values among the occupational groups cited. This inventory seems much more appropriate for stimulating discussions about values in relation to careers than for selection and classification. The items are transparent and are open to faking, particularly when an individual is aware that the results will be used for selection.

Reliability studies include split-half reliabilities ranging from .84 to .95 and test-retest reliabilities (intervals of one and two months) ranging from .77 to .93. External validation was accomplished by examining scores of groups of individuals whose characteristics were fairly well known, such as engineering students, nurses, clergy, and teachers. High and low scores for the group studies corresponded with prior expectations.

The manual needs to include more suggestions for illustrations of the use of the results than it now does. Case studies would be helpful for illustrating how to apply the results in a variety of counseling situations. This instrument would also be much more useful for career counseling than it now is if additional data were available on differences in values among occupational groups. See Rabinowitz (1984) and Anastasi (1988) for in-depth reviews.

Case of a Veteran Seeking a Career

Carl reported to the counseling center, seeking assistance in making a career choice. He was 26, was married, and had one child. He had spent over three years in the military and saw action in the Persian Gulf war. He grew up in a town of about 25,000 and was active in student affairs in high school. His father was employed in a local bank. He reported that his family had been supportive during his youth and active in their church. Carl spent his first year in college taking courses that are generally required of most students. His grades were outstanding, and his favorite course was philosophy.

Carl informed the counselor that he had been struggling with what he should do in the future. On the one hand, he wanted a career that would provide him with financial security, while on the other hand, he wanted to make a contribution to humanity. As the discussion continued, the counselor realized that values were an important consideration for Carl. The counselor suggested that a value inventory might help Carl clarify his goals. Carl agreed and took the Study of Values.

Carl's profile is shown in Figure 8-3. Considering these scores, the counselor viewed Carl as placing a high value on the search for truth and knowledge, on relating to people with sympathy and unselfishness, and on actively seeking unity in the world around him. Conversely, he placed a low value on economic gains and having power over others. The aesthetic value was average.

The counselor compared Carl's scores with the mean and standard deviation of college males reported in the manual (Allport et al., 1970, p. 12). Carl's score was well beyond the first standard deviation on the social and religious scales.

Carl admitted that he had always felt a strong identification with religious activities and the welfare of others. Although he had earlier reported a strong need to provide well for his family, his highest priority was to make a contribution to society. He stated that this test provided him with the stimulation to assess his true values, and he was satisfied that the results were accurate—that is, they expressed his values at this time. However, his family's welfare would remain a primary consideration.

The counselor talked over these value considerations with Carl a number of times during Carl's college career. Carl finally decided in his junior year to enter seminary training.

SUGGESTIONS FOR CAREER DEVELOPMENT

Many of the following suggestions for fostering the career development of students and adults can be modified and used interchangeably to meet the needs of both groups. These suggestions should not be considered exhaustive of all possibilities of using assessment results to enhance career development but rather as examples from which exercises can be developed to meet local needs and needs of other groups.

For Schools:
- Using the subtests from selected values inventories, ask students to identify occupations that they consider would meet the needs of individuals who have these values. Compare theirs with each group.
- Using an identified value and its definition, have students develop a list of work environments and occupations that may satisfy the selected value. Compare the results with their scores and discuss.
- Have students interview workers and compare their values with their own. Share results.
- Ask students to compare the results of a work values inventory with their interests and abilities. Develop a selected list of occupations that meet requirements of all variables.
- Form discussion groups with peers who have opposite and/or same values.
- Have students discuss how values can influence likes and dislikes of certain occupations. Use identified values or examples.
- Have students compare their work values with their parents' occupations. Share their conclusions in groups.

For Adults:
- Ask adults to identify relevant values that have contributed to the desire for career change.
- Ask adults to identify and describe values that influenced their initial career choice. Contrast and compare these values with current ones.
- Ask adults to share and describe how their values have influenced their search for meaning in life. Use currently held values as examples.
- Ask adults to describe how their values are integrated into lifestyle preferences. Discuss major decisions.

- Ask adults to describe and identify how their values have developed. Relate relevant experiences.
- Ask adults to identify and share the importance of identifying values in career decision making. Give examples.
- Ask adults to describe how the purposes behind one's actions are influenced by value orientation. Use currently held values as examples.
- Ask adults to describe how values determine a person's interests in social groups. Compare social groups in different work settings with their values.
- Ask adults to compare their work values with work environments.
- Ask adults to identify and discuss how their values determine work ethics, orientation, and adjustment.
- Ask adults to describe and discuss how their values have the potential for fulfilling their needs and desires. Give examples.
- Ask adults to describe how values in general and specific work values influence career choices. Give examples of each.

OTHER VALUE INVENTORIES

The value inventories listed below should be evaluated for their use in career counseling. These instruments may stimulate discussions of values and their relationship to career decision making.

Rokeach Values Survey. Both of the two parts of this instrument contain an alphabetical list of 18 values defined by short phrases. Individuals are required to rank-order the two lists. Part 1 consists of "terminal" values: freedom, happiness, national security, true friendship, and so forth. Part 2 contains "instrumental" values: ambition, cheerfulness, courage, obedience, and so forth. This instrument has been used with individuals ranging in age from 11 through adulthood. It is recommended as a general measure of value.

The Campbell Organizational Survey. This instrument provides a measure of an overall index for the individual's satisfaction with the working environment. It is a part of an integrated battery that includes several other surveys (discussed in Chapter 6 with the Campbell Interest and Skill Survey). Some of the scales include measures of the following: the work itself, working conditions, co-workers, supervision, and job security.

Ohio Work Values Inventory. This inventory consists of 77 items yielding scores on 11 work values: altruism, object orientation, security, control, self-realization, independence, money, task satisfaction, solitude, ideas/data orientation, and prestige. Its use is designed for grades 4 through 12.

Career Orientation Placement and Evaluation Survey. This instrument, for junior high through community college, presents results for 7 work values on a bipolar scale as follows: investigative versus accepting, practical versus carefree, leadership versus supportive, orderliness versus noncompulsive, recognition versus privacy, aesthetic versus realistic, and social versus self-concern.

Hall Occupational Orientation Inventory. This inventory has three levels: grades 3–7, high school and college, and adults who are disabled. It is based on Maslow's hierarchy of needs. It yields 22 scores—for example: esteem, self-actualization, aspiration, co-worker concern, risk, creativity, and independence.

The Values Scale. This instrument, a research edition in developmental stage, is a measure of intrinsic and extrinsic life-career values. Examples of its 20 scales are: ability utilization, economic rewards, lifestyle, personal development, and cultural identity. This instrument has the potential of becoming a very valuable career development counseling tool.

Rating Scales of Vocational Values, Vocational Interests, and Vocational Aptitudes. This assessment instrument is designed to integrate values, interests, and aptitudes.

Individuals rate 60 activities as to their worthwhileness, interest to them, and aptitude required. This instrument may be used to foster discussion of the activities rated.

Temperament and Values Inventory. See Chapter 7 for full description of this inventory.

SUMMARY

In this chapter the relationship between individual values and career selection and satisfaction has been stressed. Because values tend to remain fairly stable over the life span, general values and work values need to be considered in career counseling. The value assessment instruments discussed in this chapter measure value constructs involved in an individual's relationship with other people, associated with everyday living, inherent in personality types, and associated with the satisfactions men and women seek in their work.

QUESTIONS AND EXERCISES

1. What are the similarities and differences between personality and value inventories? How do these similarities and differences affect their use in career counseling?
2. An individual indicates a high priority for financial independence but also aspires to a relatively low-paying job. What would be your strategy in counseling this person?
3. What are the arguments for and against using a value inventory as a selection instrument for job placement?
4. How would you justify the use of value inventories for individuals who indicate an interest in social service occupations?
5. What are the distinctions between work values and general values? How can both be used in career counseling?

Chapter Nine

Using Career Maturity Inventories

The concept of career maturity has evolved from developmental approaches to career guidance and career education programs. Super (1953, 1990), Miller-Tiedeman and Tiedeman (1990), and Gottfredson (1981) among others have made significant contributions toward an understanding of the importance of developmental approaches in career counseling. Super (1990) especially has emphasized that career choice is a continuous process through life. At different stages of life different developmental tasks must be accomplished to reach maturity.

The degree of an individual's career maturity is determined by the individual's location in the developmental process. To determine the particular stage of development, Super (1990) identifies six dimensions. He feels these dimensions are relevant to and appropriate for adolescents, but they have become the basis for all career maturity inventories: orientation to vocational choice—an attitudinal dimension determining whether the individual is concerned with making a vocational choice; information and planning—a competence dimension concerning the specificity of career information the individual has and the amount of planning the individual has done; consistency of vocational preferences—a dimension providing an index of an individual's consistency of preferences; crystallization of traits—a dimension indicating an individual's progress toward forming a self-concept; vocational independence—a dimension indicating an individual's independence in making decisions about work; and wisdom of vocational preferences—a dimension concerning the individual's ability to make realistic preferences consistent with personal goals. Individuals who score high on all dimensions are considered to be vocationally mature. In addition, for career-counseling purposes, the counselor is provided with an index of career maturity based on several dimensions.

The concept of career maturity covers not only these individually accomplished developmental tasks but also the behavior manifested in coping with the tasks of a given period of development—choosing certain courses, engaging in certain extracurricular activities, obtaining work experience. Career maturity inventories therefore measure the degree of vocational development, vocational attitude, and competence in coping with vocational developmental tasks. Knowing when individuals are competent and attitudinally ready to undertake career-related activities and to make important decisions concerning their education or vocation is an important part of career counseling and career education programs (Mitchell & Krumboltz, 1990).

Just as in an individual's vocational development, there are critical decision points in career education programs. One of the major uses of career maturity inventories is in making these assessments of the effectiveness of career education programs.

In this chapter four career maturity inventories are reviewed. For each inventory, the career maturity dimensions are identified and the use of the results for career counseling and career education programs is emphasized.

CAREER MATURITY INVENTORY (CMI)

The CMI, formerly called the Vocational Development Inventory, is divided into two parts: an attitude scale and a competence scale. Both scales are applicable to males, females, minorities, and other special groups and can be hand or computer scored. Normative data for both scales cover grades 6–12. (Norms are also available for grade 13.) The two scales can be administered and interpreted separately; however, the author suggests the use of both scales for maximum usefulness in assessing career maturity.

The attitude scale is designed to measure whether the individual is concerned about making a vocational choice. The attitude section of the inventory is in a true/false format and consists of a screening form (A-2) and a counseling form (B-1). The screening form yields only one total score; the counseling form yields a score for each of five subscales: decisiveness in career decision making, involvement in career decision making, independence in career decision making, orientation to career decision making, and compromise in career decision making. The reading level for the attitude scale is approximately sixth grade. The suggested time limits are 20 minutes for the screening form and 30 minutes for the counseling form. The attitude dimensions measured are listed in Table 9-1, which provides sample items and defines the variables for each dimension. The information contained in this table is valuable not only for understanding what is being measured by the attitude section, but also for interpreting the attitude dimensions for career counseling and for career education program evaluations.

Internal consistency for the attitude scale was calculated by the KR-20 for item data from grades 6–12 and yielded ranges from .65 to .84 with a mean coefficient of .74. A test-retest (one-year interval) measure of stability yielded a coefficient of .71 for grades 6–12. Content validity was established by evaluation of items by ten expert judges. Criterion-related validity was established by comparing scores on the attitude scale with other criteria of career maturity such as

TABLE 9-1.
Variables in the Attitude Scale of the CMI*

Dimension	Definition	Sample Item
Involvement in the choice process	Extent to which individual is actively participating in the process of making a choice	"I seldom think about the job I want to enter."
Orientation toward work	Extent to which individual is task- or pleasure-oriented in attitudes toward work and values placed on work	"Work is dull and unpleasant." "Work is worthwhile mainly because it lets you buy the things you want."
Independence in decision making	Extent to which individual relies on others in the choice of an occupation	"I plan to follow the line of work my parents suggest."
Preference for career choice factors	Extent to which individual bases choice on a particular factor	"Whether you are interested in a job is not as important as whether you can do the work."
Conceptions of the choice process	Extent to which individual has accurate or inaccurate conceptions about making a career choice	"A person can do any kind of work as long as he or she tries hard."

*From *Career Maturity Inventory* devised by John O. Crites. Reprinted by permission of the publisher, CTB/McGraw-Hill, Del Monte Research Park, Monterey, CA 93940. Copyright © 1973, 1978 by McGraw-Hill, Inc. All rights reserved. Printed in the U.S.A.

Super's (1990) indices of vocational maturity and Gribbons and Lohnes's (1968) description of readiness for vocational planning. The author of the test concludes that criterion-related validity should be considered tentative because the number of cases in the study was small.

The competence test measures the specificity of information the individual has concerning careers and the planning skills needed for career decision making. It contains items in multiple-choice format and consists of five parts: knowing yourself, knowing about jobs, choosing a job, looking ahead, and solving problems. Internal consistency for the competence scale was calculated by the KR-20 for each subtest for grades 6–12. The reported range was .72 to .90 with the exception of the problem-solving scale for the sixth and seventh grades. Few data are reported for establishing the validity of this scale. However, the author contends that content validity is ensured by the detailed analysis of the items selected.

The format of the competence subtest knowing yourself, which requires individuals to judge and appraise hypothetical characters, poses an interesting question. Can we assume that individuals who are capable of appraising others or judging what others should do are good self-appraisers? Because this appears to be the basic assumption of the author, data should be reported to support this assumption.

The results of a study by Westbrook, Cutts, Madison, and Arcia (1980) do not support the multidimensional structure of the CMI. Their findings suggest that the variables measured by the CMI are positively related to each other. Frary (1984) agrees with this conclusion. He states that the subtests of the CMI do not measure distinct constructs. Until further research is done, counselors are warned to use this inventory with some caution.

Interpreting the CMI

The results of the CMI are provided on a profile as shown in Figure 9-1. One of the limitations of the inventory is the single score yielded by the attitude subtest (Westbrook & Mastie, 1973). Because this scale measures several indices of attitudinal development, meaningful results could be communicated by additional part scores.

The degree of career maturity may be determined by evaluating responses to the inventory and from each scale score report. This information can be used for counseling purposes. For example, if a review of the responses on the attitude scale indicates an individual lacks independence in career decision making, counseling programs designed to encourage independent thought and recognition of personal assets should be considered. Likewise, a finding of a lack of occupational information (competence scale 2) or of poor planning skills (competence scale 4) suggests specific counseling procedures.

Patterns on the CMI profile also provide relevant information for evaluating career maturity and deciding on counseling approaches. For example, an individual's results may be relatively high on the attitude scale but low on the competence scale for looking ahead. In this case, the individual may be ready to make a career decision, but does not have the planning skills necessary to follow through.

Individual responses may also be evaluated for counseling considerations. For example, individuals who have difficulty in assessing their assets and liabilities might profit from counseling sessions in which they can clarify their characteristics and traits.

The CMI can be administered to a wide range of individuals, which increases its utility. The items have been drawn primarily from actual counseling cases. The author acknowledges that longitudinal research is needed to provide further measures of career development aspects. For in-depth reviews of this instrument, refer to Katz (1982) and Frary (1984).

Case of a Prevocational Training Program

A prevocational training program was designed for adults residing in small towns and rural areas within a 50-mile radius of a university in south central Texas. The major purpose of the program was to assist disadvantaged adults in preparing for employment.

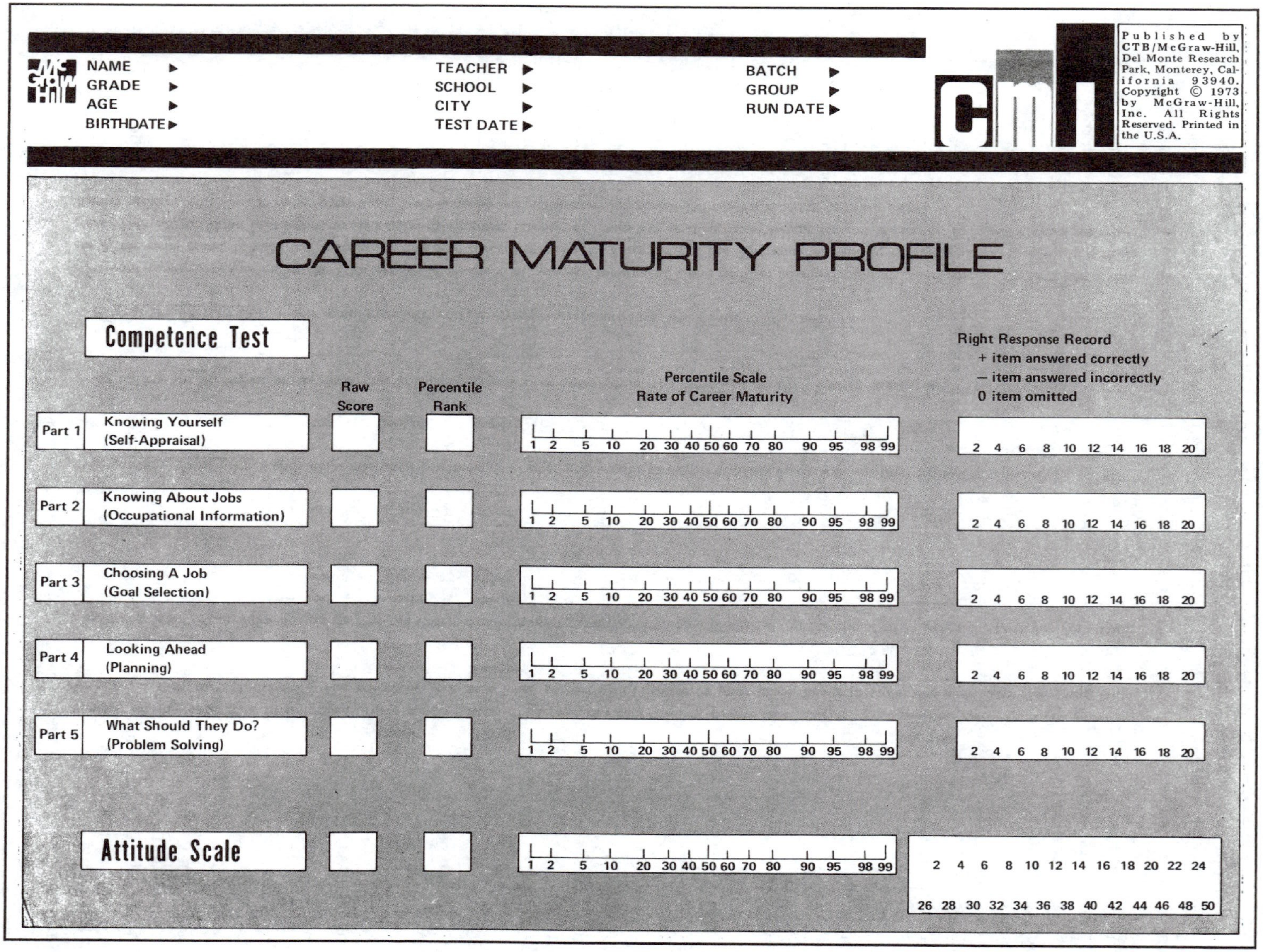

FIGURE 9-1.

Career Maturity Inventory Profile.
From *Career Maturity Inventory* devised by John O. Crites. Reprinted by permission of the publisher, CTB/McGraw-Hill, Del Monte Research Park, Monterey, CA 93940. Copyright © 1973, 1978 by McGraw-Hill, Inc. All rights reserved. Printed in the U.S.A.

The instructor was interested in knowing which components of the program were most effective in improving perceptions of and dispositions toward the world of work and in improving knowledge of occupations and planning skills. The CMI was selected as an evaluation tool because it could answer these questions. Garcia, Zunker, and Nolan (1980) report that pretest and post-test scores on the CMI showed changes in a positive direction on the attitude scale. Specifically, the results suggested significant improvement in the graduates' orientation toward work and perception of the world of work. However, the competence test revealed that the classes were not having a significant effect on the class members' planning skills.

This information made the instructor aware of program deficiencies and suggested ways to improve certain parts of the program. Learning experiences designed to enhance knowledge of occupational and career decision-making skills were added to the program. For example, time was devoted to research in the university career development resource center, and information was given to individual clients concerning jobs in general and in the community. This case illustrates how a career maturity inventory may be used in evaluating program effectiveness and in identifying parts of programs that are in need of improvement.

CAREER BELIEFS INVENTORY (CBI)

The CBI was designed as a counseling tool to help clients identify faulty beliefs that interfere with career decision making and subsequent career development. It consists of 96 items and is answered by using a 5-point rating scale from strongly agree to strongly disagree. The results are reported by 25 scales and an index to estimate response accuracy. The 25 scales are organized under five headings as follows: my current career situation, what seems necessary for my happiness, factors that influence my decisions, changes I am willing to make, and effort I am willing to initiate.

Each of the 25 scales provides a description of the meaning of a low score, the meaning of a high score, and the possible reason why it may be useful to explore low scores. This information can be very helpful to counselors when initiating discussion with clients. For example, under factors that influence decisions and the Control scale, it is suggested that the counselor find out who is exerting the most influence on the client in the decision-making process and how and why. All suggestions that are given as a result of low scores provide examples for developing intervention strategies.

The instrument is untimed and is recommended for eighth graders through adults. The directions are very clear and easily followed. Scoring may be done in Palo Alto, California, or Washington, D.C.

Interpreting the CBI

The results may be interpreted to groups or individually. A six-step model is recommended for interpretation:

1. Listen to the client's concerns and communicate your understanding of the client's situation.
2. Use the results to identify possible categories of beliefs and explore how they may be blocking progress. Low scores are the best indicators of problems.
3. Use probing procedures to tease out specific beliefs.
4. Have clients elaborate on identified beliefs, especially what would be required to disconfirm them.
5. If an identified belief is most important to a client, elicit steps to test the accuracy of the belief.
6. Have clients plan actions to take if beliefs are found to be inaccurate.

Case studies are given as examples of how the results can be used most effectively. Also included in the manual is the rationale for the CBI. Before using this instrument counselors should become familiar with Krumboltz's social learning theory of career decision making (Mitchell & Krumboltz, 1990).

The norms for this instrument were developed from 7500 people in the United States and Australia. Percentile ranks and standard scores are given for employed and unemployed adults, male and female employed adults, full-time adult students, undergraduate college students, high school students, and junior high school students. Test-retest reliabilities are provided for high school and college students and range from the .30s to mid .70s. Alpha reliability coefficients were given for all groups in the norm sample and had approximately the same ranges as the test-retest reliabilities. Although several validity studies were conducted between scales and satisfaction ratings and between other inventories such as the Strong Interest Inventory, The Self-Directed Search, and the Myers-Briggs Type Indicator, the manual points out that there is no single meaningful criterion against which one can validate career beliefs. In summary, this instrument was developed for providing information about career beliefs, which can be used in career counseling but not as the basis for selection or classification.

Case of the Reluctant Decision Maker

Bev was accompanied to a community counseling center by a friend who was also a client for career counseling. Bev needed a great deal of support and encouragement before she agreed to make an appointment.

Bev quit high school when she was in the 10th grade to work in a fast-food establishment. She recently completed a high school equivalency course and received a diploma. Now 22, she continued to live with her parents. She had four siblings. Her father was a factory worker, and her mother a homemaker. She asked for help to find a better job.

The counselor discovered that Bev had taken part in a career-counseling program while in the high school equivalency program.

Bev: Yes, I took several tests before I finished my training.
Counselor: Do you recall the kind of tests?
Bev: One was for interests and the other one was an aptitude test.
Counselor: Good! What did you decide after going over the results?
Bev: Well, I decided to think about two or three different jobs, but I didn't get anywhere.
Counselor: Explain more fully.
Bev: I thought the counselor there was supposed to tell me more about what I should do and what I'm qualified for.

As Bev and the counselor continued their discussion it became apparent that she had some faulty beliefs about career decision making. She evidently thought that someone would decide for her or provide a recipe for choosing a job with little effort on her part. In addition, the counselor suspected that there were some underlying reasons why she was not taking appropriate actions to solve her problems, but this would have to be confirmed by additional data and observation.

Bev: I just was not able to decide, and I really needed more help.
Counselor: Could you tell me more about the help you needed?
Bev: I don't know—I just couldn't see myself in those jobs. I thought there would be steps you take to find out. I just don't know about all those jobs. My family makes fun of me when I talk about more school.
Counselor: Tell me more about your family.
Bev: They all have low-paying, labor-type jobs and think that I should be like them—just get by and shift from one job to another. Some of the time I think they are right—maybe I'm not cut out to do any other kind of work.

After further discussion, the counselor confirmed some faulty beliefs that might prevent Bev's progress in the decision-making process. The counselor based such opinions on the following observations that appeared to form a pattern of thinking and viewing the world that could inhibit Bev's career development.

> Apparent anxiety about career planning
> Lack of flexibility in decision making
> Lack of willingness to consider new occupations
> Self-observation generalizations that were blocking her efforts to make a decision
> Faulty beliefs about career decision making and occupational environments
> Lack of family support

Counselor: Bev, we can help you make a career decision, but first we both should learn more about your career beliefs. Would you be interested in taking an inventory that would help us understand more about your beliefs and your assumptions about careers.

Bev: Sure, I guess so, but I don't understand how it would help.

Counselor: Let me explain how we will use the results. We can find out about some of the factors that influence your decisions, what may be necessary to make you feel happy about your future, and the changes you are willing to make. Discussing these subjects should help in clarifying your role and my role in the career decision-making process.

The results of the CBI indicated low scores on several scales, especially on acceptance of uncertainty and on openness. Low scores on these scales indicate that excessive anxiety leads to viewing career decision making as overwhelming and suggest that Bev has fears about the reactions of others.

After the counselor explained the inventory, the following dialogue took place:

Counselor: Bev, could you tell me the reasons why you are uncertain about your career plans?

Bev: Nobody in my family has ever had much schooling. I guess it's not in me to go for more education or training.

Counselor: So you believe that you cannot be successful in higher education because your family has not.

Bev: Yes, I suppose that's true.

Counselor: Could you tell me why you feel this way?

Bev: They don't think I can do it.

Counselor: How did you do in the courses for the high school equivalency?

Bev: I made good grades—above "C" in every course and I got two "A"s.

Counselor: What does this tell you about your ability to do academic work?

Bev: OK, I was successful here but that doesn't mean I could do the same in college.

Counselor: You are right. There are no guarantees, but we have known for a long time that past academic performance is a good indicator of future performance in school.

Bev: But my brother and mom keep telling me we aren't the kind to go to college.

Counselor: If I provide you with some information about your chances of making a "C" or better in community college, would you be willing to talk with your family about the options you are considering for the future?

After receiving agreement from Bev to talk with her parents about further education and her desire to change jobs, the counselor planned to have Bev discuss the reasons why her parents feel the way that they do and the effect this has had on thinking about her future plans. The counselor hoped to lead Bev into recognizing that faulty beliefs about her own future were affecting her ability to make decisions in her own best interests.

Each of the scales that Bev scored low on were discussed in a similar manner—that is, faulty beliefs were identified and discussed, followed by specific plans of action that she would take if the belief proved to be inaccurate.

In this case the CBI provided the stimulus for discussing relevant problems that inhibited a client from making choices in her best interests. Bev's counselor will need to spend considerable time in attempting to change faulty beliefs that have been ingrained through socialization for a considerable period of time. The client must actively participate in this process to deal appropriately with questions of changes.

CAREER DEVELOPMENT INVENTORY (CDI)

Form IV of the CDI consists of two parts. The first part measures two attitudinal aspects of career development (planfulness and exploration) and two cognitive aspects (career decision making and career and occupational information). The second part measures knowledge of the individual's preferred occupational group. The first part can be administered in 40 minutes and the second part in 20 minutes. Separate sex norms are provided for grades 9–12. The inventory can be hand scored or computer scored.

The planfulness scale measures how much time the individual has devoted to planning career-related activities, such as courses in school. The exploration scale indicates whether the individual has used educational and occupational information resources. The career decision-making scale measures knowledge of the principles of career decision making. Career and occupational information, the fourth scale, is a measure of the individual's knowledge of and perspectives on the world of work.

The second part of the inventory consists of a single test, knowledge of preferred occupational groups. First, the individual selects a preferred occupational group from 20 families of related occupations. Second, the individual selects for this group the most appropriate level of education or training, the duties, the personal characteristics required for entry and getting established, the rewards and satisfactions, and so forth.

Interpreting the CDI

The CDI yields two different kinds of data useful for counseling purposes. First, a composite score provides a multidimensional measure of vocational maturity. This score is useful as a single measure of vocational maturity, although the authors make it clear that not all dimensions of vocational maturity are measured.

Second, five trait scores indicate specific strengths and weaknesses and provide an evaluation of the individual's readiness to make career decisions. These scores are useful for determining further developmental experiences necessary to increase readiness for decision making.

The CDI is useful as a diagnostic measure in that it indicates an individual's readiness to make educational and occupational choices. The results provide an index of attitudes toward career planning, knowledge of occupations, and skills necessary for career decision making. Curriculum and guidance programs may also be evaluated using the CDI for their effectiveness in supporting attitudes and in teaching skills necessary in the career decision-making process. Earlier forms of this instrument have been reviewed by Bingham (1978), Ricks (1978), and Hilton (1982).

Case Test Questions in Group Counseling

The career counselor in a high school and one of the teachers reviewed the results of the CDI that had recently been administered to junior and seniors in their school. Their major goal was to establish programs for students based on needs indicated by the CDI results. Typical of the programs was the one developed for students with particularly poor scores on the planning section of the inventory. The students volunteered for participation in the program.

Both the teacher and the counselor were concerned with the students' lack of knowledge of working environments and their naive and nonchalant attitudes concerning the world of work. They wanted to provide a program that would help these students take a realistic approach to career planning. They agreed on a group counseling approach in order to reach all these students in a short period of time. The strategy was to use selected items from the CDI section measuring planfulness to stimulate group discussion. Several specific tasks were identified as the major objectives: clarify career planning attitudes, evaluate time spent thinking about and planning careers, identify courses associated with potential career plans, increase awareness of relevant activities associated with career planning, and clarify reasons for considering work environments in relation to careers. The following dialogue illustrates how the strategy of using CDI questions was employed to meet the specific objectives.

Counselor:	The major goal of this counseling session is to encourage each of you to devote more time to career planning. We will begin our session by discussing some of the questions in the CDI. Each of you has an inventory booklet for this purpose. (The counselor continued by presenting sample questions that she had previously identified. One of the questions dealt with the purpose of learning about actual working conditions of jobs being considered.)
Jan:	If you don't know anything about a job, how can you be expected to choose it?
Roberto:	Yeah, you have to know what the requirements are to make a decision about it.
Tom:	You should also know where you will be working — I mean, what places and how.
Rosa:	I remember that my brother told me he never would have taken the job he has if he had known more about it. He gets all dirty, and the other guys talk rough and threaten him. He is trapped in that job, and he can hardly wait to find another job.
Counselor:	Very good! You have illustrated why it is important to thoroughly investigate the requirements of occupations you may be considering and the kind of people you will be associating with in those occupations. Now, let's look at another question. Jan, what was your answer for question 1: "Taking classes that will help me decide what line of work to go into when I leave school or college"?
Jan:	I'm not sure, but I believe I answered, "Not giving any thought to doing this." [Pause] I really haven't thought about it much. I guess I'm just enjoying myself now and not considering the future.
Bertha:	I heard that more and more women are going to have to work to support their families, so I believe we have to plan for jobs in the future like the boys do.
Rosa:	I agree. The sooner we get started thinking about the jobs, the better prepared we will be.
Tom:	We guys had better get started, too!

The counselor provided the opportunity for each member of the group to respond to other key questions from the CDI. After the implications of the questions were discussed, the counselor reiterated the need for thinking about and planning various career-related activities. This case illustrates the use of inventory questions to create discussion topics related to identified goals and specific tasks.

NEW MEXICO CAREER EDUCATION TEST SERIES (NMCETS)

The NMCETS is a good example of a vocational maturity test designed to assess specific objectives for career education programs for grades 9–12. This criterion-referenced test consists of six subtests—five competence scales and one attitude scale: career planning, career-oriented activities, knowledge of occupations, job application procedures, career development, and attitude toward work. Each test has general objectives and subobjectives stated in behavioral terms. Questions were derived from a review of the objectives of a national sample of career education programs.

The range of the subtest coefficients for grades 9 and 12 was .52 to .87 with the average near .66. According to Bodden (1978) these reliabilities are low primarily because of the small number of items used in the subtests. The authors claim validity on the basis of gains in the students' vocational readiness in grades 9–12. Independent t-tests of 9th and 12th grade means were statistically significant, which lends support to the author's claim that the inventory assesses incremental program effects.

This test should be considered experimental. There are some limitations to the test. The authors fail to provide adequate information on the counseling implications of the test results. In addition, the norms on this test are based completely on samples of students drawn from the public schools in New Mexico. The test is in need of further research and comprehensive normative data. Finally, the philosophical basis of the attitude scale should be scrutinized and its appropriateness for the target population carefully analyzed. The correct responses on this scale appear to be based on the authors' particular philosophy without sufficient evidence of validity. This instrument has been reviewed by Bodden (1978), Prediger (1978), and Westbrook (1978).

Interpreting the NMCETS

Percentile and stanine norms for each of the six tests are provided for 9th and 12th grades. These scores aid in use of the test as a diagnostic tool for counseling. However, the authors suggest this test may be best used as a criterion-referenced measure of the effectiveness of career education programs in reaching established goals. Another important use of the NMCETS is in needs assessments for career education programs. This instrument seems to have great potential for prescribing specific activities. The dimensions measured by this instrument provide a solid foundation on which to base career education programs.

COGNITIVE VOCATIONAL MATURITY TEST (CVMT)

The CVMT is primarily a cognitive test of an individual's knowledge of occupations. Specifically, it measures knowledge of how to make realistic occupational choices; knowledge of work conditions, training requirements, and duties of various occupations; knowledge of sources of career information, planning skills, occupational and industrial trends, and employment-seeking skills. The authors emphasize that the test does not attempt to measure attitudes toward work (Westbrook & Parry-Hill, 1973). The test consists of 120 multiple-choice items; administration time is approximately 60 minutes. The reading levels for the subtests range from grades 1.4 to 2.2.

The test is divided into six subtests: fields of work (knowledge of occupations), job selection (knowledge of individual characteristics required for jobs), work conditions (knowledge of characteristics of work environments), education required (knowledge of specific requirements of jobs), duties (knowledge of duties performed in jobs), and attributes (knowledge of specific skills required). Each subtest yields its own score.

Internal consistency was established by KR-20 for all subtests grades 6–9. The coefficients range from .67 to .91. The criterion validity was based on data from a sample of ninth graders whose vocational choices were in their fields of interest and whose aptitude scores were considered appropriate for their career choice. These students tended to score higher on the subtests than did their counterparts, whose career choices were not in accord with their interests or aptitudes.

Interpreting the CVMT

Westbrook and Mastie (1973) suggest that the CVMT has value as a diagnostic test. It is also appropriate for evaluating needs for career education programs and the effectiveness of career education programs that have objectives that match the six areas measured. However, their general evaluation of the CVMT suggests that the instrument is in need of further research and the current norm table should be used with a great deal of caution. In addition, content and construct validity of the subtests need to be researched and established. More data are also needed on the stability of the test. The measures of cognitive domain need refinement and expansion.

In the meantime, the CVMT may be used effectively as a criterion-referenced measure. For example, the CVMT may be used to assess individual readiness for career planning by evaluating the difference in scores obtained and projected or expected scores. It may also be used for assessing career program needs.

Case of Needs Analysis for Program Development

The counselor at Jones High School received permission to participate in a follow-up survey of graduates sponsored by a national testing firm. The survey included those students who had graduated from Jones High within the last five years. The results of the survey pointed to a general weakness on the part of the high school in preparing students for making career decisions and in general in preparing them for the world of work. The counselor presented these results to the administration and later in a faculty meeting. He gained the support of the faculty and the administration for developing programs to prepare students for entering the labor market.

Although the committee formed to develop these programs was aware of the results of the recently completed survey, the members unanimously agreed that an analysis of current student needs would provide guidelines for building developmental programs. The CVMT was chosen primarily because of its six criterion-referenced measures. The committee agreed that this instrument could serve both as an indicator of needs and as an evaluation tool when used as a posttest. Financial limitations dictated that the test could be administered only to the freshman class.

The results of the CVMT indicated a general weakness among students in fields of work, work conditions, and attributes required. The committee decided to concentrate their efforts on these identified needs. Specifically, they decided to sponsor specially designed seminars and to solicit the help of a selected group of teachers in developing modules that could be incorporated into classroom instruction. An example of a counseling component designed to enhance the students' knowledge of occupations had these technique options: published printed materials, microfiche systems, computer information systems, and files. The specific tasks to be accomplished were: identify sources of occupational information, identify work worlds and how they relate to lifestyle, identify and assess occupational opportunities, relate identified skills and work experience to specific occupational requirements, evaluate how well occupations fulfill needs, relate identified goals to occupational choice, identify educational/training needs for specific occupations, and identify expectations of future work and lifestyle.

The case of Jones High illustrates how the CVMT can identify specific needs of individuals—information that can then be used to develop programs. As an evaluation tool for program effectiveness the CVMT identifies weaknesses and strengths of the strategies used.

OTHER MEASURES OF CAREER MATURITY AND DEVELOPMENT FOR FUTURE USE

Adult Career Concerns Inventory. This inventory, a research edition in developmental stage, is a measure of Super's (1990) hierarchy of life stages: exploration, establishment, maintenance, and disengagement. Another scale, career change status, has been added. An individual's career state and vocational maturity are assessed by this instrument.

The Salience Inventory. This instrument, a research edition in developmental stage, is designed to measure five major life roles: student, worker, homemaker, leisurite, and citizen. Use of the inventory results provides counselors an evaluation of an individual's readiness for career decisions and the individual's exposure to work and occupations.

SUMMARY

The career maturity of adolescents, according to Super, is a stage of development with six dimensions: orientation to vocational choice, information and planning, consistency of vocational preferences, crystallization of traits, vocational independence, and wisdom of vocational preferences. These dimensions have become the foundation on which career maturity inventories are built. Thus, career maturity inventories measure degree of vocational development, attitudes toward work, and competence in coping with vocational developmental tasks. Career maturity inventories provide measures of the individual's readiness to enter certain career-related activities and are used to assess the effectiveness of career education programs.

QUESTIONS AND EXERCISES

1. What are career maturity inventories designed to measure?
2. Defend or criticize the following: Career maturity is easily measured. Defend your position with illustrations.
3. At what stage in the educational process can career maturity inventory results be used in career-counseling programs? Illustrate with three examples.
4. How would you justify the use of a career maturity inventory to evaluate career education programs?
5. What are the advantages of using questions taken directly from a career maturity inventory to stimulate group discussion?

Chapter Ten
Combining Assessment Results

In each of the preceding chapters the discussion of assessment was of necessity limited to one type of inventory or test. I do not want to give the impression, however, that segregating individually measured characteristics and traits is good practice. On the contrary, career counselors should consider the totality of individual needs. Each measured characteristic provides a rich source of information for stimulating discussion about goals and for enhancing self-understanding. The career counselor's aim is to encourage combining this information in the career-planning process.

In this chapter a counseling case illustrates the use of a conceptual model for using assessment results in a university counseling center. Additionally, a combined assessment program, The American College Testing (ACT) Career Planning Program, is reviewed and discussed. Examples of the use of such an instrument for career counseling are presented. Use of a combination of assessment results is also illustrated by cases that utilize the results of several tests and inventories discussed in preceding chapters. Finally, the use of a computerized assessment program is illustrated.

USING A MODEL FOR COMBINING ASSESSMENT RESULTS

In the following illustration of a conceptual model for using assessment results both major and minor components of the model are identified to demonstrate a sequential order of events. Although this is a contrived situation, it closely resembles an actual counseling case at a university counseling center.

Marvin, a 20-year-old college sophomore, was referred to the counseling center by one of his instructors. He informed the receptionist that he needed help choosing a major. Bob, a career counselor, was assigned to Marvin's case by the receptionist.

Step 1. Analyzing Needs

A. Establishing the Counseling Relationship

Counselor:	Hi, Marvin. I'm Bob. Come into my office and let's talk. I see that you were referred by Mr. Goss.
Marvin:	Yes, sir. He's my math instructor.
Counselor:	I know Mr. Goss well. He's a great professor, isn't he?
Marvin:	I really like him! I guess because he's so fair to everyone and he's real easy to talk to.
Counselor:	Right. Most students have told me that. Do you live in the city, Marvin?
Marvin:	No. I live out on Hunter Road.

Counselor: That's a nice area. Now, let's see how we can help you. You mentioned to the receptionist you need help in choosing a major.

Marvin: Yeah. I just can't decide. But, let me tell you the whole story. Do you have the time?

Counselor: You bet. We'll take as much time as we need.

(Marvin informed the counselor that he was interested in forestry but wasn't able to attend a college that offered forestry as a major because he was financially unable to live away from home and felt he should not leave his aged parents. He was somewhat disappointed but seemed to accept the reality of the situation.)

B.   Accept and Adopt the Counselee's View

Counselor: I understand your concern. That's not the ideal situation for you, perhaps, but let's follow up on your interest in forestry. Tell me something about that.

Marvin: Well, I like to be outdoors—growing up in the woods and all—our house is right on a river and I've fished and hunted all my life. I just like it outside. I probably couldn't make it being penned up in an office all day long.

Counselor: Okay, you like the outdoors and that's a good point we need to keep in mind when you are considering college majors or careers. What else can you tell me about forestry?

(The counselor's question was an attempt to determine if Marvin had investigated the nature or work involved in forestry. Also, the counselor wanted to measure the depth of Marvin's commitment to this kind of work.)

Marvin: Okay, see, I read up some on forestry in a career book and it sounded just like the kind of work I'd like. You know, watch the growth of trees and how they survive. And I also looked at some college catalogs to find out which ones offered it as a major. That's about when I realized I couldn't go with forestry because I just can't leave my parents now.

(Following further discussion of forestry, the counselor was satisfied that Marvin was indeed committed and he concluded that occupations related to forestry would be a good point for discussion in the future.)

C.   Establish Dimensions of Lifestyle

Counselor: Earlier, you mentioned that you like to hunt and fish. What other leisure activities do you enjoy?

Marvin: Oh, I collect rocks and I go horseback riding, plus I like to watch basketball, and I play a little tennis.

Counselor: Do you belong to any clubs on campus?

Marvin: Yes, I'm a member of the science club, and I've thought about joining a fraternity.

(During these discussions the counselor made occasional notes reflecting pertinent information about Marvin. Included in the notes are the following statements:

Expressed an interest in forestry

Likes the outdoors

Grew up in a country home

Has given considerable thought to a career

Commitment to outdoor work seems firm

Interested in science

Likes to be around animals

Collects rocks

Likes team sports

Some interests are fairly well crystallized

Is disappointed about inability to pursue forestry degree, but has accepted the situation fairly well . . .)

D.   Specify Needs

Counselor: Let's get back to your reason for coming here. You mentioned that you wanted help in choosing a major that is available at this university.

Marvin nodded.

Counselor:	Okay, one of the first things we can do is to further explore your interests. For example, you stated a strong need to work outdoors and a definite interest in forestry. Would you like to explore other interests and link them to possible major and career options?
Marvin:	Right. That's what I came here for. I'd like to take one of those interest tests.
Counselor:	I believe this would be a good first step, and we can arrange for you to take an interest inventory during your next appointment. But before we decide on a specific interest inventory, tell me how you are doing academically in college.

Marvin informed the counselor that he had maintained a high B average in all of his course work. He explained that he did best in math and science courses.

Marvin:	I've always liked math and science, and I make my best grades in these courses. So far, I have an "A" in biology, chemistry, and math.

(The counselor decided that an aptitude or achievement test was not necessary at this time since Marvin had established a good academic record. The counselor would review Marvin's transcript before the next appointment.)

Step 2.   Establishing the Purpose

Counselor:	Now, let's get back to the interest inventory. How do you think an interest inventory will help you in choosing a major?
Marvin:	Well, I hope it will give me some ideas about possible majors.
Counselor:	Right, it will. We usually expect that results will verify some previously expressed interests and will also introduce new possibilities to explore. How does this sound to you?
Marvin:	Let's go for it!
Counselor:	Great! Later we can decide if other testing is necessary. Now, let's check with the receptionist for a testing time.

Step 3.   Determining the Instrument

When selecting an interest inventory for Marvin, the counselor reviewed the notations he had made earlier and, in fact, reconstructed the entire conversation with Marvin. He concluded that Marvin could benefit most from an interest inventory that provided occupational college major scales as presented by the Kuder Occupational Interest Survey, Form DD. His rationale was that Marvin had crystallized his interest fairly well at this point in his life and was more in need of specific information such as college major scale scores and less in need of information pertaining to broad areas of interest such as general occupational themes. The counselor decided that the Kuder Occupational Interest Survey, Form DD, would also be a good instrument to provide Marvin with specific college majors to consider in the career decision-making process. Scores on college majors and occupational scales can be compared on the Kuder Occupational Interest Survey profile (see page 66).

Step 4.   Utilizing the Results

During the pre-interpretation phase the counselor reviewed the profile scores from the interest inventory. He noticed that Marvin's highest occupational scale scores were for forestry worker, civil engineer, county agricultural agent, mathematician, and veterinarian. His highest college major scale scores were forestry, mathematics, biological science, civil engineering, animal husbandry, and physical science. These results seem to verify Marvin's expressed interest in the outdoors, mathematics, and sciences.

In reviewing Marvin's transcript of earned college credits, the counselor found that Marvin's grade point average was a high "B." Marvin had done extremely well on mathematics and science courses, earning grades of "A"s. His outstanding performance in mathematics and science courses linked well with his interest in mathematics, civil engineering, and biological and physical sciences.

Marvin reported promptly for the next counseling session. After asking Marvin what had transpired since their last meeting, the counselor presented the profile of interest scores.

Counselor: As you recall, in our discussion of interest inventories, we agreed that we could get some suggestions for college majors from the results. I believe you will be pleased to find that there are a number of majors indicated for your consideration. But, remember, that this information is only one factor we should consider in the career decision-making process.

Marvin: Right.

The counselor explained the occupational major scale scores as in the following example.

Counselor: The asterisk by this list of college majors (pointing to the profile) indicates that your responses were very similar to responses of satisfied individuals who are majoring in these fields of study. Your highest scores in mathematics on the college major scales are typical of satisfied people who are majoring in mathematics. According to these results, a major in mathematics should be one of the majors for you to consider.

Marvin: (pause) Yeah, I do like math, but I'm not really all that interested in being a mathematician. What do they do besides teach?

Counselor: Good question. I think you will find our career library helpful in answering questions like this one. In fact, I think it would be a good idea for us to make a list of all the college majors and related careers you might want to explore further.

(Marvin agreed that he would be interested in researching several majors suggested from the results of the interest inventory. The counselor also discussed how interests in certain college subjects could be related to the occupational scales on the interest inventory.)

Counselor: One of your highest interests on the occupational scales is civil engineering. Can you link high interests in college major scales to this occupation?

Marvin: Oh, I see. Yeah, civil engineers have to be sharp in mathematics.

Counselor: That's right. The point is, if you don't want to be a mathematician, you can link this interest and your proficiency in math to a number of occupations.

(Using this procedure to discuss the results of the interest inventory, the counselor assisted Marvin in developing a list of majors and occupations he would research in the career library. It was agreed that Marvin was to do his research within a 30-day period. After three weeks, Marvin came in for an appointment.)

Counselor: Hi, Marvin. I've been wondering how you made out. I noticed you busy at work in the career library several times.

Marvin: Yes, I went through quite a bit of material.

Counselor: Before you tell me what you found, let's review the list of majors and occupations you were to research.

Marvin: Okay, but I eliminated several right away.

(As they looked over the previously prepared list of majors and occupations, Marvin also reviewed the notes he had made from his research.)

Marvin: I still would like to be a forester, but I found that civil engineering might be a good substitute.

Counselor: Tell me more about how you came to that conclusion.

Marvin: Well, as you know, I like the outdoors and I'm pretty good in math and I read that civil engineers do spend a lot of time surveying in the open country. Also, our college offers a degree in civil engineering. This appeals to me. I think I might like a job like this, but I'm not completely sure.

Counselor:	Your conclusions sound logical. The civil engineer occupation does fit the pattern of your expressed interests we reviewed from the interest inventory, and you have a good background in math and sciences. But, you still seem to have doubts.
Marvin:	Yeah, I'd like to know more about it.
Counselor:	Would you like to talk to someone who is a civil engineer?
Marvin:	Hey, that'd be great!

(The counselor arranged for Marvin to visit a civil engineer assigned to the state highway department and one assigned to a privately operated surveying company. He also suggested that Marvin visit the chairman of the civil engineering department. Marvin opted to visit the practicing engineers first.

In addition to discussing civil engineering, Marvin and the counselor explored several other career options. However, Marvin, preoccupied with visiting the civil engineer, gave little attention to other possible alternatives.

Two weeks later Marvin was back for another counseling session after having visited the work sites of two civil engineers. Surprisingly, Marvin lacked his usual enthusiasm when he greeted the counselor.)

Counselor:	It's good to see you again, Marvin. I hope you found the visits to the engineers to be informative.
Marvin:	It was okay, I guess.
Counselor:	You don't seem to be too excited about what you found.
Marvin:	No, I'm not. I don't really think now that I'd like being a civil engineer.
Counselor:	Would you mind sharing your observations with me?
Marvin:	Well, it turns out they have to be inside and do more office work than I had thought, looking up materials, reading land titles, and plotting grades. That part of it sure doesn't appeal to me. I just have this thing about working outdoors. Also, they don't make much money, either!

(As Marvin and the counselor continued to discuss civil engineering and other occupations, it became clear to the counselor that Marvin was in need of further clarification of interests, values, and preferred lifestyles. The counselor shifted the discussion to analyzing needs.)

Counselor:	Marvin, during this conversation there have been some key factors discussed that are most important for you to consider in planning for the future. For example, you found several work requirements in civil engineering that were not to your liking. You also brought up the fact that the pay scale of civil engineers does not meet your financial requirements. The point is, that on this visit, you learned a great deal about a particular occupation and some very important factors about yourself. Would you agree?
Marvin:	You're right. I had the wrong impression about civil engineering, and I guess it took a trip out there to make that clear. Besides, when I started researching in the career library, I realized that I hadn't thought about a lot of things concerning work.
Counselor:	We all learn through experience.
Marvin:	Yeah, I guess that's right, but now what?
Counselor:	You mentioned that you learned more about yourself when you made the on-site visitation. Could you explain more fully?
Marvin:	Oh, I guess I started thinking about a lot of things, like I know now that I want to make a lot of money, you know. I need to be able to afford to buy some land, and have a nice car and even a stable full of horses. I just didn't realize that this was all a part of what I was supposed to be deciding. I suddenly realized that the decisions I make right now will have a lot to do with all this stuff in the future like for the rest of my life, even. Whew, heavy stuff.
Counselor:	Perhaps I can help you clarify more of these important factors like the ones you mentioned.
Marvin:	Yep, that's what I need, all right. I'm just not ready to make that big a decision yet.

(The counselor had returned to the first step in the model for using assessment results: analyzing needs. He was now ready to further specify needs, part of step 1.)

Counselor: What we have been discussing are values. You have verified your interests and now we have shifted to considering a most important dimension — value clarification. For example, how strongly do you value a variety of tasks on a job, such as prestige, independence, creativity, and a feeling of accomplishment?

Marvin: (pause) I never even thought of those things before.

(The counselor was now in the position to once again establish the purpose of using assessment results.)

Counselor: Would you like to learn more about your values?

Marvin: That sounds interesting.

Counselor: We have found that value clarification is an important part of career decision making. Many individuals find that the discussion of values is an enlightening experience which helps clarify expectations of life and work. I believe that an inventory that measures satisfaction one seeks from work would be helpful to you.

(Marvin agreed that value clarification would help him at this point in the decision process and an appointment was made for administering a values inventory.)

In determining the instrument the counselor decided that the Work Values Inventory (WVI) (Super, 1970) would be most helpful for Marvin primarily because the focus of attention at this point had been on values associated with work. This instrument measures 15 work values as described on pages 104–105. The counselor's strategy was to link specific work values with college majors and occupational interest patterns as measured by the previously administered interest inventory. The counselor's rationale was that Marvin was in need of a values measure that could provide direct association with work in order to stimulate discussion about satisfactions derived from work.

When the results of Marvin's scores on the WVI were available, the counselor began preparation for utilizing the results. He made notes of the three highest values—creativity, surroundings, and way of life—and the three lowest scores—supervisor relations, economic returns, and variety. Using these results, the counselor felt that he could stimulate discussion concerning work values and their relation to career choice.

When Marvin reported for his next appointment, the counselor explained the purpose of the inventory and presented Marvin with the profile of scores.

Counselor: I'd like you to study your pattern of scores and read the definition of each value. After you have finished, we will discuss the results.

Marvin spent considerable time reviewing the results of the WVI. After reading the definition of each value, he made the following comment:

Marvin: This is interesting. I'm surprised about some of the results, but yet when I think of what I really like and value, I guess I'm not all that surprised.

Counselor: Could you be more specific?

Marvin: Remember when I came back from the visit with the civil engineer, I said they didn't make enough money for me? Well, that's not really a big thing with me. I guess that I was just frustrated because civil engineers turned out to not be a good substitute for what I really want. Anyway, my low score in economic returns is right, I think.

Counselor: What about the other scores?

Marvin: Being creative and having a way of life is right on target.

Counselor: Can you relate these values to college majors and occupations as measured by the interest inventory?

Marvin: I guess you probably have opportunities to be creative in most any occupation so that's no big deal. But, the way-of-life value is something else. (Pause) You know, Bob, I've just got to follow through in some way to get what I really like. Isn't there some way I could still go into forestry?

(The depth of Marvin's commitment to forestry was once again made very clear in this discussion and others that followed. Assessment of interest and work values stimulated Marvin to consider alternative college majors and occupations, but he also came to the conclusion that his dream of becoming a forester was an overwhelming desire for which there was no substitute.)

Step 5.   *Making a Decision*

Marvin decided to continue college on a part-time basis in order to find a job from which he could save the necessary funds to attend a university that offered forestry. Even though he was reluctant to leave his parents to attend college, they encouraged him to pursue his interest.

Summary

This case illustrates how assessment results can be used at various stages in the career decision-making process and in particular how they can encourage further exploration and clarification. In Marvin's case, assessment results were used when the need was established. An interest inventory focused attention on career alternatives that Marvin had not considered and reinforced his expressed interest in outdoor work. When Marvin and the counselor agreed that value clarification was an important dimension to consider in the career decision-making process, a values inventory was used. In each instance, the purpose of assessment results was clearly established. As Marvin experienced a greater sense of awareness, he was greatly assisted in the career decision-making process by the use of carefully selected assessment inventories.

ACT Career Planning Program (CPP)

The CPP consists of several components designed to provide a comprehensive career guidance model for use in high schools and postsecondary institutions. The CPP is also recommended for use as a basic part of career development minicourses and as an organizing theme for displaying and filing occupational information in a career center. In addition, the CPP provides cooperative guidance programs for feeder high schools and postsecondary institutions. Specifically, joint career guidance programs can be offered by the high school and postsecondary institutions through CPP-designed materials and follow-up career days. The CPP ability measures can also be used for placement in mathematics, English, and reading programs.

The CPP assessment instruments consist of a Vocational Interest Profile (VIP), ability measures, experience scales, and a background and plans section. Testing time is two and one-half hours. All scoring is done by computer except for the ability measures, which can be self-scored. Local norms can be generated for the ability measures.

For the VIP, which measures interest in eight occupational areas, estimates of reliability by alpha coefficients for men range from .84 to .93; for women the range is .80 to .90. Test-retest correlations (60-day intervals) range from .62 to .79 for men and from .72 to .88 for women. The correlations indicate that the VIP is sufficiently stable for use in career counseling. The CPP manual presents evidence that the VIP scales successfully discriminate among students enrolled in a variety of educational and training programs.

The six ability measures assess reading skills, numerical skills, language usage, mechanical reasoning, clerical skills, and space relations. Reliability estimates for the ability measures were calculated by KR-20 and test-retest (two-week intervals). The KR-20 reliability estimates range from .77 to .99 with a median of .83. The median test-retest correlations range from .73 to .87. Validity was established by comparing the relationship between test results and course performance in various educational programs. Each ability test appears to be appropriate for assessing specific skills.

The experience scales provide a summary of work-related experience in the eight occupational interest areas on the VIP. The background and plans section includes information on educational and vocational plans, biographical information, information on educational needs, and local items supplied for a specific institutional program or service. Estimates of reliability by alpha coefficients for men range from .74 to .88; for women the range is .65 to .86. Healy (1978) and Geisinger (1984) provide additional information for evaluating this instrument.

Interpreting the CPP

The CPP profile reports scores for eight career clusters as shown in Figure 10-1. Sample educational programs that prepare people for careers within each of the clusters are listed. Abilities considered essential for meeting the requirements of jobs within each cluster are also listed. This organization of career clusters is built around Holland's (1985) career typology.

Another part of the profile, shown in Figure 10-2, reports relevant experiences of the individual within each career cluster. These experiences are rated as none, few, some, and many, as compared with a national norm. The eight interest measures and the six ability measures are assigned stanine scores marked on a graph divided into lower quarter, middle half, and upper quarter. An estimated ACT composite score range is also projected; it can be used when higher education is being considered.

The CPP profile report can be self-interpreted. A student handbook offers a concise explanation of scores and a systematic procedure for interpreting the results. Various alternatives and references are given for each major step in career exploration. A counselor can complement the reported information, as many students need assistance in making the most meaningful interpretations of the data reported. For this purpose the CPP *Counselor's Guide* (American College Testing Program, 1980) is provided.

Case of an Ex-Navy Deckhand Considering Community College

Abe was considering the possibility of attending the local community college after four years in the Navy. He asked the counselor for information on the CPP, which he had read about in a brochure. This program appealed to Abe because, as he put it, "I want to know more about myself so that I'll have a better idea of what to do in the future." He added that his experience as a deckhand in the Navy convinced him that he wanted something different as a career, but he needed help in finding the right job.

After a rather lengthy discussion, the counselor decided that Abe would probably gain insight into career planning by using the CPP student booklet entitled *Planning* (American College Testing Program, 1976). This booklet outlines the steps in career planning, provides self-awareness exercises, and gives information on job groups and educational programs. The counselor's rationale was that after Abe had completed the tests and planning exercises, productive counseling sessions would be possible.

Abe's profiles from the CPP are shown in Figures 10-1 and 10-2. The counselor noted a fairly consistent pattern of scores. For example, the educational program preferences, art and architecture, listed in item 9, were in agreement with the long-term goal of applied arts. The counselor also noted that Abe's highest ability score was in space relations and his highest interest area was creative arts. Space relations, a skill of visualizing objects in space, is important for applied arts and architecture. However, Abe had no work experiences in this area, probably because he had been working for only a few years.

Abe was not surprised by the results: "I always like to draw, and I have daydreamed about a job of illustrating for an advertising firm. I guess that I was afraid to admit this to anyone and especially to myself. But I really don't know much about the requirements, training, or pay in commercial art."

CAREER CLUSTERS

ACT CAREER PLANNING PROGRAM

STUDENT REPORT

DATE SCORED:
EDUCATIONAL LEVEL
RACIAL/ETHNIC BACKGROUND

1. BUSINESS SALES & MANAGEMENT

SAMPLE EDUCATIONAL PROGRAMS

Agriculture Business
Business Administration
Finance & Credit
Hotel/Restaurant Management
Sales & Retailing

| BUSINESS CONTACT INTERESTS | LOW |
| BUS. CONTACT EXPERIENCES | NONE |

SOME IMPORTANT ABILITIES*

LANGUAGE USAGE	LOW
NUMERICAL SKILLS	LOW
CLERICAL SKILLS	MED

2. BUSINESS OPERATIONS

SAMPLE EDUCATIONAL PROGRAMS

Accounting
Data Processing
Office Machine Operation
Office Management
Secretarial Science

| BUSINESS DETAIL INTERESTS | MED |
| BUS. DETAIL EXPERIENCES | NONE |

SOME IMPORTANT ABILITIES*

NUMERICAL SKILLS	LOW
CLERICAL SKILLS	MED
LANGUAGE USAGE	LOW

8. SOCIAL & PERSONAL SERVICES

SAMPLE EDUCATIONAL PROGRAMS

Child Care
Home Economics
Physical Education & Recreation
Police Science
Social Work, Teaching

| SOCIAL SERVICE INTERESTS | MED |
| SOCIAL SERVICE EXPERIENCES | FEW |

SOME IMPORTANT ABILITIES*

| LANGUAGE USAGE | LOW |
| NUMERICAL SKILLS | LOW |

3. TRADES, CRAFTS, & INDUSTRIES

SAMPLE EDUCATIONAL PROGRAMS

Appliance, Auto, Other Repair
Carpentry
Farming
Food Service
Welding

| TRADES INTERESTS | MED |
| TRADES EXPERIENCES | FEW |

SOME IMPORTANT ABILITIES*

MECHANICAL REASONING	MED
NUMERICAL SKILLS	LOW
SPACE RELATIONS	HIGH

9. YOUR CAREER PLANS

EDUCATIONAL PROGRAM PREFERENCES YOU REPORTED

CAREER CLUSTER NUMBER

1st   ART
2nd   ARCHITECTURE

LONG-TERM CAREER GOAL YOU REPORTED
APPLIED ARTS

SOME CAREER SUGGESTIONS (BASED ON YOUR INTEREST SCORES)

YOUR INTERESTS SUGGEST YOU LIKE TO WORK MOSTLY WITH IDEAS. JOBS IN REGION 09 (SEE WORLD OF WORK MAP ON BACK) OFTEN INVOLVE THESE KIND OF WORK ACTIVITIES.

7. CREATIVE & APPLIED ARTS

SAMPLE EDUCATIONAL PROGRAMS

Architecture
Art & Photography
English & Literature
Interior Decorating
Journalism

| CREATIVE ARTS INTERESTS | HIGH |
| CREATIVE ARTS EXPERIENCES | NONE |

SOME IMPORTANT ABILITIES*

Consider your ability to express thoughts or feelings in clear or inventive ways, and your specific skills in fields such as art, music, writing, etc.

4. TECHNOLOGIES

SAMPLE EDUCATIONAL PROGRAMS

Computer Programming
Engineering (Civil, Elec., Mech., etc.)
Engineering Technical (2 years)
Mechanical Drawing
Pilot Training

| TECHNOLOGY INTERESTS | MED |
| TECHNOLOGY EXPERIENCES | FEW |

SOME IMPORTANT ABILITIES*

MECHANICAL REASONING	MED
NUMERICAL SKILLS	LOW
SPACE RELATIONS	HIGH

6. HEALTH SERVICES/SCIENCES

SAMPLE EDUCATIONAL PROGRAMS

Dental Assistant
Medical Technology (Lab Work)
Nursing
Physical/Occupational Therapy
X-Ray Technology

| HEALTH INTERESTS | LOW |
| HEALTH EXPERIENCES | NOT ASSESSED |

SOME IMPORTANT ABILITIES*

| NUMERICAL SKILLS | LOW |
| MECHANICAL REASONING | MED |

5. NATURAL & SOCIAL SCIENCES

SAMPLE EDUCATIONAL PROGRAMS

Biological Sciences
Law School
Math
Physical Sci. (Chem., Physics, etc.)
Social Sci. (History, Psych., Econ.)

| SCIENCE INTERESTS | LOW |
| SCIENCE EXPERIENCES | NONE |

SOME IMPORTANT ABILITIES*

NUMERICAL SKILLS	LOW
LANGUAGE USAGE	LOW
MECHANICAL REASONING	MED

*NOTE: Reading is an important ability in each Career Cluster.

FIGURE 10-1.
Career-cluster portion of CPP profile.
From *The ACT Career Planning Program.* Copyright © 1977 by The American College Testing Program. Reprinted by permission.

EXPERIENCES RELATED TO INTERESTS	INTERESTS	NAT'L STA-NINE (1-9)	LOWER QUARTER	MIDDLE HALF	UPPER QUARTER
			5 10 25	40 60 75	90 95
NONE	BUSINESS CONTACT		–XX–		
NONE	BUSINESS DETAIL		–XX–		
FEW	TRADES			–XX–	
FEW	TECHNOLOGY			–XX–	
NONE	SCIENCE		–XX–		
NOT ASSESSED	HEALTH		–XX–		
NONE	CREATIVE ARTS				
FEW	SOCIAL SERVICE		–XX–		

ADDITIONAL NORMS STANINES	ABILITIES	NAT'L STA-NINE	LOWER QUARTER	MIDDLE HALF	UPPER QUARTER
			5 10 25	40 60 75	90 95
5	MECHANICAL REASONING			–XX–	
4	NUMERICAL SKILLS		–XX–		
9	SPACE RELATIONS				–XX–
5	READING SKILLS			–XX–	
4	LANGUAGE USAGE		–XX–		
5	CLERICAL SKILLS			–XX–	

ADDITIONAL NORMS FOR

INSTITUTIONAL CHOICE

5 10 25 40 60 75 90 95
1 2 3 4 5 6 7 8 9

Score Bands—The —XX— on the charts show how your scores compare to those of the nationwide group. *Bands are used because tests are not exact measures.* When two bands do not overlap, chances are good that one score is higher than the other.

N—An N means you did not answer enough questions.

Placement Information—If your English or math composite is 3 or less, ask your counselor about how you can improve these skills.

ACT Composite Range—This estimates what your score would be if you took the ACT Assessment. The average score for students thinking about attending college is 17 to 21.

PLACEMENT INFORMATION		
BASIC SKILLS	ASKED HELP?	STANINE ON
STUDY SKILLS	**	
READING SKILLS	**	
ENGLISH COMPOSITE	**	
MATH COMPOSITE	**	
ESTIMATED ACT COMPOSITE RANGE:		

PERCENTILE RANK: A percentile rank of 40 means that 40% of students had scores below this point.

STANINES: Stanines are a special type of scale which is divided into 9 equal parts. Stanine bands are numbered 1 (low) through 9 (high), with 5 being the average score for a norm group.

FIGURE 10-2.
Relevant-experience and abilities portion of CPP profile.
From *The ACT Career Planning Program.* Copyright © 1977 by the American College Testing Program. Reprinted by permission.

Abe felt that he had gained valuable information by using the planning exercises. He explained that he learned that he must evaluate all aspects of his personal characteristics and traits: "The job value exercises in the planning booklet made me think about factors that I never considered before. After working for a while, a person starts thinking about working conditions, and this exercise helped put these considerations in perspective."

Abe was directed to regions 9 and 10 of the world-of-work map, shown in Figure 10-3. He recalled listing visual arts and creative arts as job groups to explore. He noticed that the results of the interest inventory suggested that his interests were similar to those of individuals who liked working with ideas.

As Abe and the counselor reviewed the CPP results, they considered combinations of scores in relation to educational and occupational requirements. If Abe were to decide on commercial art or architecture, a four- or five-year college program would be required. His lower scores in mathematics and reading plus his low high-school grades in related subjects indicated possible problems. The counselor called Abe's attention to this possibility and noted that he had asked for help in reading and mathematics on the background and plans section of the profile. The counselor recommended that he seek assistance in upgrading these skills. Abe also indicated a need for financial aid and employment. Because employment would require considerable time, the counselor suggested that Abe learn to plan his schedule well and budget his time wisely.

In this case, the CPP provided Abe with the incentive to explore the results and link them to educational and occupational requirements. The counselor also obtained information for helping Abe meet specific educational requirements and personal needs. For example, the counselor encouraged Abe to investigate potential specific careers within an identified occupational group, to enter special programs for improving basic skills and for learning how to budget time, and to seek financial assistance and employment from the college financial aid office.

WORLD-OF-WORK MAP

FIGURE 10-3.
World-of-work map for the CPP.
From *The ACT Career Planning Program.* Copyright © 1977 by the American College
Testing Program. Reprinted by permission.

COMBINING SEPARATE TESTS AND INVENTORIES

The preceding section provided an example of a program specifically designed for multidimensional assessment results. Another way to obtain such results is to combine several tests and inventories. Let's look at three cases in which the results of more than one test or inventory are combined. In the case of Carol, the results of an interest inventory and a career development inventory were used to assist her in career planning. In the case of Art, the results of the DAT, the KOIS, and the WVI were combined to provide information designed to stimulate career exploration. In the case of Harry, achievement and aptitude test results were combined with the results of an interest inventory to enhance the self-awareness so vital to career decision making and educational planning. In the case of Flo, computerized inventories measuring abilities, interests, and values were used to help her decide on a career direction.

Case of a High School Senior Lacking in Career Orientation
Carol was both confused and infuriated by her poor scores on the Career Development Inventory (CDI)—specifically, low scores on the decision-making scale. She felt she was as ready as anyone to make a career decision. "What's all this nonsense about self-evaluation?" she asked herself as she waited outside the counselor's office. "After all, I have been in school almost 12 years, my

grades are good, and I'm ready to go to college. Or am I ready to go to college? Maybe I should go to work? Oh well, I'm just like the rest of my classmates: I'll know what to do when I graduate."

The counselor sensed that Carol was upset. He realized that Carol had rarely received what she conceived of as low scores on a test. She had been a model student throughout her school career. With emotional overtones, Carol immediately brought up the issue of low scores. The counselor acknowledged her concerns and suggested that they evaluate her scores by studying the content of the inventories.

The counselor explained that the CDI was different from tests on which one received grades; the CDI was used primarily as a counseling tool to help students in developing skills for career planning and decision making. This information seemed to have little bearing on Carol's emotional state. The counselor allowed considerable time for Carol to express her feeling of frustration. She eventually returned to the content of the inventories.

As the profile was discussed, the counselor asked Carol if she would like to look at some of the item responses. The counselor and Carol started with the results of the career-planning and decision-making scales.

Carol: I missed quite a few of the questions dealing with understanding how to make career deci-
            sions. I don't know what that means.
Counselor: Okay, let's look at some of the items.

This review revealed that Carol had difficulty recognizing various aspects of work and working conditions. Although Carol was threatened by her answers on the items, she recognized the differences between her responses and those considered appropriate. As Carol became increasingly defensive, however, the counselor decided to set up another meeting to give himself time to plot strategy and create a more productive atmosphere.

Carol seemed relaxed at the beginning of the second conference. The counselor hoped that she would be able to accept suggestions for programs that could help her. He began by informing Carol that career decision making was a learned skill and knowledge of working conditions came with experience.

While discussing the results of an interest inventory, Carol commented that she had low scores here, too. The counselor agreed that Carol had a flat profile, but again he emphasized that this was not a test used to give grades for high scores. In fact, the counselor commented that the results of the CDI and the interest inventory were somewhat similar because she had admitted to having little knowledge about the world of work and had narrow, well-defined interests. This, he stated, could be the primary reason for the "low scores" or flat profile. Finally, he explained that she had difficulty in responding to questions and choices on the interest inventory because of her lack of involvement in work activities; she simply had very little knowledge of occupations and work environments.

The combined results of the interest inventory and the CDI pointed out problems Carol would have in career planning. As she recognized her lack of knowledge of occupations and lack of career decision-making skills, she became convinced that action was necessary. The counselor was now in a position to suggest methods to overcome her inexperience including visits to workplaces. In this case, the results of two inventories provided both Carol and the counselor with specific information to be used in planning intervention strategies to overcome recognized deficits.

Case of a High School Senior Attempting to Decide Whether to Go to College or to Work

During the fall semester of his senior year in high school, Art made an appointment to see the career counselor for help in planning his future. He informed the counselor that he thought about going to college "like everyone else," but he also thought about going to work after graduation. His parents were indifferent about his plans and left these decisions to him. After a rather lengthy conversation concerning Art's likes, dislikes, and options, Art agreed with the counselor that a battery of tests and inventories would help with decision making. Specifically, Art was to take the DAT to help him understand his abilities and then relate these abilities to his interests as measured by the KOIS and his values as measured by the WVI.

As the counselor reviewed the results of the DAT, shown in Figure 10-4, she questioned whether Art currently possessed the aptitude necessary for college work. She was particularly concerned about the low scores in verbal reasoning and numerical ability, as these two scores provide a fairly reliable index for predicting academic success. She was aware that colleges vary in their requirements and did not want to eliminate this option, but at the same time, Art's low scores had to be considered in their discussion. She also noticed that his highest score was in mechanical reasoning.

The results of the KOIS were valid (V score above .45). The highest occupational scores (males) were for engineer, mechanical engineer, industrial, and auto mechanic. His highest college major scores (males) were for engineering, mechanical engineering, civil engineering, and physical education. The counselor wondered whether Art's apparent interest in occupations that

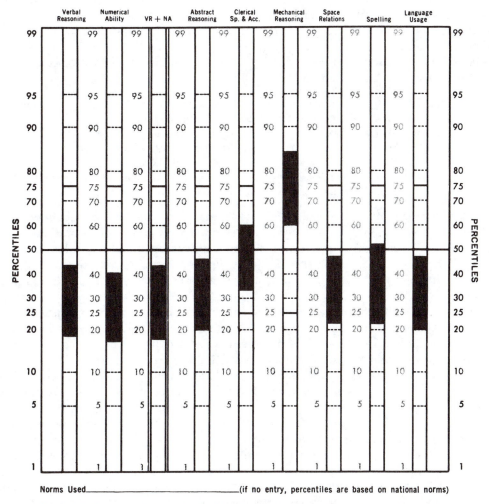

Norms Used_____(if no entry, percentiles are based on national norms)

*F — first (fall) semester testing and percentiles; S — second (spring) semester testing and percentiles.

FIGURE 10-4.
Art's DAT profile.
From *Differential Aptitude Test* by G. K. Bennett, H. G. Seashore, and A. G. Wesman, 1974. The Psychological Corporation. Reprinted by permission.

require a college degree reflected a current interest Art had in attending college, rather than his true interests, especially in light of his low aptitude for college work.

On the WVI, Art's highest scores were in supervisory relations (values a friendly supervisor), associates (values working with desirable people), way of life (values a desirable lifestyle), and surroundings (values a pleasant environment). His lowest scores were in intellectual stimulation (values independent thinking), independence (values independent actions), and aesthetics (values artistic endeavors). These results were of particular interest to the counselor because Art placed a high value on the working environment but a low value on intellectual stimulation.

Art seemed somewhat embarrassed by the DAT scores but stated that he did not consider himself a good student. The counselor then asked about his interest in attending college. Art replied: "Well, all of my friends are going to college, and I figure that I ought to go, too. I got through high school somehow, and I ought to be able to make it in college." These remarks indicated that Art did not know what college would be like. His reason for going to college reflected little knowledge of college requirements and a lackadaisical attitude toward exploring other options available to him.

When the counselor mentioned his high score on mechanical reasoning, Art expressed an interest in mechanics and other jobs such as television repair and electric engine repair. The counselor followed this expression of interest with a description of occupations in technical fields—auto mechanics and related trades. Her purpose was to introduce several career options Art had not considered.

The counselor then moved on to the results of the WVI. A discussion of values as related to work environments held Art's attention.

Art: Yeah, I like to work around people who are friendly and visit a lot. The way I see my life is a job 8-to-5, five days a week, and a chance to go fishing and hunting.

Counselor: Okay, now that you have come to that conclusion, we should examine other parts of the inventory. Your lowest score was in intellectual stimulation, which means that you do not place a high value on work that permits independent thinking.

Art: I guess that's right. That doesn't interest me. I just want a job that's not too complicated. I don't care about being independent, and I'm not interested in artistic things.

The counselor then linked the results of the assessment instruments to occupational requirements. She suggested that Art attempt to develop a list of occupations that would be related to his high mechanical reasoning score. Next, he was to relate these occupations to his interests and work values. The counselor helped Art begin this assignment by suggesting several occupations to consider, including jobs that would require apprentice training and for which technical training courses were offered.

Art reported for the next counseling session early. He seemed eager to get started. He said: "Do you think everybody should go to college? I've been thinking that maybe college isn't for me. This assignment you gave me helped me see that I'm actually more interested in jobs that require some education and training, but not necessarily a four-year program."

The counselor asked Art to explain how he arrived at this conclusion. Art replied: "When we started talking about my values, I realized that I was thinking about college because most everyone else was. That isn't really me; besides, my grades and test scores are not very high."

The counselor and Art continued their discussion and reached some tentative conclusions. Art would not give up the idea of college completely, but he would explore other options also. He therefore looked into occupations that require college training as well as into technical occupations and trades.

In this case the combined test results provided the stimulus for considering career options from several perspectives. Measuring aptitudes, interests, and work values provided Art with information he had never considered for career exploration. The discussions of the results helped Art relate his characteristics and traits to occupational and educational information. He was stimulated to explore several different options and gained an understanding of the complexities of the world of work.

Case of a High School Senior with a Poor Attitude toward School

Being the last one to enter the classroom and the first one to leave typified Kwok's attitude toward school. Most teachers wondered why he bothered to stick around for his senior year. Perhaps it was the good time he was apparently having, or maybe it prevented him from having to go to work. The counselor had made numerous attempts for two years to get Kwok interested in coming in for counseling, but Kwok managed to evade the counselor's office. Thus, the counselor was quite surprised when Kwok's name appeared on the appointment list.

Kwok further amazed the counselor when he asked for help in planning what to do after high school. He informed the counselor that he began thinking about his future because of the results of a test he had taken. He explained that the entire class had been required to take several tests and that his teacher informed him that he had scored high on the aptitude test. The counselor and Kwok set up another meeting in a few days so that the counselor could gather the test data. In the meantime, the counselor suggested that Kwok take an interest inventory. The counselor was interested in maintaining Kwok's enthusiasm as well as in obtaining a measure of his interests.

The counselor discovered that Kwok did indeed do well on the DAT, which had been administered to all seniors. The counselor was surprised to find that his scores were above the 90th percentile for verbal reasoning and numerical ability. Abstract reasoning and mechanical reasoning also were significantly high (above the 75th percentile). The counselor wondered why Kwok let all this talent go to waste during his school career.

Achievement test scores reflected Kwok's poor academic performance. Most scores were below the 50th percentile (national group) with the exception of mathematics reasoning, which was at the 75th percentile. The counselor concluded that even Kwok's high aptitude could not make up for the academic work he had not done.

The SDS provided insights into Kwok's modal personal style; enterprising was his dominant personality type. An enterprising person, according to the SDS description, is adventurous, extroverted, and aggressive—a good description of Kwok. Although Kwok didn't use these characteristics in academic endeavors, he was considered a leader by his peer groups. His summary code, ECS (enterprising, conventional, social), suggested that he would prefer sales jobs such as insurance underwriter, real estate salesperson, and grain buyer (Holland, 1987b).

In the next session Kwok told the counselor that he was planning to attend college and devote much more of his energy to college courses than he had to high school courses. The counselor took this opportunity to point out the discrepancies between Kwok's aptitude test scores, and his grades and achievement test scores. He emphasized that Kwok had the potential for making much better grades than he had in the past. Kwok was quick to agree that he had goofed off and would have to pay the price now. The counselor suggested that Kwok enroll in a summer course sponsored by the community college learning resource center to upgrade his basic skills and improve his study habits.

Kwok was undecided about a career because he had given little thought to his future. The SDS results provided him with several specific occupations to consider.

Kwok: I think I would like sales work of some kind or to have my own business. Do you think I should study business?

Counselor: That may be a good possibility. However, I think you should take the time to research what is offered in a typical school of business at a university. But first, let's consider what's involved in career decision making.

The counselor continued by emphasizing the importance of self-understanding in career planning. He discussed the significance of modal personal style as identified by the SDS. Kwok recognized that the results of the aptitude and achievement measures also contributed to his self-understanding; they provided stimulus for further discussion. As a result, Kwok was challenged by the counselor to devote time to researching the world of work in relation to his personal characteristics. Kwok thanked the counselor for helping him establish some direction and set up several appointments to discuss and evaluate the careers he was exploring on the basis of his personal characteristics.

Case of a Divorced Woman Searching for a Career Direction

Flo had been encouraged by her sister and friends to attend a job club at the nearby woman's center. She experienced immediate support from the job club group and found that other divorced women with children were in the process of deciding future alternatives. Eventually, Flo was given an appointment with a volunteer counselor. She related information about her background to the counselor who summarized it as follows:

Marital status: divorced for eight months after a 10-year marriage.

Children: four children, ages nine, seven, four, and two.

Financial situation: child support payments and state welfare assistance.

Work experience: had never worked outside the home.

Educational level: high school graduate—grades were above average in the "A" and "B" categories and she was on the honor role several times.

Strongest and most interesting subjects: science courses such as chemistry and biology.

Living accommodations: renting an apartment owned by her sister who lives next to her. Good schools are nearby.

Occupations considered: none seriously because she was devoted to raising her children. In high school she had considered being a nurse, M.D., or dentist. She expressed an interest in helping others and working with people, but at this point in her life, did not have a career preference or direction.

The woman's center was fortunate enough to have the computerized career guidance system for adults, DISCOVER (ACT, 1989). This computer-based career information and planning system was designed to assist adults through a systematic career exploration and decision-making process. It contains large databases that provide up-to-date information about occupations and educational opportunities and contains inventories that measure interests, abilities, and work-related values.

The interest inventory available was the Unisex Edition of the American College Testing Program (ACT, 1989) that contains 15-item scales corresponding to Holland's (1985) six interest types shown in parentheses: business operations (conventional), social service (social), technical (realistic), arts (artistic), and science (investigative). These scores can be translated into work-related activity preferences and basic work tasks (people, data, things or ideas) associated with occupations as depicted on the world-of-work map on page 141.

The self-rating ability inventory consists of 15 abilities important to career planning. Individuals are to rate abilities on a scale of 1 to 5 for meeting people, helping others, sales, leadership, organization, clerical, mechanical, manual dexterity, numerical, scientific, creative/artistic, reading, language usage, and space.

The values inventory consists of a list of 9 defined values: creativity, economic security, helping others, recognition, earnings, independence, responsibility, vanity, and working with people. The individual is required to prioritize values according to the importance of each value in a job.

Under the counselor's direction Flo entered the DISCOVER system with the approach that she was completely undecided, eventually deciding that she would take the ability, interests, and value inventories.

The counselor explained: "The results of the ability inventory will provide a summary of how your abilities relate to work tasks. The interest inventory can help you identify jobs to explore, and the values inventory will help you become aware of values that are important to you."

The results of the interest inventory indicated the following occupational preferences:

Dental assistant
Medical assistant
Nursing–psychiatric aide
Proofreader
Singer
Stunt performer

As Flo considered each occupation, she stated: "Everything from stunt performer to dental assistant—will there be others?"

The counselor replied, "This list of occupations has only those that you can consider at this time, but I'm sure there'll be other occupations that you want to review."

The results of the ability inventory indicated that Flo would enjoy working with ideas and people. A copy of how her abilities related to work tasks is as follows:

How Abilities Relate to Work Tasks[1]

On the next display you are going to see a "great chart." Down the left side of the display are the names of 15 very important abilities . . . such as Reading, Numerical, Language, etc.

Across the top are the names of work tasks, such as working with PEOPLE, PEOPLE and DATA, DATA and THINGS, etc. Under those work tasks you will see that four key abilities have been marked in each column with one of these two symbols:

   o   means that this ability is very important for this kind of work task

   *   means that this ability is very important AND YOU HAVE IT!

You may want to print this chart and discuss it with your counselor. It will give you a good summary of where your abilities fit related to these four work tasks.   Press NEXT

How Abilities Relate to Work Tasks

ABILITIES	P	P/D	D/T	T	T/I	I/P
Meeting	*					
Helping	*					
Sales		o				
Leadership		o				
Organization				o		
Clerical				*		
Mechanical				o		
Manual				o		
Numerical		*		*	*	*
Scientific					*	
Artistic						o
Literary						o
Reading	*				*	
Language	*	*		*	*	*
Space				o		o

P = people   D = data   T = things   I = ideas

Press NEXT.

From the experience you've had, it appears that you may want to consider working with ideas and people. . . .

The counselor and Flo discussed the definition of ideas as a work task dimension that suggests individuals prefer working with abstractions, being creative, and implementing new methods of doing tasks. The people dimension was explained simply as being involved with interpersonal processes such as helping or serving people. Flo commented that the results came as no surprise as she had considered herself as being a people person who was interested in people activities.

Flo and the counselor decided that she would discuss abilities and work tasks in more depth at a later time. For now, she would continue with the values inventory. The results of value ratings were as follows:

---

[1]This and following computerized material in this section from the DISCOVER programs, college and adult version. American College Testing Program, Iowa City, Iowa. Reprinted by permission.

You have selected the following values:

A.	Creativity	Medium
B.	Recognition	High
C.	Helping Others	High
D.	Economic Security	Medium
E.	Working with People	High
F.	Variety	Low
G.	Independence	Low
H.	Responsibility	Medium
I.	Earnings	Medium

The counselor explained the results of the values inventory by pointing out that one way to interpret her scores was to think of values as a way to explain purposes behind one's action. Also, people express values in what they do, how they behave, and the various kinds of goals they establish. The results of Flo's value inventory helped her to reinforce her desires to be involved in people activities.

In the next counseling session the results of the three inventories were carefully evaluated and discussed.

Flo: This has been a completely new experience for me. During my marriage I never considered working because my husband had a marvelous income and I was happy with raising a family. I'm excited about a future career role, but I still want and have the responsibility of raising my children.

Counselor: Let's look at some options to accomplish both of those goals.

In the sessions that followed, Flo and the counselor discussed several occupational options from the list presented by the computerized career guidance system. Other occupations were added for exploration purposes. Flo found more information from the computerized database concerning work tasks, employment outlook, income potential, and paths of training. She had verified and learned some new things about herself from the results of the inventories that she had completed. She kept these results in mind as she explored occupations and felt that the major benefit from talking with the counselor and using the computerized career guidance system was the fact that she was able to develop a frame of reference to use in career decision making. As she read job descriptions from the computer's file, she was able to evaluate each one of them from the vantage point of how she could accomplish the job training requirements and still care for her four children. Flo eventually decided to choose dental assistant primarily because of the availability of training at a nearby community college. For the time being, she would aspire to this occupation, but she recognized that the future might provide opportunities in the field of dentistry. She had for the first time in her life developed a potential career direction.

SUMMARY

In this chapter combinations of assessment results were discussed as a useful way of helping individuals consider their characteristics and traits in career counseling. This chapter emphasizes that assessment results should not be used in isolation; counselors and clients should consider the totality of individual needs. Assessment results taken from different types of tests and inventories provide useful information in the career decision-making process.

QUESTIONS AND EXERCISES

1. Following the steps of the conceptual model for using assessment results discussed in Chapter 2, develop a counseling case that illustrates each step.
2. How would you determine which instruments to use if you were requested to recommend tests and inventories for a group of tenth graders interested in career exploration?

3. Defend the following statement: Multidimensional assessment results are more effective in career counseling than are the results of only one instrument.
4. How would you explain to an individual the differences in norms when using a combination of assessment results, some of which are based on local norms and others on national norms?
5. Illustrate how assessment results from two different instruments can support each other and how they can point out conflicts.

Chapter Eleven
Using Assessment for the Academically Disadvantaged and Disabled

Since the early 1970s attention has been focused on rehabilitation services for the physically and mentally disabled and career-counseling programs for the disadvantaged. The major goal of these services and programs is to maximize each individual's potential for employment. Legislation that requires equal access to training and employment for the disabled and disadvantaged has led to intense scrutinization of assessment methods and procedures. The diverse needs of disabled and disadvantaged individuals require specially designed assessment instruments to assist them in career planning.

The challenge of meeting their needs is complicated by the fact that both disabled and disadvantaged people have a wide variety of ethnic and racial backgrounds. It has been claimed that many tests are discriminatory because their norms are based on white, male, middle-class individuals and, therefore, do not account for the unique characteristics of minorities and the special needs of the disabled. The issue of test discrimination will no doubt affect the future research efforts of numerous individuals in the counseling profession.

In the first part of this chapter examples of tests and inventories specially designed for the academically disadvantaged are reviewed. In the second part specially designed measuring instruments for the disabled are discussed. Specifically, two achievement tests and one interest inventory for academically disadvantaged and disabled individuals are reviewed. Also, a prevocational information battery that measures skills considered important for employability and one work-sample test for use with the disabled are reviewed. Sample cases illustrate the use of assessment for these groups. The tests described in this chapter may be supplemented when appropriate with some of the inventories and tests discussed previously.

BASIC OCCUPATIONAL LITERACY TEST (BOLT)

BOLT is an achievement test designed to measure the reading and arithmetic skills of educationally disadvantaged adults. It is published by the U. S. Department of Labor, Manpower Administration, for use by various governmental agencies, including state employment agencies. BOLT is used primarily to assess skills for occupational training or occupational entry.

The reading skills part of the test consists of two subtests: reading vocabulary and reading comprehension. Arithmetic skills are assessed by two subtests: arithmetic computation and arithmetic reasoning. The reading passages and arithmetic problems are considered to be of interest to and within the experience of the educationally disadvantaged.

The test has four levels of difficulty: advanced, high intermediate, basic intermediate, and fundamental. The Wide Range Scale is used as a pretest to determine which level should be administered to each individual. Alternate forms are available for each level of difficulty. This instrument has been reviewed by Cronbach (1978), Tuckman (1978), and Bass (1984).

Reliability coefficients obtained by KR-20 range from .61 to .82 with a median of .76. Local validation between test scores and job performance ratings is suggested for the most effective use of the test. Tuckman (1978) suggests that this test appears to be a good one for predicting job outcome.

Interpreting BOLT

BOLT test results are expressed in standard scores and General Educational Development (GED) levels. Standard score units cannot be compared with GATB standard scores because of the restricted norm sample of educationally disadvantaged adults. However, the standard scores used in BOLT are on the same scale for all levels and therefore can be compared across all four forms. Thus, retest results for an individual can be compared with original test results even though the retest is at a higher level.

The GED functional levels used for interpretation range from 1 to 6. Level 1 is the expected functional level in reasoning, mathematics, and language development for grades 1–3; level 2 for grades 4–6; level 3 for grades 7–8; level 4 for grades 9–12; level 5 for college freshmen and sophomores; and level 6 for college juniors and seniors. A detailed explanation of all levels may be found in the DOT.

Using GED levels as a frame of reference, the counselor can determine whether an individual's functional level is appropriate for an occupation under consideration. In some cases the counselor may recommend remedial training to meet job requirements. Thus, the functional levels primarily provide guidelines for educational planning and career exploration. An example of the BOLT score report is shown in Figure 11-1.

Career counselors can locate the nearest agency where this instrument is available. Most state employment agencies or rehabilitation offices should be able to provide it.

PRINT NAME: PAGE, Charlie G. (Last, First, Middle Initial)
Address: General Delivery, Anytown, U.S.A.

Classification
Sex: ☒ M ☐ F   ☒ Age 40 to 64

BASIC OCCUPATIONAL LITERACY TEST

Test Date	Test Form	Raw Score	Standard Score	GED Level	Retest Date	Retest Form	Raw Score	Standard Score	GED Level	Wide Range Scale Scores
4/2/80	RV3A	3	69	1						Reading
4/2/80	RC3A	2	71	1						
4/2/80	AC4A	3	70	1						Arithmetic
4/2/80	AR3A	3	63	1						

COMMENTS: Instructions had to be repeated several times. Charlie worked very slowly and seemed to feel out-of-place. He needed constant encouragement

TEST RECORD CARD
NONREADING APTITUDE TEST BATTERY AND BASIC OCCUPATIONAL LITERACY TEST
For sale by the Superintendent of Documents, U.S. Government Printing Office

U.S. DEPARTMENT OF LABOR
U.S. GOVERNMENT PRINTING OFFICE : 1978 O—267-690

Washington, D.C. 20402 (in 100's)
Stock No. 029-000-00139-1

Manpower Administration
MA Form 7-23 (R-9/71)

FIGURE 11-1.
BOLT profile.
From *Basic Occupational Literacy Test*, 1973. U.S. Government Printing Office.

Case of an Older Man with Little Education

Mr. Page, at age 52, reported to the rehabilitation counselor, needing a job. He had worked for a long time on a large cattle ranch near his home. But the ranch had been sold and was now being developed for housing, leaving Mr. Page without a means of support. He had quit school during his early elementary years and had little job experience other than working cattle and tractor maintenance.

Because of Mr. Page's limited educational background, the counselor decided to use BOLT to assess his reading and arithmetic levels. The pretest, Wide Range Scale, was administered to determine the level of BOLT to use; the fundamental form of BOLT was selected. The results may be seen in Figure 11-1. They indicated that Mr. Page was functioning at level 1. The counselor reviewed the description of that level in the DOT. As the counselor suspected, Mr. Page would probably be able to carry out only simple instructions and needed a highly structured job with little or no variation in tasks. Most instructions would have to be given to him orally or demonstrated. Mr. Page's educational disadvantage was severe, and the counselor realized that this would place restrictions on his potential for employment.

Mr. Page was a proud and sensitive individual, and the counselor had to approach job considerations with a great deal of diplomacy. He asked Mr. Page to describe some of the skills he had learned on the ranch to determine whether any of them could be applied in local work settings. Because Mr. Page lacked information concerning jobs other than those he had on the ranch, it was difficult for him to relate the skills he had obtained in his previous work to other occupations. However, Mr. Page admitted his lack of occupational information and told the counselor that he knew that he didn't have much schooling. He said he would be willing to take a job where he would be required to learn something new. Eventually, three job possibilities were agreed on—custodian, tractor mechanic's helper, and assembly line worker in a local factory. The counselor explained each of these jobs in detail, and a visit to the sites helped Mr. Page decide to apply for the job as a tractor mechanic's helper.

In this case the test results identified Mr. Page's functional level. Even though the counselor suspected that Mr. Page's functional level was low, he wanted an objective measure. The counselor had learned from experience that many clients had studied on their own and through experience were able to function at higher levels than that indicated by their formal education. In many other cases the opposite was true: Individuals functioned below their formal educational levels. The test also provided a starting point for considering jobs. Both the counselor and Mr. Page were able to take into account Mr. Page's current limitations in the job search.

ADULT BASIC LEARNING EXAMINATION (ABLE)

ABLE was designed to measure the general educational level of adults who have not completed high school. It is used to determine achievement ranging from the primary grade level to the 12th grade level. It may be used for educational planning or training for job placement. Three levels have been developed: level I (grades 1–4), level II (grades 5–8), level III (grades 9–12). Two forms are available for each level. Levels I and II are not timed. Level III is timed, but the time limits allow most individuals to complete the test. Split-half reliabilities are satisfactory; they tend to be in the .80s and .90s for each subtest. Correlations between ABLE and the Stanford Achievement Test subtests are primarily in the .70s.

ABLE measures achievement in vocabulary, reading, spelling, and arithmetic. The test was not designed to be a diagnostic instrument in that the results do not reveal specific weaknesses in any of the areas tested. The test was constructed to cover typical adult problems, tasks, and activities. For example, newspaper articles are used in the reading section of the test. The authors report that the questions in the test help to establish rapport between the individual and the counselor because they are common problems encountered by many adults.

Interpreting ABLE

The authors of ABLE strongly suggest that local normative samples be established whenever possible for meaningful interpretation. This point is well founded; because of the great diversity in the adult population, normative samples for adults should be carefully scrutinized before making any significant career decisions based on test scores. Every effort should be made to find a norm population that closely matches the individual being tested in ethnic background, experience, and training.

Table 11-1 provides some descriptive information on adult samples; this information should be carefully considered for all achievement test designed for adult use. The ABLE manual does an excellent job in describing the adult population used in the development of ABLE. In addition, each subgroup is clearly described—for example, the high school equivalency candidates in a particular section of a state. The descriptive information on sex, age, race, socioeconomic status, and education background should allow a counselor to determine whether the local adult population matches the test sample closely enough to provide meaningful interpretations of the test results.

An important characteristic of the ABLE test results is that they correspond to Stanford Achievement Test results—that is, scores from ABLE can be converted to Stanford Achievement Test score equivalents. Comparing Stanford results with ABLE results provides the counselor with the vast amount of information on school achievement available from research conducted with the Stanford Test.

ABLE is well constructed and meets its primary goal of measuring levels of achievement of adult groups. Reviews of ABLE are provided by Anastasi (1988), Fitzpatrick (1992), and Williams (1992).

Case of a School Dropout Seeking Work

Gus had a poor educational background. During his school years the truant officer was constantly after him. Gus disliked school so much that he ran away from home and got a job for several years as an able seaman in the Merchant Marine.

The counselor tried to make Gus feel comfortable when he reported for his first session. It was apparent that Gus felt out of place. Gus needed placement in a local job because he had the responsibility of taking care of his aging parents and maintaining their home. However, the counselor was concerned about Gus's educational background and decided that some measure of his academic abilities was necessary. The counselor planned to administer the ABLE to determine whether Gus had the educational background required for employment in a local firm. Because ABLE provides measures of spelling, reading, and numerical competence, the counselor had discovered that a total battery score provided a fairly reliable estimate of an individual's ability to perform in local industry. Fortunately, the counselor had collected data from and developed local norms based on individuals placed in this firm.

When Gus was approached about the possibility of taking an achievement test, he was intimidated. The counselor explained that the test was designed to cover typical adult problems, tasks, and activities and was not like a test that a student would take in high school. She also added that the scores would help her to determine whether Gus was capable of working at a local firm. Gus's anxiety was somewhat lowered by this explanation; he was particularly interested in placement in the local firm, for he had heard that working conditions were fairly good and that the pay was reasonable. Working there, he reasoned, would provide him with an outside income to maintain a home.

The results of ABLE indicated that Gus's chances of success in the local firm were fairly good; he scored in the fifth stanine with the local norms developed by the counselor.

Counselor: Your scores are in the average range compared with others from our community who have taken this test during the last eight years. This indicates to me that you have a fairly good

TABLE 11-1.
Adult Samples for Achievement Tests

Number of Cases:	Each subtest should have an adequate number of samples that match the group in characteristics to be tested.
Sex and Age:	Each subtest should contain balanced numbers from each sex. Age distributions by percentage of representation from age ranges should resemble the group to be tested. For example, what percentage of the sample was in the 50-and-over range, and what was the median age range?
Race:	There should be an adequate number of ethnic groups represented in each subtest. The standard group should consist of the same ethnicities or races as the examinees.
Educational Level:	Determine the median grade level of the standard group. Each educational level should contain adequate samples of both sexes and ethnic groups.
Place of Residence:	The sample group should be representative of the persons with whom the examinees are compared. The backgrounds of the sample members should be consistent with potential users.
Socioeconomic Status:	Socioeconomic backgrounds should be consistent with potential users. Should one use assessment results whose scores were developed from a predominantly male urban white middle class for a female who is an ethnic minority from a rural poor background?

In summary, seek the answers to the following questions:

Is the sample representative of my clients?

Does the sample include enough cases?

Does the sample group consist of the sort of person with whom my clients can be compared?

Is the sample appropriately subdivided?

---

chance of being successful in the local firm we have discussed. However, if you want to move up in the firm, you will need further training in the basics such as reading and arithmetic.

Gus: It has been a mighty long time since I have taken a test like this. I don't know what to say except that I was able to do a little studying on my own when I wasn't doing my chores, and I would like very much to improve my reading, spelling, and arithmetic skills.

The counselor explained to Gus that even though the test was a fairly good indication of his ability to compete in the local firm, he would have to adjust to a working environment that was different from the one he was accustomed to. She explained that he now would be working with people whose values might be quite different from his. The counselor offered to help Gus adjust to the new working environment and to provide him with suggestions for upgrading his educational skills.

In this case, results from ABLE not only were used as a link to local employment, but also provided a basis for discussing adjustments to a new working environment. In addition, the test results provided an opening for the counselor to discuss the importance of upgrading basic educational skills for occupational mobility.

WIDE RANGE INTEREST-OPINION TEST (WRIOT)

The WRIOT is a pictorial interest inventory developed for measuring interests and attitudes of the academically disadvantaged and the severely disabled. The 450 pictures are presented in groups of three (150 combinations); the individual chooses the most liked and the least liked. The activities portrayed in the pictures come from a wide range of unskilled, technical, professional, and managerial occupations. The WRIOT is untimed and may be administered to groups or individually. The authors report that the time for individual administration is approximately 40 minutes and for group administration 50–60 minutes. Scoring is done either by hand or by computer.

Split-half reliability coefficients by the Cureton formula (Guilford, 1954) for each scale in the 1979 edition range from .83 to .95 for males and from .82 to .95 for females. Validity was established by correlations between the WRIOT and the Geist Picture Interest Inventory. Most correlations are high and within satisfactory ranges. However, additional validity studies are needed for women, mental retardates, and ethnic minority groups.

Interpreting the WRIOT

The results are organized into 18 interest clusters and 8 attitude clusters. These are shown in the computer format in Figure 11-2. The manual provides a definition of each interest cluster with information on correlations with other clusters by sex, job title, and lists of positive and negative items as related to the cluster. The eight attitude clusters are similarly defined. Norms for all scales are available by sex and age (from age 5 on up). Means and standard deviations by sex and age are also provided for each interest and attitude cluster.

The results are reported by standard score (mean = 50, S.D. = 10) for each cluster and attitude scale. The profile reports scores by five categories ranging from very low (20–31) to very high (69–80). Scores of 50 or more are considered positive interests and attitudes; below 50, negative. The authors suggest that the individual consider the entire profile of scores (both negative and positive measures) in career exploration.

The manual for the WRIOT has been well prepared in that each scale is clearly defined. Additional information on using the test with mental retardates and individuals who have reading problems is needed because this instrument was designed especially for nonreaders. The difficulty in hand scoring the test most likely will make it mandatory for most users to have it computer scored. This instrument has been reviewed by Zytowski (1978).

Case of a High School Student Lacking Basic Education Skills
Shortly after Arturo's arrival at Central High, his teacher referred him to the counselor's office for the purpose of placement in a proper educational program. The teacher reported that Arturo had a low reading level and could not compete with the students in her class. She had talked briefly to Arturo about his background but did not have the time to investigate the reasons for his lack of educational achievement. The counselor discovered that because Arturo's family had moved around a great deal in the last ten years, he had missed a significant amount of schooling.

When the counselor mentioned tests, Arturo said that he had taken a series of tests at the school he had previously attended. The counselor called the school and asked for the test results. The achievement test indicated that Arturo was performing very much below grade level in all areas. He was particularly low in language skills, having a third-grade reading level. The counselor discovered that Arturo's mother could speak only Spanish and his father knew little

PROFILE FOR WRIOT
WIDE RANGE INTEREST — OPINION TEST
JOSEPH F. JASTAK, Ph.D. — SARAH JASTAK, Ph.D.

NAME _____ AGE _____ SEX _____ DATE _____ EXAMINER _____

SCORE RAW	T	CLUSTER	VERY LOW 20-31	LOW 32-37	BELOW AVG. 38-43	AVERAGE 50 44-49	51-56	ABOVE AVG. 57-62	HIGH 63-68	VERY HIGH 69-80	DESCRIPTION (Scores and Graph explained on back)
		A ART		– – – – – –							is skilled in arts and crafts
		B LITERATURE	– – – – –								reads, writes, communicates by word
		C MUSIC		– – – –							plays, composes, and enjoys music
		D DRAMA	– – – – – – – – –								goes to stage plays; acts out own feelings
		E SALES			– – –						gets people to buy things and ideas
		F MANAGEMENT	– – – – –								directs the work of others
		G OFFICE WORK	– – – – – – – – – – – – – –								types, files, does paper work
		H PERSONAL SERVICE		– – – – – – – – – –							caters to individual needs and comforts
		I PROTECTIVE SERVICE		– – – –							safeguards people, property, country
		J SOCIAL SERVICE		– – – – – – – –						works in education, health, employment
		K SOCIAL SCIENCE	– – – – – – – –								studies the actions of people and groups
		L BIOLOGICAL SCIENCE	– – – –								studies the bodies of living things
		M PHYSICAL SCIENCE	– – – – – – – – – – – – –							studies the motion of bodies in space-time
		N NUMBER			– – – –						works with numbers; knows algebra; computes
		O MECHANICS						+++++			designs, builds, and maintains machines
		P MACHINE OPERATION						+++++			operates machines, processes materials
		Q OUTDOOR						+++++			works on farm, in forest, in garden, at sea
		R ATHLETICS		– – – – – – – – – –							takes part in group or individual sports
		S SEDENTARI-NESS		– – – – –							sits mainly in one place on the job
		T RISK			– – – – –						takes on dangerous and risky jobs
		U AMBITION					+++++				wants to improve self, income, status
		V CHOSEN SKILL LEVEL			– – – – – – – –						works at shown level of difficulty
		W SEX STEREOTYPE				+++++++					prefers work formerly done by persons of own sex
		X AGREEMENT		– – – – – – – – – – –							likes/dislikes pictures most people like/dislike
		Y NEGATIVE BIAS		– – – – – –							motivated by dislikes
		Z POSITIVE BIAS					+++++++++				motivated by likes

Copyright 1978 By Jastak Associates, Inc.   1526 Gilpin Avenue   Wilmington, DE 19806

FIGURE 11-2.
WRIOT profile.
From *Wide Range Interest-Opinion Test* by J. F. Jastak and S. Jastak. Copyright © 1978 by Jastak Associates, Inc. Reprinted by permission.

English. Arturo stated that he forgot the English he learned at school after spending a summer at home. Arturo explained that he had some interest in academic subjects but was more interested in finding a job because his family needed an additional source of income. However, Arturo was unable to specify a vocational choice.

The counselor selected the WRIOT as an instrument that might provide some stimulus for discussion of future occupations. Because this inventory measures interests by having the individual respond to activities portrayed in pictures, Arturo's poor reading ability did not handicap him.

Arturo's profile is shown in Figure 11-2. As expected, Arturo had little interest in academic subjects but did show a high interest in mechanics, machine operations, and outdoor activities. The counselor was pleased to see that Arturo scored on the positive side of the ambition scale, which supported his claim of wanting to improve his vocational skills and income. Arturo agreed with the high score on the sex stereotype scale in that he basically preferred work traditionally done by men. The results also indicated that Arturo was highly motivated by his likes as opposed to being motivated by his dislikes.

Arturo responded positively to the results and indicated that he felt that they were a fairly good measure of his interests. He added that he much preferred to work with his hands as opposed to reading or writing. The counselor turned to the mechanics scale description and reviewed some of the key positive items, as shown in Figure 11-3. The counselor noticed that the positively keyed items include upholstering, assembling, repairing, servicing, and construction work. The job titles for this scale include automobile mechanic, cabinet maker, carpenter, concrete layer, construction worker, draftsman, electrician, gas station attendant, television repairer, roofer, and machine assembler. The counselor pointed out to Arturo that he also had a high level of interest in machine operations and was interested primarily in outdoor work. Arturo stated that he liked working with machines and working outdoors, but he had never given a great deal of thought to specific jobs. The counselor presented some of the occupations from the list as a point of reference for discussion. Arturo obviously needed additional information about requirements, environments, and skills needed for career exploration. Specific occupations selected for further investigation by Arturo included electrician's helper, auto mechanic, sheet metal worker, and machine operator.

The counselor pointed out that certain academic skills would be required in these jobs and that it would therefore be necessary for Arturo to apply himself in the academic area as well as in specific training programs. The counselor suggested that Arturo visit the vocational-technical training division of the school to learn about the jobs he had elected to explore.

The results of this interest test provided the opportunity for the counselor to help Arturo identify and clarify his interests through activities portrayed in pictures. His motivation for career exploration was also significantly increased by the discussion of the test results. In addition, the results were easily linked to occupational groups and to specific occupations. Finally, the counselor was able to emphasize academic requirements in addition to specific occupational requirements.

SOCIAL AND PREVOCATIONAL INFORMATION BATTERY (SPIB)

The SPIB was developed to measure five long-range goals that are considered to be relevant for educationally and mentally retarded (EMR) students in junior and senior high school. These goals are identified with specific objectives as follows: employability (job search skills and job-related behavior), economic self-sufficiency (banking, budgeting, and purchasing), family living (home management and physical health care), personal habits (hygiene and grooming), and communication (responding appropriately to safety, emergency, and general information signs). The entire test consists of 277 items, which are mostly true/false and are administered verbally.

Mechanics

O – Mechanics

Cluster Items

The following items are consistently liked by persons wishing to engage in **Manual Building** and **Repair** activities and are therefore positively correlated with this cluster.

Female	Key Positive Items	Male
2 A. upholster chair		2 A. upholster chair
6 C. put up steel girders		6 C. put up steel girders
20 C. repair telephone lines		20 C. repair telephone lines
41 B. repair TV sets		31 B. assemble machines
43 A. repair record players		41 B. repair TV sets
47 B. make cabinets		43 A. repair record players
48 B. cut out dress patterns		47 B. make cabinets
65 A. construct field fences		50 C. repair steeples
73 C. do masonry work		61 B. service cars
78 C. repair office machines		71 C. install traffic lights
82 C. build roofs		73 C. do masonry work
95 C. build bridges		78 C. repair office machines
106 C. do carpentry work		82 C. build roofs
110 C. pour concrete floors		95 C. build bridges
141 A. make candy		106 C. do carpentry work
		110 C. pour concrete floors
		139 B. install electric fixtures
		140 C. lay bricks

Female	Secondary Positive Items	Male
5 B. do plumbing work		5 B. do plumbing work
17 B. bake pastry		10 C. polish floors
32 C. repair appliances		29 B. work as ship
37 C. skin dive		steward-stewardess
61 B. service cars		46 B. set type for print
70 A. work on airplanes		48 B. cut out dress patterns
71 C. install traffic lights		49 C. sell hardware
75 B. run steamroller		57 C. paint house
84 B. wrap packages		66 A. drive dump truck
87 C. operate a bulldozer		67 C. spray trees
91 C. trim hedges		74 B. run a mixing machine
101 C. check soil temperature		84 B. wrap packages
128 A. saw lumber		87 C. operate a bulldozer
142 C. repair shoes by machine		91 B. operate cranes
149 A. do welding		112 B. examine leaf etchings
		122 A. operate street cleaner
		141 B. run duplicating machine
		142 C. repair shoes by machine
		145 C. operate power hammer

The following items are consistently disliked by persons wishing to engage in **Manual Building** and **Repair**. Their negative choices are positively correlated with this cluster.

Female	Key Negative Items	Male
2 C. sell appliances		5 C. broadcast the news
20 B. explain sales graph		20 B. explain sales graph
32 A. massage person's back		22 B. sell real estate
50 A. chauffeur		33 A. conduct orchestra
58 B. pitch baseballs		42 B. carry trays in restaurant
75 C. serve as congressperson		49 A. sell fire, burglary insurance
86 B. drill recruits		70 B. file archives, records
87 B. act as army general		71 A. work as bartender
88 C. work as receptionist		83 B. guide tours
89 B. attend executive meetings		85 B. collect coins
95 B. advise on bank loans		87 B. act as army general
114 C. prepare newspaper ads		107 C. speak at club
127 C. argue before jury		134 B. sell theater tickets
142 A. run city as mayor		141 C. sing in opera
149 B. sell stocks and bonds		142 A. run city as mayor
		149 B. sell stocks and bonds

Definition

Choices in this cluster express preferences for the designing, building, assembling, erecting, maintaining, and repairing of three-dimensional structures.

Significant Correlations with other clusters:

Females: Positive: art (A), machine operation (P), outdoor (Q)

Negative: literature (B), sales (E), management (F), office work (G), protective service (I), social service (J), social science (K), number (N)

Males: Positive: art (A), physical science (M), machine operation (P), risk (T)

Negative: literature (B), music (C), drama (D), sales (E), management (F), personal service (H), social service (J), social science (K), number (N)

Job Titles

Titles may recur in clusters positively correlated with this one.

airplane mechanic
automobile designer
automobile mechanic
automotive engineer
beekeeper
boiler inspector
boiler mechanic
bookbinder
bridge builder
building inspector
cabinet maker
camera repairperson
carpenter
civil engineer
combustion engineer
concrete layer
construction foreperson
construction inspector
construction worker
dental technician
die designer
die maker
draftsman, draftswoman
electrical engineer
electrician
electricians helper
factory foreperson
farm foreperson
fence builder
gas station attendant
gift wrapper

gunsmith
hardware salesperson
heating repairperson
house painter
industrial engineer
leaf examiner
machine assembler
manufacturing foreperson
masonry worker
mechanic
mechanical engineer
medical lab technician
office machine repairperson
pattern cutter
phonograph repairperson
plumber
radio operator
radio technician
recording engineer
refrigeration engineer
roofer
ship steward, stewardess
steel worker
telephone repairperson
television repairperson
toolroom manager
traffic light installer
typesetter
x-ray technician

FIGURE 11-3.

Description of mechanics scale on the WRIOT.
From *Wide Range Interest-Opinion Test* by J. F. Jastak and S Jastak. Copyright 1978 by Jastak Associates, Inc. Reprinted by permission.

Reliability estimates obtained by KR-20 for each subtest ranged from .65 to .82 with a median of .75. Test-retest reliabilities over two-week intervals are approximately the same. Meyers (1978) considers the validity acceptable because these scales provide more adequate information for placement and identification of needs than could generally be expected from subjective ratings and appraisals. Overton (1992) suggests that the norms underrepresent minorities.

Interpreting the SPIB

Three norm-referenced groups are available for interpreting the results of the SPIB: junior high school students, senior high school students, and combinations of junior and senior high school students.

The authors suggest a task-analysis method of evaluating specific competencies in each domain measured by the SPIB. For this evaluation method, each content area is divided into subcontent areas. For example, for job-related behavior, the subcontent areas are: knowledge of role and duties of a supervisor, knowledge of appropriate communications, knowledge of what constitutes job completion, and recognition and knowledge of appropriate relations with fellow employees. Each subcontent area also provides the basis for developing instructional activities and for measuring the outcome of the instructional activities.

SPIB results give the career counselor some indication of the readiness of the disabled individual to enter the job market. In addition, the information obtained from this battery can be used to establish counseling programs that assist individuals in making an adequate adjustment to the work environment.

Case of a Group Program Based on SPIB Results

The teacher of EMR students made an appointment in early October to see the counselor. She informed the counselor that several of her students would be ready for placement at the end of the school year. However, the SPIB administered at the beginning of the fall term indicated that some students did not have appropriate job-related behaviors and job-search skills. The teacher requested help from the counselor in developing modules that would simulate work environments in order to teach the students about supervisor-worker relationships, the importance of communication on the job, and factors affecting job performance.

Additional modules would be developed to teach students how to prepare resumés, how to conduct themselves in interviews, and how to increase their knowledge of sources of occupational information. The following outline is for the module designed to promote an understanding of supervisor-worker relationships:

Module I: To promote understanding of supervisor-worker relationships.

Objective: To understand the role of the supervisor.

Strategy: Worker-supervisor simulation.

Participants: Two students.

Materials: Eighteen pencils, six rubber bands.

Activity:
1. Worker is given orders by supervisor to secure six pencils together with rubber bands.
2. Supervisor inspects work, makes suggestions and gives constructive criticism, changes orders to secure five pencils together.
3. Classmates, as observers, identify supervisor as boss and identify the supervisor's activities as praising, criticizing, suggesting, instructing, inspecting, and assigning duties.

In this case, the SPIB results identified the need for an educational program and provided the specific data for forming instructional units. A post-test provides data for evaluating the effectiveness of the program and for determining the need for additional programs.

MICRO-TOWER

The Micro-Tower system of vocational evaluation was developed by ICD Rehabilitation and Research Center of New York City. The original instrument, Tower, is an acronym for Testing, Orientation, and Work Evaluation in Rehabilitation. Tower consists of 94 individually administered work samples. Micro-Tower consists of 13 work samples that can be administered to a group over a three-to-five-day period. The Micro-Tower work samples are performance tests that measure aptitudes for a number of unskilled and skilled occupations. These aptitudes are grouped into five broad areas, each measured by specific tests: motor—electronic connector assembly, bottle capping and packing, lamp assembly; clerical perception—ZIP coding, record checking, filing, mail sorting; spatial—blueprint reading, graphics illustration; numerical—making change, payroll computation; and verbal—want ad comprehension, message taking.[1]

The reading level required is third to fourth grade. The work samples can be administered to an individual who is sitting down but do require the use of at least one hand. The individual is required to understand spoken English.

A unique feature of the Micro-Tower system is the involvement of the clients in group discussions designed to explore interests, values, lifestyles, and so forth. A separate manual outlines specific procedures and variations for the discussion groups. One of the major objectives of the discussion groups is to improve the clients' motivation for job placement. Discussion groups are also used before the test in an effort to make the testing situation as nonthreatening as possible.

Interpreting Micro-Tower

Several kinds of normative data are available, including data for a general rehabilitation population, Spanish-speaking individuals, left-handed individuals, the physically disabled, the psychiatrically disturbed, the brain damaged, individuals with cerebral palsy, students in special education, the socially disadvantaged, former drug abusers, former alcoholics, adult offenders, males, and females. The variety of norms available for interpretation increases the usefulness of this instrument.

Interpretive materials for the Micro-Tower system are elaborate and thorough. The results are reported on a graph that ranges from weak to strong for the general aptitudes and specific work samples. Additional information for the counselor includes: a report of behavioral observations during testing, a summary of the client's interests and performance; a client data sheet; a summary report, which includes a narrative of the test results; a recommendation summary sheet, which covers areas such as special training; a list of referral recommendations; and a list of vocational recommendations.

The Micro-Tower system grew out of a need for a work evaluation instrument that could be administered to a group in a relatively short period of time. The evaluation system may also be used as a screening device to determine which clients would benefit from an extensive evaluation of specific aptitudes. A manual converts Micro-Tower scores into estimates of the DOT aptitude levels. Several other work-sample tests such as Micro-Tower have been developed, sometimes on a local basis, to meet the specific needs of the disabled.

Both Micro-Tower and SPIB point out the need for specially developed norms or criterion-referenced objectives based on specific population samples. A growing number of the tests and inventories on the market today have developed normative data from disadvantaged and disabled population samples. One hopes that additional assessment instruments will be developed in the future to meet the needs of these special groups.

---

[1]Adapted from Micro-Tower, ICD Rehabilitation and Research Center, New York. Copyright © 1977. Reprinted by permission.

Case of a Brain-Damaged Individual Seeking Employment

The rehabilitation counselor was pleased to see Rex after his long stay in the hospital after a car accident. Rex had substantial head injuries and brain damage. The counselor was particularly concerned about Rex's motor coordination. Rex had been a construction foreman before his accident and was now ready to seek employment again. He had stated earlier that he desired a change of jobs and had agreed that several local industries might provide opportunities for him.

Previous testing revealed that Rex had average intelligence and had maintained his previous academic achievement levels. The counselor arranged for Rex to take the Micro-Tower tests of motor coordination: electronic connector assembly (to assess finger dexterity); bottle capping and packing (to assess manual dexterity); and lamp assembly (to assess manual assembly skills). The counselor felt that these tests were most essential for determining whether Rex was able to handle the tasks required in the local industries under consideration. The results of the test were to be judged as satisfactory (based on level of performance for productive workers in the industries) or unsatisfactory.

On the electronic connectors test (placing metal pins into discs) Rex's performance was satisfactory compared with that of workers in the local industries. The scorer observed that Rex's performance was somewhat affected by his lack of speed, but he was able to complete most of the tasks. On the bottle capping and packing test, Rex's performance was also judged satisfactory. The scorer observed that his manual dexterity was good and that Rex was able to learn these tasks quickly. On the lamp assembly test, which requires the use of a screwdriver, wire stripper, and long-nose pliers in assembling a lamp, Rex's average performance was judged satisfactory for meeting local job requirements. The counselor felt that this work sample was crucial because it closely resembled the kinds of tasks required in a number of local industries.

Rex seemed pleased with his performance: "I was really under pressure before I took those tests. I just didn't know if I could handle it. Now I feel more confident that I can take on another job."

The counselor informed Rex that his physician felt that he would continue to show improvement in tasks requiring fine visual-motor coordination. In the meantime, the counselor suggested that they consider how his physical condition would affect his personal relationships in a new working environment and the conflicts that might arise when he returned to work with a disability.

In this case the test results provided vital information for evaluating the motor coordination of a disabled individual. The results also provided specific information concerning Rex's ability to handle certain tools and to perform tasks that could be related to similar tasks in several local firms. This case illustrates how tests such as Micro-Tower can be used to assist the disabled in evaluating their level of performance and linking their performance with occupational requirements.

OTHER INSTRUMENTS

The diverse needs of the disabled and educationally disadvantaged necessitate specially designed assessment instruments. Those listed below are examples of the kinds of instruments that may serve some of the purposes of assessment for the disabled and disadvantaged.

Tests of General Ability. These tests are appropriate for students from culturally deprived backgrounds as measures of general intelligence and basic learning ability. All items are pictorial, and the examiner's manual has been translated into Spanish. One part of the test measures an individual's ability to recognize relationships and to understand meanings of pictures and basic concepts. The second part of the test measures reasoning ability.

Chicago Non-Verbal Examination. This intelligence test is designed specifically for individuals with reading difficulties or those who have been reared in foreign-language environments. The test is administered either verbally or in pantomime. Standardization samples include 70% native and 30% foreign-born students.

Tests of Adult Basic Education. The four levels of this test are designed to identify the need for instruction in basic skills. The subtests are reading vocabulary, reading comprehension, arithmetic reasoning, and arithmetic fundamentals.

California Occupational Preference Survey. This test has been translated into Spanish and is designed primarily to assist individuals in defining broad areas of interest.

Geist Picture Interest Inventory. A special edition of this interest inventory for Spanish-speaking and bilingual males uses pictures of occupational activities. The general interest areas are persuasive, clerical, mechanical, musical, scientific, outdoors, literary, computational, artistic, social service, and dramatic. This inventory may be used with many other male groups besides Spanish-speaking and bilingual males.

J.E.V.S. Worksample System. J.E.V.S. is a work-sample system similar to the Micro-Tower system discussed in this chapter. It is designed primarily for the vocational assessment of rehabilitation clients. The battery helps the counselor evaluate an individual's skills, behaviors, and interests.

Vocational Evaluation System. This is a work-sample test for vocational assessment of adults. It assesses more than 20 work activities, including bench assembly, drafting, woodworking, welding, medical service, and soil testing.

SUMMARY

Legislation that requires equal access to training and employment for the disabled and disadvantaged has encouraged the development of specially designed assessment instruments. These instruments must meet the needs of individuals from many ethnic and racial backgrounds. In this chapter the counselor has been encouraged to carefully evaluate the reference groups from which the assessment data have been derived. Norm groups should match the individuals being tested in cultural background and other characteristics.

QUESTIONS AND EXERCISES

1. Why is it important to have specially developed norm data for the disabled and disadvantaged?
2. Explain how you would use aptitude test results for the disabled when special norms for the disabled are not available.
3. An individual states that he has been turned down for jobs because of his low educational achievement. He claims that he can read, spell, and do some arithmetic. He is now confused about what kind of job he wants. While considering other counseling needs, what kind of assessment instruments would you use?
4. Should pictorial interest inventories for nonreaders include activities that depict high-level jobs requiring college degrees? Explain your answer.
5. Explain how you could most effectively interpret test data to a disabled individual who is applying for a job in a local industry. Under what conditions would the results be most meaningful?

Chapter Twelve

Using Nonstandardized Self-Assessment Inventories

In recent years career-counseling programs have incorporated self-assessment techniques to identify individual characteristics and traits. Self-assessment inventories include a variety of self-scored questionnaires, checklists, and rating and ranking formats that evaluate specific characteristics for use in career counseling. For example, Bolles (1978) uses self-assessment of developed skills as a vital step in career decision making. Fogel (1974) has employed self-assessment techniques in a group guidance program designed to increase certainty about career goals. Self-estimates of ability as they are related to Holland's (1985) six modal personal styles and matching work environments are an integral part of the Self-Directed Search. Harrington and O'Shea (1992) recommend the use of self-estimates of ability in their system of career decision making. Lathrop (1977) emphasizes self-estimates of skills and abilities as an important step in finding an ideal job. McKinlay (1990) has developed a questionnaire for identifying skills and interests; results are used to obtain appropriate career information from a computerized system. Zunker (1994) suggests methods of self-assessment of skills for adults.

Super's (1990) emphasis on self-concept has encouraged the development of programs for increasing self-awareness. For example, life-planning workshops (Thomas, 1972) incorporate self-assessment exercises for increasing self-awareness in order to stimulate career exploration. Tyler (1961) developed a vocational card sort as a technique for increasing self-awareness. Dinkmeyer and Caldwell (1970) recommend the use of an autobiography for developing self-awareness. Other career development programs that assess self-awareness include those by Jones (1981) and Figler (1990).

A number of research projects suggest that self-estimates of ability are valid in that individuals tend to function in ways that are consistent with their self-perceptions (Baird, 1969). In a study of National Merit Scholars, the best predictors of college achievement were high school grades and self-estimates of scholastic ability (Holland & Astin, 1962). Baird (1969) found that the best predictors of grade point average among college freshmen were self-ratings of scholastic ability. A study of high school students by Payne (1962) revealed a high degree of predictive validity for achievement based on self-concepts. Other research studies of secondary students by Binder, Jones, and Strowig (1970), Wylie (1963), and Bowen (1968) also produced evidence that self-estimates of ability are efficient predictors of achievement.

Despite this evidence of the validity of self-assessment in general, the self-assessment methods discussed in this chapter do not meet the criteria for standardized instruments. They are designed primarily to stimulate discussion of career options and to supplement or raise questions about information obtained in other ways. Because the validity and reliability of the instruments reviewed here have not been established, the results must be used with caution. The counselor interested in measuring personal characteristics related to the entire spectrum of jobs should use a standardized interest or ability inventory.

Several methods of self-assessment are discussed in this chapter. By discussing these instruments I do not intend to imply that self-assessment techniques should replace standardized tests and inventories. Career decision making is a process in which all aspects of individuality should receive consideration. When career-counseling programs incorporate all relevant information, including self-estimates, the chances of career decision making being dominated by any one source are decreased.

DIMENSIONS OF LIFESTYLE ORIENTATION SURVEY (DLOS)

The DLOS (Zunker, 1977) is a counseling tool designed to assist individuals in determining their lifestyle orientations: preferences for career style, family style, leisure style, place of residence, and work environment. The results of the survey may be used in a variety of counseling programs, but the survey is designed primarily to facilitate discussion in groups or individually with a counselor about important career and life decisions.

Students determine individual lifestyle dimensions by choosing those preferred from a list of 80; they also answer several questions concerning desired geographic locations; an essay is optional. In the first part of the survey, as shown below, students read a list of phrases and respond to them.

> **Directions:** This is not a test, but an inventory to help you in thinking in terms of a lifestyle after graduation from college. The first part contains a list of statements concerning such matters as job style, leisure style, membership style, home study, and family styles. You are to read through the list very carefully and rate each of the items according to the following scale:
>
> 1 = unimportant to me
> 2 = moderately important to me
> 3 = of great importance to me

Samples of the items are as follows:

1. Live in a moderate-sized home of three to four bedrooms in a suburban area
2. Eat at restaurants that are relatively inexpensive
3. Be socially prominent
4. Rent a modest home
5. Compete strongly to move up the financial ladder
6. No "rat race"—have a minimum of material possessions

After completing the first section of the survey, the individual chooses a region of residence, a state of preference or a foreign country, and community preference from lists provided.[1] Items marked "of great importance" provide relevant information for discussion. For example, a preference for living in different parts of the country or for "a job that is easygoing with little or no pressure" is clarified and considered in the decision-making process.

When significant discrepancies are found between lifestyle needs, such as financial expectations, and the realities of potential careers, the individual is required to establish priorities for lifestyle needs. Through discussion individual priorities can be clarified, and realistic alternatives and options can be developed.

For example, Mike's completed DLOS indicated a strong orientation toward financial compensation. During group discussion he examined the potential financial rewards of careers he was considering. He learned that some of the careers would probably not provide the salary he expected. In explaining to the group why he had selected those careers for consideration, he

---

[1] In each case the individual can indicate undecided or no preference.

became aware that lifestyle needs other than financial rewards—for example, having time for his family and obtaining satisfaction from his job—were important to him. Through further discussion he was able to establish priorities for his needs.

Susan, too, found that she had some lifestyle needs that conflicted with career goals. DLOS results indicated a strong orientation toward raising a family, having time for leisure activities, and having a job with little pressure. However, she was considering careers that involved much pressure, long hours, and considerable dedication. During the discussion she identified these striking differences and decided to give further thought to career requirements before deciding which of her needs were most important. The approach of the counselor was not to disparage any of the identified needs, but to promote an understanding of potential conflicts and further clarification of lifestyle orientations and career requirements.

These examples illustrate how consideration of lifestyle factors can assist in setting career goals. Lifestyle orientation is a factor that might be ignored in career planning because students may have difficulty in projecting their needs into the future. The DLOS stimulates clarification of individual lifestyle orientation and thereby enhances the individual's capacities for effective planning. A copy of the DLOS is included in Appendix C.

CAREER SELF ASSESSMENT (CSA)

Snodgrass (1980) developed the CSA for analyzing career plans. Specifically, the inventory introduces the basic elements of career planning and aids individuals in determining their progress in this area. The inventory was built around Super's (1990) theory of self-concept (originally published in 1953); individuals are encouraged to evaluate their interests, values, abilities, personalities, and other specific characteristics. For example, individuals indicate their reasons for selecting a college major or career by responding to questions such as the following:

2) If you stated your major in number 1 . . . can you state why you selected what major? If you have not made a choice, move to question number 6.
   a) It sounded interesting.
   b) I didn't know what else to choose.
   c) It will prepare me for a job.
   d) It will prepare me for a career I have thoroughly researched and planned; it is required.
   e) I felt that I was supposed to choose a major as soon as possible.
   f) Other _____

3) How certain are you that you have selected a major most appropriate for you?
   a) very certain
   b) certain
   c) somewhat certain
   d) not very certain
   e) not certain at all

4) How satisfied are you with your major selection?
   a) very satisfied
   b) satisfied
   c) somewhat satisfied
   d) not very satisfied
   e) not satisfied at all
   f) too early to tell

5) Did you know what the field was about before you selected your major?
   Yes_____   No_____

In other questions the individual is challenged to state why a career has been selected. Examples of such questions follow:

10) List below the three primary factors that were considered before making your (career) choice. _____

_____

_____

11) From what resources did you learn about this field (e.g., career brochures, pamphlets, books, people working in the field)?

12) How much do you feel you know about this field?
    a) very much
    b) I have general information about it.
    c) not very much
    d) very little[2]

The inventory also requires the individual to indicate assistance needed in career planning. The individual is then directed to either group or individual counseling programs or to the career resource center.

The CSA is a well-designed instrument for introducing the basic elements of career planning. Informal evaluation of it has been positive. The instrument should promote stimulating discussions about the relationship between college majors and careers. Ideally, individuals should also learn how to make rational decisions about college majors and careers.

Case of a University Freshman Who Needs to Establish Career Objectives[3]

Erik, a university freshman, was involved in a course project that required him to complete the CSA and then discuss it with a counselor in the career resource center. During the discussion, Erik told the counselor that he had to choose a major and, even though he didn't know much about it, business seemed as practical as anything else. Erik told the counselor that he had not given much thought to his career goals; he had just assumed he would go into business. He then indicated that he realized he had chosen his career without much forethought and perhaps he should give some consideration to other options.

Reviewing the CSA further, the counselor noted that Erik had had some difficulty completing the section that required him to list personal characteristics such as interests, skills, values, and personality traits. Erik told the counselor that he found it difficult to describe himself in those terms but that he realized it would be helpful to know more about himself in order to choose a suitable career. The counselor and Erik agreed that self-awareness would be a good starting point for career planning. Erik then made an appointment to continue career counseling the following week. This example illustrates the use of the CSA in helping students establish objectives.

QUICK JOB HUNTING MAP

Bolles (1985) has devised a self-assessment method for identifying functional and transferable skills. The purpose of the Quick Job Hunting Map is, first, to assist individuals in identifying functional skills they have used in the past; second, to identify the skills the individual enjoys using; and finally, to recognize how learned skills can be transferred to meet the requirements of selected occupations. The Quick Job Hunting Map is divided into three categories: people, information, and things. Each category is defined and a sample of skills associated with each category is given.

---

[2]From *Career Self Assessment* by G. Snodgrass. Southwest Texas State University, unpublished document, 1980. Reprinted by permission.

[3]Adapted from *Career Self Assessment* by G. Snodgrass. Southwest Texas State University, unpublished document, 1980, p. 3. Reprinted by permission.

The individual is instructed to write seven brief stories about past experiences that involved accomplishments, solving problems, and skills used that were enjoyed. With the seven stories the individual uses the Quick Job Hunting Map to identify skills with people (such as dealing patiently with difficult people or caring for the disabled), information (such as computing data or surveying for research), and things (such as monitoring a machine or photographing). For example, under information, the Quick Job Hunting Map lists 15 skills, one of which is shown below, and an additional skills-verbs bank to assist the individual with the skill identification process (Bolles, 1985, pp. 24–25).

Computing

Dealing with numbers, performing simple or complex arithmetic.
    counting
    taking inventory
    calculating
    solving statistical problems
    auditing
    keeping accurate financial records
    reporting
    maintaining fiscal controls
    budgeting
    projecting
    purchasing
    operating a computer competently with spreadsheets and statistics (and, by extension, with all computer applications: word processing, databases, graphics, and telecommunications)

Additional Skills-Verbs Bank:
    Performing rapid and accurate manipulation of numbers, in one's head or on paper
        preparing financial reports
        estimating
        ordering
        acquiring

The individual is then instructed to go through the complete list of skills identified by seven narratives of past experiences, choose skills liked best, and prioritize them. Eventually, the individual chooses the top three or four skills in which he or she is proficient and likes doing under each of the three categories: people, information, and things. These lists of skills are used to identify occupations for further consideration. Additional help in the job search is given in the form of specific suggestions for job site visits and for finding additional information. The Quick Job Hunting Map is a thorough method of identifying a variety of skills. However, the time necessary to complete the map may limit use in some career-counseling programs.

GUIDE TO CAREER PLANNING AND DEVELOPMENT

A career development manual was designed by Hanson (1976) in association with the Lawrence Livermore Laboratory in California. The manual is divided into three sections. The first section contains exercises and suggestions for self-evaluation of personal values and goals. Interests are identified by using the Strong Interest Inventory. The second section contains self-assessment techniques for identifying satisfying and dissatisfying events in one's life and analyzing abilities used during these events. The third section contains self-assessment techniques for defining the ideal job and relating personal qualities to job requirements. The purpose of the manual is to have individuals focus on career objectives. All data from the self-assessments are placed on a profile, which is used in career exploration.

An example of the personal values section follows. Individuals are instructed to rank-order the phrases according to their own values. The top six values are used with other data when considering career objectives.[4]

Recognition	to be acknowledged	1. _____
Duty	to dedicate myself to what I call responsibility	2. _____
Expertness	to become an authority	3. _____
Independence	to have freedom of thought and content	4. _____
Pleasure	to enjoy life; to be happy and content	5. _____
Power	to have control over others	6. _____
Leadership	to become influential and to lead other people	7. _____
Affection	to obtain and to share companionship and affection	8. _____
Parenthood	to raise a fine family; to have heirs	9. _____
Acceptance	to be received with approval	10. _____
Financial success	to earn a great deal of money	11. _____
Health	to enjoy physical well-being	12. _____
Service	to contribute to the satisfaction of others	13. _____
Self-realization	to optimize personal development	14. _____
Security	to have a secure and stable position	15. _____
Prestige	to become well known and to have status	16. _____
Stability	to have the ability or strength to withstand change	17. _____
Professional accomplishment	to attain work goals	18. _____
Intimacy	to be close to others	19. _____

Overall, this guide is well prepared and concise, and it clearly ties together the steps used in career planning. However, the list of values should be explained and their relationship to work environments and job satisfactions clarified.

COMMUNITY COLLEGE GROUP COUNSELING PROGRAM

Fogel (1974) emphasizes self-assessment techniques in a career development program for community college students. The program is based on Super's (1990) belief that interests, values, and other individual traits are important aspects of vocational development (originally published in 1953). Thus, a major goal of the program is the development of self-awareness to improve the participants' ability to choose a career. Self-assessments of interests, strengths (skills), personality, and values are an integral part of the program.

An example of the interest assessment component of this program follows:[5]

Check the areas that represent your real interests.

When I really have my free choice I prefer to:
— Work with things (fix my car, make a dress, etc.)
— Work with business (think of a money-making scheme, be involved in business and selling, etc.)
— Do something systematic and predictable (make something similar to what I have made before, keep my work in order, etc.)
— Do something to help others (do volunteer work, be a camp counselor)
— Do something where I'll get recognition from others (speak in public, act as an officer or leader, etc.)
— Do something outdoors (hike, garden, work with a harvest crew, etc.)

---

[4]From *Guide to Career Planning and Development* by M. C. Hanson. Copyright 1976 by Lawrence Livermore Laboratory. Reprinted by permission.
[5]From *Development of a Replicable Group Vocational Counseling Procedure for Use with Community College Students* by A. J. Fogel, 1974. Unpublished doctoral dissertation, University of California, Los Angeles. Reprinted by permission.

— Work with people and communicate ideas (play in a musical group, join a discussion, etc.)

— Do something scientific (work on a collection, read about some part of science, etc.)

— Do something creative (plan a project I've never done before, write a story or paint, etc.)

— Work with machines or processes (take and develop photos, operate an electric drill, sewing machine, etc.)

— Do something where I get tangible results (make jewelry or a fish pond, etc.)

— You name it; what other interests would you like to express in your work?

_____

_____

Which three interests do you consider to be most important to use in your work?

(1) _____   (2)_____

(3) _____

Are you sure these are your interests?_____

How can you find out if you're not sure?

Would others agree that the three interests you listed are right for you?

_____

Two problems are apparent. First, only one item is used to assess interest in a whole category, such as an interest in things, an interest in business, an interest in helping others. This limitation offers doubts about the reliability of the instrument. Authors of standardized instruments find that it is necessary to have several items to measure adequately a personal trait or characteristic. Second, the rationale used to select interest categories is not clear. It would perhaps have been wiser to select items that could be classified under systems such as Holland's, the DOT, or Kuder's. However, the instrument should stimulate discussion of interests as they are related to the activities listed.

SUMMARY

In this chapter several nonstandardized self-assessment methods have been discussed. Evidence indicates that self-estimates of ability are valid. Many self-assessment questionnaires and checklists have been developed to evaluate specific characteristics that are of interest in career counseling. The use of self-assessment is encouraged in order to lessen the chances that career decision making will be dominated by any one source. Nonstandardized self-assessment devices have limitations but are useful for stimulating discussion and for supplying supplementary information for career exploration.

QUESTIONS AND EXERCISES

1. What are the major advantages of using self-assessment measures in career counseling?
2. What strategy would you use to introduce measures of interests and values after using the Career Self Assessment?
3. Develop a strategy for interpreting the results of an instrument for assessing lifestyle orientations. Explain how you would use information on dimensions of lifestyle with other data.
4. What are the advantages and disadvantages of an instrument such as the Quick Job Hunting Map?
5. Build a self-assessment instrument for measuring values of high school seniors. Explain how you would incorporate this instrument into a career-counseling program.

Appendix A
List of Tests and Publishers

Academic Promise Test

The Psychological Corporation
555 Academic Court
San Antonio, TX 78204

Adult Basic Learning Examination (ABLE)

The Psychological Corporation
555 Academic Court
San Antonio, TX 78204

Adult Career Concerns Inventory

Consulting Psychological Press, Inc.
3803 Bayshore Drive
Palo Alto, CA 94303

American College Testing (ACT)

American College Testing Program
P.O. Box 168
Iowa City, IA 52240

American College Testing (ACT) Career
Planning Program (CPP)

American College Testing Program
P.O. Box 168
Iowa City, IA 52240

Armed Services Vocational Aptitude
Battery (ASVAB)

U.S. Department of Defense
Washington, DC 20301

Basic Occupatonal Literacy Test (BOLT)

U.S. Department of Labor
Manpower Administration
Washington, DC 20210

Basic Skills Assessment Program

Educational Testing Service
P.O. Box 6736
Princeton, NJ 08541-6736

Brainard Occupational Preference
Inventory

The Psychological Corporation
555 Academic Court
San Antonio, TX 78204

California Occupational Preference Survey	Educational and Industrial Testing Service P.O. Box 7234 San Diego, CA 92017
California Test of Personality	Publishers Test Service 20 Ryan Ranch Road Monterey, CA 93940
Campbell Organizational Survey	NCS Assessments P.O. Box 1416 Minneapolis, MN 55440
Career Ability Placement Survey	Educational and Industrial Testing Service P.O. Box 7234 San Diego, CA 92107
Career Assessment Inventory	NCS/Interpretive Scoring Systems P. O. Box 1416 Minneapolis, MN 55440
Career Beliefs Inventory	Consulting Psychologists Press 3803 E. Bayshore Drive Palo Alto, CA 94303
Career Development Inventory	Consulting Psychologists Press 3803 E. Bayshore Drive Palo Alto, CA 94303
Career Interest and Skills Survey	NCS Assessments P.O. Box 1416 Minneapolis, MN 55440
Career Maturity Inventory (CMI)	CTB-Macmillan-McGraw-Hill Book Co. 20 Ryan Ranch Road Monterey, CA 93940
Career Self Assessment (CSA)	Gregory Snodgrass Counseling Center Southwest Texas State University San Marcos, TX 78666
Career Skills Assessment Program (CSAP)	College Entrance Examination Board 888 Seventh Avenue New York, NY 10019
Chicago Non-Verbal Examination	The Psychological Corporation 555 Academic Court San Antonio, TX 78204
Children's Personality Questionnaire	Institute of Personality and Ability Testing, Inc. P.O. Box 188 Champaign, IL 61820

Cognitive Vocational Maturity Test (CVMT)	Department of Psychology North Carolina State University Raleigh, NC 27607
College Entrance Examination Board Scholastic Aptitude Test	Educational Testing Service P.O. Box 6736 Princeton, NJ 08541-6736
Comprehensive Test of Basic Skills	CTB-Macmillan-McGraw-Hill Book Co. 20 Ryan Ranch Road Monterey, CA 93940
Cooperative English Test	Addison-Wesley Testing Service Reading, MA 01864
Cooperative Mathematics Test	Addison-Wesley Testing Service Reading, MA 01864
Cooperative Science Test	Addison-Wesley Testing Service Reading, MA 01864
Cooperative Social Studies Test	Addison-Wesley Testing Service Reading, MA 01864
Coopersmith Self-Esteem Inventory	Consulting Psychologists Press 3803 E. Bayshore Drive Palo Alto, CA 94303
Diagnostic Reading Scales	CTB-Macmillan-McGraw-Hill Book Co. 20 Ryan Ranch Road Monterey, CA 93940
Differential Aptitude Test (DAT)	The Psychological Corporation 555 Academic Court San Antonio, TX 78204
Early School Personality Questionnaire	Institute of Personality and Ability Testing, Inc. P.O. Box 188 Champaign, IL 61820
Edwards Personal Preference Schedule (EPPS)	The Psychological Corporation 555 Academic Court San Antonio, TX 78204
Flanagan Aptitude Classification Test	Science Research Associates, Inc. 155 North Wacker Drive Chicago, IL 60606
Geist Picture Interest Inventory	Western Psychological Services 12031 Wilshire Boulevard Los Angeles, CA 90025

General Aptitude Test Battery (GATB)

U.S. Government Printing Office
Washington, DC 20402

Guilford-Zimmerman Aptitude Survey

Sheridan Psychological Services
P.O. Box 6101
Orange, CA 92667

Guilford-Zimmerman Temperament
Survey

Sheridan Psychological Services
P.O. Box 6101
Orange, CA 92667

Hall Occupational Orientation Inventory

Scholastic Testing Service, Inc.
480 Meyer Road
P.O. Box 1056
Bensonville, IL 60106

Harrington/O'Shea Systems for Career
Decision-Making—Revised (CDM-R)

Career Planning Associates
P.O. Box 273
Needham, MA 02192

Iowa Test of Basic Skills

Riverside Publishing Co.
8420 Bryn Mawr
Chicago, IL 60631

Jackson Vocational Interest Inventory

Research Psychological Press, Inc.
P.O. Box 984
1110 Military St.
Port Huron, MI 48061-0984

Jenkins Activity Sequence

The Psychological Corporation
555 Academic Court
San Antonio, TX 78204

J.E.V.S. Worksample System

Vocational Research Institute
Jewish Employment and Vocational Service
1624 Locust Street
Philadelphia, PA 19103

Kuder Occupational Interest Survey (KOIS)

CTB-Macmillan-McGraw-Hill Book Co.
20 Ryan Ranch Road
Monterey, CA 93940

Mastery: Survival Skills Test (SST)

Science Research Associates, Inc.
155 North Wacker Drive
Chicago, IL 60606

Metropolitan Achievement Test
High School Battery

The Psychological Corporation
555 Academic Court
San Antonio, TX 78204

Micro-Tower

ICD Rehabilitation and Research Center
340 East 24th Street
New York, NY 10010

Minnesota Counseling Inventory	The Psychological Corporation 555 Academic Court San Antonio, TX 78204
Minnesota Importance Questionnaire	Vocational Psychology Research N620 Elliot Hall University of Minnesota Minneapolis, MN 55455-0344
Minnesota Vocational Interest Inventory	The Psychological Corporation 555 Academic Court San Antonio, TX 78204
Myers-Briggs Type Indicator	Consulting Psychologists Press 3803 E. Bayshore Drive Palo Alto, CA 94303
New Mexico Career Education Test Series (NMCETS)	Monitor Book Co. 195 South Beverly Drive Beverly Hills, CA 90212
Non-Sexist Vocational Card Sort (NSVCS)	C. R. Dewey Route 4, Box 217 Gainseville, FL 32601
Occupational Aptitude Survey and Interest Schedule	PRO-ED 8700 Shoal Creek Blvd. Austin, TX 78758
Ohio Vocational Interest Survey	The Psychological Corporation 555 Academic Court San Antonio, TX 78204
Ohio Work Values Inventory	Publishers Test Service 20 Ryan Ranch Road Monterey, CA 93940
Omnibus Personality Inventory	The Psychological Corporation 555 Academic Court San Antonio, TX 78204
Personal Values Inventory	Colgate University Testing Service Hamilton, NY 13346
Primary Mental Abilities Test	Science Research Associates, Inc. 155 North Wacker Drive Chicago, IL 60606
Rating Scales of Vocational Values, Vocational Interests, and Vocational Aptitudes	Educational and Industrial Testing Service P. O. Box 7234 San Diego, CA 92107

Rokeach Values Survey	Halgen Tests 837 Persimmon Sunnyvale, CA 94087
The Salience Inventory	Consulting Psychologists Press 3803 E. Bayshore Drive Palo Alto, CA 94303
Self Description Inventory	NCS/Interpretive Scoring Systems P. O. Box 1416 Minneapolis, MN 55440
Self-Directed Search (SDS)	Consulting Psychologists Press 3803 E. Bayshore Drive Palo Alto, CA 94303
Sixteen Personality Factor Questionnaire (16PF)	Institute for Personality and Ability Testing P.O. Box 188 Champaign, IL 61820
Social and Pre-Vocational Information Battery (SPIB)	CTB-Macmillan-McGraw-Hill Book Co. 20 Ryan Ranch Road Monterey, CA 93940
Stanford Achievement Test	The Psychological Corporation 555 Academic Court San Antonio, TX 78204
Stanford Diagnostic Arithmetic Test	The Psychological Corporation 555 Academic Court San Antonio, TX 78204
Strong Interest Inventory (SII)	Stanford University Press Stanford, CA 94305
Study of Values	Houghton Mifflin One Beacon Street Boston, MA 02138
Survey of Interpersonal Values (SIV)	Science Research Associates, Inc. 155 North Wacker Drive Chicago, IL 60606
Temperament and Values Inventory (TVI)	NCS/Interpretive Scoring Systems P. O. Box 1416 Minneapolis, MN 55440
Tests of Adult Basic Education	CTB-Macmillan-McGraw-Hill Book Co. 20 Ryan Ranch Road Monterey, CA 93940

Tests of General Ability	Guidance Testing Associates 6516 Shirley Avenue Austin, TX 78752
Thorndike's Dimension of Temperament	The Psychological Corporation 555 Academic Court San Antonio, TX 78204
The Value Scale	Consulting Psychologists Press 3803 E. Bayshore Drive Palo Alto, CA 94303
Vocational Evaluation System	Singer Education Division Career Systems 80 Commerce Drive Rochester, NY 14623
Wide Range Achievement Test (WRAT)	Jastak Associates, Inc. P.O. Box 4460 Wilmington, DE 19807
Wide Range Interest-Opinion Test	Jastak Associates, Inc. P.O. Box 4460 Wilmington, DE 19807
Wide Range Scales	U.S. Department of Labor Manpower Administration Washington, DC 20210
Work Values Inventory (WVI)	Riverside Publishing Co. 8420 Bryn Mawr Avenue Chicago, IL 60631
Writers Skills Test	Educational Testing Service P.O. Box 6736 Princeton, NJ 08541-6736

Appendix B
Code of Fair Testing Practices in Education

*Prepared by the Joint Committee
on Testing Practices*

The Code of Fair Testing Practices in Education states the major obligations to test takers of professionals who develop or use educational tests. The Code is meant to apply broadly to the use of tests in education (admissions, educational assessment, educational diagnosis, and student placement). The Code is not designed to cover employment testing, licensure or certification testing, or other types of testing. Although the Code has relevance to many types of educational tests, it is directed primarily at professionally developed tests such as those sold by commercial test publishers or used in formally administered testing programs. The Code is not intended to cover tests made by individual teachers for use in their own classrooms.

The Code addresses the roles of test developers and test users separately. Test users are people who select tests, commission test development services, or make decisions on the basis of test scores. Test developers are people who actually construct tests as well as those who set policies for particular testing programs. The roles may, of course, overlap as when a state education agency commissions test development services, sets policies that control the test development process, and makes decisions on the basis of the test scores.

The Code presents standards for educational test developers and users in four areas:

A. Developing/Selecting Tests
B. Interpreting Scores
C. Striving for Fairness
D. Informing Test Takers

Organizations, institutions, and individual professionals who endorse the Code commit themselves to safeguarding the rights of test takers by following the principles listed. The Code is intended to be consistent with the relevant parts of the *Standards for Educational and Psychological*

The Code has been developed by the Joint Committee on Testing Practices, a cooperative effort of several professional organizations, that has as its aim the advancement, in the public interest, of the quality of testing practices. The Joint Committee was initiated by the American Educational Research Association, the American Psychological Association, and the National Council on Measurement in Education. In addition to these three groups, the American Association for Counseling and Development/Association for Measurement and Evaluation in Counseling and Development, and the American Speech-Language-Hearing Association are now also sponsors of the Joint Committee.

This is not copyrighted material. Reproduction and dissemination are encouraged. Please cite this document as follows:

Code of Fair Testing Practices in Education. (1988). Washington, D.C. Joint Committee on Testing Practices (Mailing Address: Joint Committee on Testing Practices, American Psychological Association, 1200 17th Street, NW, Washington, D.C. 20036.)

Testing (AERA, APA, NCME, 1985). However, the Code differs from the Standards in both audience and purpose. The Code is meant to be understood by the general public; it is limited to educational tests; and the primary focus is on those issues that affect the proper use of tests. The Code is not meant to add new principles over and above those in the Standards or to change the meaning of the Standards. The goal is rather to represent the spirit of a selected portion of the Standards in a way that is meaningful to test takers and/or their parents or guardians. It is the hope of the Joint Committee that the Code will also be judged to be consistent with existing codes of conduct and standards of other professional groups who use educational tests.

A. Developing/Selecting Appropriate Tests*

Test developers should provide the information that test users need to select appropriate tests.

Test users should select tests that meet the purpose for which they are to be used and that are appropriate for the intended test-taking populations.

Test Developers Should:

1. Define what each test measures and what the test should be used for. Describe the population(s) for which the test is appropriate.

2. Accurately represent the characteristics, usefulness, and limitations of tests for their intended purposes.

3. Explain relevant measurement concepts as necessary for clarity at the level of detail that is appropriate for the intended audience(s).

4. Describe the process of test development. Explain how the content and skills to be tested were selected.

5. Provide evidence that the test meets its intended purpose(s).

6. Provide either representative samples or complete copies of test questions, directions, answer sheets, manuals, and score reports to qualified users.

7. Indicate the nature of the evidence obtained concerning the appropriateness of each test for groups of different racial, ethnic, or linguistic backgrounds who are likely to be tested.

Test Users Should:

1. First define the purpose for testing and the population to be tested. Then, select a test for that purpose and that population based on a thorough review of the available information.

2. Investigate potentially useful sources of information, in addition to test scores, to corroborate the information provided by tests.

3. Read the materials provided by test developers and avoid using tests for which unclear or incomplete information is provided.

4. Become familiar with how and when the test was developed and tried out.

5. Read independent evaluations of a test and of possible alternative measures. Look for evidence required to support the claims of test developers.

6. Examine specimen sets, disclosed tests or samples of questions, directions, answer sheets, manuals, and score reports before selecting a test.

7. Ascertain whether the test content and norms group(s) or comparison group(s) are appropriate for the intended test takers.

*Many of the statements in the Code refer to the selection of existing tests. However, in customized testing programs test developers are engaged to construct new tests. In those situations, the test development process should be designed to help ensure that the completed tests will be in compliance with the Code.

8. Identify and publish any specialized skills needed to administer each test and to interpret scores correctly.

8. Select and use only those tests for which the skills needed to administer the test and interpret scores correctly are available.

B. Interpreting Scores

Test developers should help users interpret scores correctly.

Test users should interpret scores correctly.

Test Developers Should:

9. Provide timely and easily understood score reports that describe test performance clearly and accurately. Also explain the meaning and limitations of reported scores.
10. Describe the population(s) represented by any norms or comparison group(s), the dates the data were gathered, and the process used to select the samples of test takers.

11. Warn users to avoid specific, reasonably anticipated misuses of test scores.

12. Provide information that will help users follow reasonable procedures for setting passing scores when it is appropriate to use such scores with the test.
13. Provide information that will help users gather evidence to show that the test is meeting its intended purpose(s).

Test Users Should:

9. Obtain information about the scale used for reporting scores, the characteristics of any norms or comparison group(s), and the limitations of the scores.
10. Interpret scores taking into account any major differences between the norms or comparison groups and the actual test takers. Also take into account any differences in test administration practices or familiarity with the specific questions in the test.
11. Avoid using tests for purposes not specifically recommended by the test developer unless evidence is obtained to support the intended use.
12. Explain how any passing scores were set and gather evidence to support the appropriateness of the scores.

13. Obtain evidence to help show that the test is meeting its intended purpose(s).

C. Striving for Fairness

Test developers should strive to make tests that are as fair as possible for test takers of different races, gender, ethnic backgrounds, or handicapping conditions.

Test users should select tests that have been developed in ways that attempt to make them as fair as possible for test takers of different races, gender, ethnic backgrounds, or handicapping conditions.

Test Developers Should:

14. Review and revise test questions and related materials to avoid potentially insensitive content or language.

Test Users Should:

14. Evaluate the procedures used by test developers to avoid potentially insensitive content or language.

15. Investigate the performance of test takers of different races, gender, and ethnic backgrounds when samples of sufficient size are available. Enact procedures that help to ensure that differences in performance are related primarily to the skills under assessment rather than to irrelevant factors.

16. When feasible, make appropriately modified forms of tests or administration procedures available for test takers with handicapping conditions. Warn test users of potential problems in using standard norms with modified tests or administration procedures that result in noncomparable scores.

15. Review the performance of test takers of different races, gender, and ethnic backgrounds when samples of sufficient size are available. Evaluate the extent to which performance differences may have been caused by inappropriate characteristics of the test.

16. When necessary and feasible, use appropriately modified forms of tests or administration procedures for test takers with handicapping conditions. Interpret standard norms with care in the light of the modifications that were made.

D. Informing Test Takers

Under some circumstances, test developers have direct communication with test takers. Under other circumstances, test users communicate directly with test takers. Whichever group communicates directly with test takers should provide the information described below.

Under some circumstances, test developers have direct control of tests and test scores. Under other circumstances, test users have such control. Whichever group has direct control of tests and test scores should take the steps described below.

Test Developers or Test Users Should:

17. When a test is optional, provide test takers or their parents/guardians with information to help them judge whether the test should be taken, or if an available alternative to the test should be used.

18. Provide test takers the information they need to be familiar with the coverage of the test, the types of question formats, the directions, and appropriate test-taking strategies. Strive to make such information equally available to all test takers.

Test Developers or Test Users Should:

19. Provide test takers or their parents/guardians with information about rights test takers may have to obtain copies of tests and completed answer sheets, retake tests, have tests rescored, or cancel scores.

20. Tell test takers or their parents/guardians how long scores will be kept on file and indicate to whom and under what circumstances test scores will or will not be released.

21. Describe the procedures that test takers or their parents/guardians may use to register complaints and have problems resolved.

Note: The membership of the Working Group that developed the Code of Fair Testing Practices in Education and of the Joint Committee on Testing Practices that guided the Working Group was as follows:

Theodore P. Bartell
John R. Bergan
Esther E. Diamond

Richard P. Duran
Lorraine D. Eyde
Raymond D. Fowler

John J. Fremer
(Co-chair, JCTP and
Chair, Code
Working Group)

Edmund W. Gordon
Jo-Ida C. Hansen
James B. Lingwall
George F. Madaus
  (Co-chair, JCTP)
Kevin L. Moreland
Jo-Ellen V. Perez

Robert J. Solomon
John T. Stewart
Carol Kehr Tittle
  (Co-chair, JCTP)
Nicholas A. Vacc
Michael J. Zieky

Debra Boltas and Wayne Camara of the American Psychological Association served as staff liaisons.

Dimensions of Lifestyle Orientation Survey

Vernon G. Zunker
College Research Form

Name _____ Date _____

This is not a test, but an inventory to help you think in terms of a lifestyle after graduation from college. The lifestyle preferences you have are important to consider in the future decisions you make about your life. The first part requests some demographic information for research and standardization purposes. In the second part, you are asked to rate your feelings about a list of statements concerning such matters as job style, leisure style, membership style, home style, and family style. The third part requests information about the kind of place in which you would like to live. The last part (optional) asks you to share some of your subjective thoughts and feelings about the lifestyle you would like to have.

Please follow the directions for each section of the inventory. When you have finished, return the inventory and answer form to your counselor or instructor.

Directions for Parts I and II
Be sure to make your marks as dark as possible, and avoid letting your marks stray in the other option spaces.

I.   Student Information

Complete the following information items by marking the appropriate option for each on your answer sheet.

1. sex
    (1) male
    (2) female

2. age
    (1) 17–18
    (2) 19
    (3) 20
    (4) 21
    (5) 22 or older

3. marital status
    (1) married
    (2) single

4. college classification
    (1) 0–29 hours completed
    (2) 30–59 hours completed
    (3) 60–89 hours completed
    (4) more than 90 hours completed
    (5) graduate or graduate student

5. racial/ethnic background
    (1) Asian
    (2) Black
    (3) Caucasian
    (4) Hispanic
    (5) other

6-7-8.   For items 6, 7, and 8 mark the 3 digits of the code for your major using the major code list on page 2

GO TO PART II

MAJOR CODES

APPLIED ARTS AND TECHNOLOGY

112   Agriculture
113   Agriculture Business
114   Home Economics
115   Industrial Technology, Arts
121   Criminal Justice

EDUCATION

211   Elementary Education
212   Secondary Education
213   Bi-lingual Education
215   Education Administration
214   Counseling and Guidance
221   Special Education
222   Speech Pathology and Audiology
223   Physical Education
224   Recreational Administration
225   Health Education
231   Occupational Education
232   Vocational Teacher Education

HEALTH PROFESSIONS

311   Nursing
312   Medical Technology
313   Medical Record Administration
314   Hospital and Health Sciences Administration
315   Nutrition
321   Occupational Therapy
322   Physical Therapy
323   Respiratory Therapy
324   Public Health

BUSINESS ADMINISTRATION/MANAGEMENT

331   Business, Management, Marketing
332   Accounting, Finance
333   Computer Information Systems, Data
       Processing
334   Industrial Relations, Personnel
335   Business Education
341   Public Administration
342   Systems Analysis
343   Hotel and Restaurant Administration

HUMANITIES/ARTS/COMMUNICATION

411   Archaeology
412   Architecture
413   Art, Fine Arts, Design
414   Commercial Art
415   Art History
421   Foreign Language, Linguistics
422   Dramatic Arts

423   Philosophy
424   Religion, Religious Studies
425   Music, Music Performance
431   Music Education
432   Speech, Communications Studies
433   English, Literature
434   Journalism
435   Folklore

LIBERAL ARTS/SOCIAL SCIENCES

441   American Studies
442   Anthropology
443   Economics
444   Geography, Planning
445   History
451   Library Science
452   Political Science, International Relations
453   Psychology
454   Sociology
455   Social Work

SCIENCES

511   Astronomy
512   Anatomy, Physiology
513   Biology
514   Biomedical Sciences, Biochemistry, Biophysics
515   Chemistry
521   Computer Science
522   Engineering
523   Environmental Science, Ecology
524   Forestry
525   Genetics
531   Geology
532   Mathematics
533   Metallurgy
534   Meteorology
535   Oceanography
541   Petroleum Land Management
542   Pharmacy, Pharmacology
543   (Pre)-Medicine, Dentistry, Veterinary
544   Physics, Nuclear Physics
545   Statistics

UNDECIDED/OTHER

111   Undecided
551   Pre-Law
555   Other

II. Lifestyle Survey

Read the list below and rate each of the items according to the following scale:

> 1 = unimportant to me
> 2 = moderately important to me
> 3 = of great importance to me

9. Eat out only on special occasions
10. Have children work for part of their own income
11. Attend religious lectures
12. Join neighborhood activities
13. Live in a moderate sized home of 3 to 4 bedrooms in a suburban area
14. Have a job which primarily offers help to others
15. Have a large family of 3 or 4 children or more
16. Entertain at home
17. Eat at restaurants that are relatively inexpensive
18. Make a significant contribution to society
19. Provide educational books and encyclopedias in my home
20. Have hobbies as leisure activities
21. Have ample opportunity to be creative in my work
22. Be required to travel to foreign countries in my work
23. See that my children receive a college education
24. Be socially prominent
25. Rent a modest home
26. Have a definite leadership role in my work
27. Take hunting or fishing trips which do not require extensive travel
28. Take simple, inexpensive vacations
29. Compete strongly to move up the financial ladder
30. No "rat race"—have a minimum of material possessions
31. Have opportunities to meet new and different people in my work
32. Strive for high-level educational attainment
33. Have a job which does not require unusually long hours
34. Be required to make decisions on my own in my work
35. Provide for private lessons in music, dance, etc., for my children
36. Be able to afford extensive traveling to far away places such as Europe and the Far East
37. Have a job in which there is flexibility to set my own hours
38. Take vacations not requiring a great deal of traveling
39. Be able to afford a housemaid
40. Participate in community volunteer work
41. Help plan community activities
42. Be a member of a local service club
43. Be comfortable, but not rich
44. Take outdoor camping vacations
45. Work for a large organization which is financially secure
46. Have a job which is easygoing with little or no pressure
47. Have a job which requires travel to numerous cities
48. Strive to be outstanding in my work
49. Rent a moderately priced apartment
50. Have a relaxed, rather happy-go-lucky existence

CONTINUED ON NEXT PAGE

51. Live in different communities before settling in one
52. Own a second home, for example, on a beach, lake, or out in the country
53. Live in a very large brick or stone home in an exclusive neighborhood
54. Have a job which is considered prestigious in my community
55. Be a member of the local conservation society
56. Have a job which provides regular challenges to overcome
57. Work actively in the PTA or similar parent–teacher groups
58. Spend time reading for leisure
59. Work outdoors most of the time
60. Have ample opportunities to take independent action in my work
61. Limit family size to 2 children or less
62. Attend team sports events
63. Delay marriage until out of college for several years
64. Live in a home of 2 or 3 bedrooms in a moderately expensive neighborhood
65. Work with a relatively new aggressive organization
66. Be able to establish a trust fund for my children
67. Spend time gardening for leisure
68. Have a job from 8–5 five days a week
69. Have a country home which is relatively private
70. Find a satisfactory permanent place to live within five years after graduation
71. Participate in golf, tennis, racquetball, etc.
72. Be a member of a country club
73. Have a legal marriage
74. Live in different parts of the country
75. Attend formal events
76. Study for advancement
77. Attend educational lectures
78. Be in charge or "boss" of an organization
79. Be able to afford summer camps for children
80. Be able to eat out in expensive, exclusive restaurants
81. Actively engage in volunteer work with the local church or synagogue
82. Be a recognized authority in my field
83. Be my own boss
84. Have a job which provides ample time to be with my family
85. Have a job which does not require weekend or evening work
86. Be able to have considerable daily contact with the general public
87. Assume a great deal of responsibility in my work
88. Move from office to office or from place to place during the work day

GO TO PART III

III. Residence Preferences

89. In what size city or town would you like to live in the future? (Circle the number below.)

(1) A metropolitan area of 500,000 population or more

(2) A large city of more than 100,000 population, but less than 500,000

(3) A medium sized city which has a population between 100,000 and 50,000

(4) A smaller city with a population between 20,000 and 5,000

(5) A town which has a population between 20,000 and 5,000

(6) A rural community of less than 5,000 population

My choice of city or town is based upon the following: _____

_____

_____

90. Indicate the geographical region in which you would like to live in the future by circling the appropriate number below and by underlining the state or area of preference. If you have no preference or are undecided, place an "X" in the square immediately below.

☐ No Preference   ☐ Undecided

Region	Names of States/Areas Included in Region
1	Connecticut, Maine, Massachusetts, New Hampshire, Rhode Island, Vermont
2	Delaware, Maryland, New Jersey, New York, Pennsylvania, West Virginia, District of Columbia
3	Illinois, Indiana, Iowa, Kansas, Michigan, Minnesota, Missouri, Nebraska, North Dakota, Ohio, South Dakota, Wisconsin
4	Alabama, Arkansas, Florida, Georgia, Kentucky, Louisiana, Mississippi, North Carolina, South Carolina, Tennessee, Virginia
5	Arizona, New Mexico, Oklahoma, Texas
6	California, Colorado, Idaho, Montana, Nevada, Oregon, Utah, Washington, Wyoming
7	Alaska, Puerto Rico, Hawaii
8	Foreign Country

GO TO PART IV

IV.   **Future Lifestyle**

Write a brief description on how you visualize your life to be ten years from now. Include the items checked by your counselor.

Description of:

1. Place of residence

2. Marital status

3. Level of education

4. Level of income

5. Leisure time activities

6. Principal occupation

7. Ideal working conditions

8. Family economic and social status

9. Type of people you would enjoy working with

10. Avocations, hobbies, and the like

Bibliography

Aiken, L. R. (1988). *Psychological testing and assessment.* Boston: Allyn and Bacon, Inc.

Allport, G. W., Vernon, P. E., & Lindzey, G. (1970). *Manual for the study of values.* Boston: Houghton Mifflin.

American College Testing Program. (1974). *Career planning program.* Iowa City, IA: Author.

American College Testing Program. (1976). *Planning.* Iowa City, IA: Author.

American College Testing Program. (1980). *Counselor's guide.* Iowa City, IA: Author.

American College Testing Program (ACT). (1989). DISCOVER for colleges and adults [Computer program]. Hunt Valley, MD: Author.

American Psychological Association. (1974). *Standards for educational and psychological tests.* Washington, DC: Author.

Anastasi, A. (1988). *Psychological testing* (6th ed.). New York: Macmillan.

Arbeiter, S., Aslanian, C. B., Schmerbeck, F. A., & Brickell, H. M. (1978). *40 Million Americans in career transition: The need for information.* New York: College Entrance Examination Board.

Baird, L. L. (1969). The prediction of accomplishment in college: An exploration of the process of achievement. *Journal of Counseling Psychology, 16,* 246–254.

Bass, A. R. (1984). Basic Occupational Literacy Test (BOLT). In D. J. Keyser & R. C. Sweetland (Eds.), *Test critiques I* (pp. 83–89). Kansas City, MO: Test Corporation of America.

Bennett, G. K., Seashore, H. G., & Wesman, A. G. (1974). *Differential Aptitude Test—Career Planning Program.* New York: Psychological Corporation.

Bennett, G. K., Seashore, H. G., & Wesman, A. G. (1974). *Handbook for Differential Aptitude Test (Forms S and T).* New York: Psychological Corporation.

Benson, A. R. (1985). Minnesota Importance Questionnaire. In D. J. Keyser & R. C. Sweetland (Eds.), *Test critiques II* (pp. 481–489). Kansas City, MO: Test Corporation of America.

Binder, D. M., Jones, J. C., & Strowig, R. W. (1970). Non-intellective self-report variables as predictors of scholastic achievement. *Journal of Educational Research, 63,* 364–366.

Bingham, W. C. (1978). Review of the Career Development Inventory. In O. K. Buros (Ed.), *The eighth mental measurement yearbook* (Vol. 2). Highland Park, NJ: Gryphon Press.

Birk, J. M. (1975). Reducing sex bias: Factors affecting the client's view of the use of career inventories. In E. E. Diamond (Ed.), *Issues of sex bias and sex fairness in career interest measurement.* Washington, DC: National Institute of Education.

Bixler, R. H., & Bixler, V. H. (1946). Test interpretation in vocational counseling. *Educational and Psychological Measurement, 6,* 145–146.

Black, J. D. (1978). Review of the Survey of Interpersonal Values. In O. K. Buros (Ed.), *The eighth mental measurement yearbook* (Vol. 1). Highland Park, NJ: Gryphon Press.

Bloxom, B. M. (1978). Review of the Sixteen Personality Factor Questionnaire. In O. K. Buros (Ed.), *The eighth mental measurement yearbook* (Vol. 1). Highland Park, NJ: Gryphon Press.

Bodden, J. L. (1978). Review of the New Mexico Career Education Test Series. In O. K. Buros (Ed.), *The eighth mental measurement yearbook* (Vol. 2). Highland Park, NJ: Gryphon Press.

Bolles, R. N. (1993). A practical manual for job-hunters and career changers: What color is your parachute? Berkeley, CA: Ten Speed Press.

Bolles, R. N. (1993). *The new Quick Job Hunting Map.* Berkeley, CA: Ten Speed Press.

Bolton, B. (1985). Work Values Inventory. In D. J. Keyser & R. C. Sweetland (Eds.), *Test critiques II* (pp. 835–843). Kansas City, MO: Test Corporation of America.

Bolton, B. F. (1978). Review of the Sixteen Personality Factor Questionnaire. In O. K. Buros (Ed.), *The eighth mental measurement yearbook* (Vol. 1). Highland Park, NJ: Gryphon Press.

Bordin, E. S. (1968). *Psychological counseling* (2nd ed.). New York: Appleton-Century-Crofts.

Borgen, R. H. (1982). USES General Aptitude Test Battery. In J. T. Kapes and M. M. Mastie (Eds.), *A counselor's guide to vocational guidance instrument* (pp. 42–47). Falls Church, VA: National Vocational Guidance Association.

Bouchard, T. J. (1972). Review of the Career Development Inventory. In O. K. Buros (Ed.), *The seventh mental measurement yearbook* (Vol 1). Highland Park, NJ: Gryphon Press.

Bowen, C. W. (1968). *The use of self-estimates of ability and measures of ability in the predication of academic performance.* Unpublished doctoral dissertation, Oklahoma State University.

Brew, S. (1987). *Career development guide for use with the Strong Interest Inventory.* Palo Alto, CA: Consulting Psychologists Press, Inc.

Brown, D. (1990). Models of career decision making. In D. Brown & L. Brooks (Eds.), *Career choice and development: Applying contemporary theories to practice* (pp. 395–422). San Francisco: Jossey-Bass.

Brown, F. G. (1982). Kuder Occupational Interest Survey—Form DD. In J. T. Kapes and M. M. Mastie (Eds.), *A counselor's guides to vocational instruments* (pp. 77–81). Falls Church, VA: National Vocational Guidance Association.

Brown, F. G. (1993). Stanford Achievement Test. In J. J. Kramer & J. C. Conoley (Eds.), *The eleventh mental measurement yearbook* (pp. 861–863). Lincoln, NE: Buros Institute of Mental Measurement, University of Nebraska–Lincoln.

Bryan, M. M. (1978). Review of the California Achievement Test. In O. K. Buros (Ed.), *The eighth mental measurement yearbook* (Vol. 1). Highland Park, NJ: Gryphon Press.

Campbell, D. P. (1974). *Manual for the Strong-Campbell Interest Inventory.* Stanford, CA: Stanford University Press.

Carlson, J. G. (1989). Affirmative: In support of researching the *Myers-Briggs Type Indicator. Journal of Counseling and Development, 67,* (8), 484–486.

Cattell, R. B. (1963). Theory of fluid and crystallized intelligence: A critical experiment. *Journal of Educational Psychology, 54,* 1–22.

Cattell, R. B., Eber, H. W., & Tatsuoka, M. M. (1970). *Handbook for the Sixteen Personality Factor Questionnaire (16PF).* Champaign, IL: Institute for Personality and Ability Testing.

Clark, E., (1989). Wide Range Achievement Test—Revised. In J. S. Conoley & J. J. Kramer (Eds.), *The tenth mental measurement yearbook* (pp. 901–903). Lincoln, NE: Buros Institute of Mental Measurement, University of Nebraska–Lincoln.

Cole, N. S., & Hansen, G. R. (1975). Impact of interest inventories on career choice. In E. E. Diamond (Ed.), *Issues of sex bias and sex fairness in career interest measurement.* Washington, DC: National Institute of Education.

College Entrance Examination Board. (1978). *Guide to self evaluation and development skills.* New York: Author.

Conoley, J. C. & Kramer, J. J. (Eds.). (1989). *The tenth mental measurement yearbook* (pp. 901–903). Lincoln, NE: Buros Institute of Mental Measurement, University of Nebraska–Lincoln.

Cooper, D. (1990). Factor structure of the Edwards Personal Preference Schedule in a vocational rehabilitation sample. *Journal of Clinical Psychology, 46,* 421–425.

Cooper, J. F. (1976). Comparative impact of the SCII and the vocational Card Sort on career salience and career exploration of women. *Journal of Counseling Psychology, 23,* 348–352.

Crites, J. O. (1977). Career counseling: A review of major approaches. In H. J. Peters & J. C. Hansen (Eds.), *Vocational guidance and career development*. New York: Macmillan.

Crites, J. O. (1982). The Self-Directed Search. In J. T. Kapes and M. M. Mastie (Eds.), *A counselor's guide to vocational guidance instrument* (pp. 88–92). Falls Church, VA: National Vocational Guidance Association.

Cronbach, L. J. (1978). Review of Basic Occupational Literacy Test. In O. K. Buros (Ed.), *The eighth mental measurement yearbook* (Vol. 1). Highland Park, NJ: Gryphon Press.

Cronbach, L. J. (1979). The Armed Services Vocational Aptitude Battery — A test battery in transition. *Personal and Guidance Journal, 57*, 232–237.

Cronbach, L. J. (1984). *Essentials of psychological testing* (4th ed.) New York: Harper & Row.

Cunningham, G. K. (1986). *Educational and psychological measurement*. New York: Macmillan.

Dawis, R. B., & Lofquist, L. (1984). *A psychological theory of work adjustment: An individual differences model and its application*. Minneapolis, MN: University of Minnesota.

Dewey, C. R. (1974). Exploring interests: A non-sexist method. *Personnel and Guidance Journal, 52*, 311–315.

Diamond, E. E. (1975). Overview. In E. E. Diamond (Ed.), *Issues of sex bias and sex fairness in career interest measurement*. Washington, DC: National Institute of Education.

Dinkmeyer, D., & Caldwell, E. (1970). *Developmental counseling and guidance: A comprehensive approach*. New York: McGraw-Hill.

Dolliver, R. H. (1967). An adaption of the Tyler Vocational Card Sort. *Personnel and Guidance Journal, 45*, 916–920.

Dolliver, R. H. (1972). Review of the Kuder Occupational Interest Survey. In O. K. Buros (Ed.), *The seventh mental measurement yearbook* (Vol. 2). Highland Park, NJ: Gryphon Press.

Dolliver, R. H. (1978). Review of the Strong-Campbell Interest Inventory. In O. K. Buros (Ed.), *The eighth mental measurement yearbook* (Vol. 2). Highland Park, NJ: Gryphon Press.

Dolliver, R. H. (1982). Combined review of card sort instruments. In J. T. Kapes and M. M. Mastie (Eds.), *A counselor's guide to vocational guidance instruments* (pp. 147–160). Falls Church, VA: National Vocational Guidance Association.

Dolliver, R. H., Irvin, J. A., & Bigley, S. S. (1978). Twelve-year follow-up of the Strong Vocational Interest Blank. *Journal of Counseling Psychology, 19*, 212–217.

Droege, R. C. (1984). The Career Decision-Making System. In D. J. Keyser & R. C. Sweetland (Eds.), *Test critiques I* (pp. 322–327), Kansas City, MO: Test Corporation of America.

Drucker, Peter F. (1992). *Managing for the future*. New York: Truman Talley Books/Dutton.

Drummond, R. (1992). *Appraisal procedures for counselors and helping professionals* (2nd ed.). New York: Macmillan.

Edwards, A. L. (1959). *Edwards Personal Preference Schedule manual*. New York: The Psychological Corporation.

Erchul, W. P. (1989). Survey of Personal Values. In J. S. Conoley & J. J. Kramer (Eds.), *The tenth mental measurement yearbook* (pp. 800–801). Lincoln, NE: Buros Institute of Mental Measurement, University of Nebraska–Lincoln.

Figler, H. E. (1990). *Path: A career workbook for liberal arts students*. Cranston, RI: Carroll Press.

Fitzpatrick, A. R. (1992). Adult Basic Learning Examination (ABLE). In J. J. Kramer & J. S. Conoley (Eds.), *The eleventh mental measurement yearbook* (pp. 19–21). Lincoln, NE: Buros Institute of Mental Measurement, University of Nebraska–Lincoln.

Fitzpatrick, J. P. (1961). Individualism in America. In D. N. Barrett (Ed.), *Values in America*. Notre Dame, IN: University of Notre Dame Press.

Fogel, A. J. (1974). *Development of a replicable group vocational counseling procedure for use with community college students*. Unpublished doctoral dissertation, University of California, Los Angeles.

Frary, R. B. (1984). In D. J. Keyser & R. C. Sweetland (Eds.), *Test critiques I* (pp. 164–167). Kansas City, MO: Test Corporation of America.

Fryer, D. (1931). *Measurement of interests*. New York: Holt, Rinehart & Winston.

Garcia, V., Zunker, V. G., & Nolan, J. (1980). *Analysis of a pre-vocational training program.* Unpublished manuscript, Southwest Texas State University.

Geisinger, K. (1984). American College Testing Program. In D. J. Keyser & R. C. Sweetland (Eds.), *Test critiques I* (pp. 11–29). Kansas City, MO: Test Corporation of America.

Ghiselli, E. E. (1963). Managerial talent. *American Psychologist, 18,* 631–642.

Ghiselli, E. (1966). *The validity of occupational aptitude tests.* New York: Wiley.

Goldman, L. (1972). *Using tests in counseling* (2nd ed.). New York: Appleton-Century-Crofts.

Gordon, L. V. (1967). *Survey of Personal Values Examiner's Manual.* Chicago: Science Research Associates.

Gordon, L. V. (1975). *The measurement of interpersonal values.* Chicago: Science Research Associates.

Gottfredson, L. (1981). Construct validity of Holland's occupational typology in terms of prestige, census, Department of Labor, and other classification systems. *Journal of Applied Psychology, 651,* 697–714.

Gottfredson, G. D., & Holland, J. L. (1989). *Dictionary of Holland occupational codes* (2nd ed.). Odessa, FL: Psychological Assessment Resources.

Gribbons, W. D., & Lohnes, P. R. (1968). *Emerging careers.* New York: Teachers College Press.

Guilford, J. P. (1954). *Psychometric methods* (rev. ed.). New York: McGraw-Hill.

Guilford, J. P. (1957). Creative abilities in arts. *Psychological Review, 64,* 110–118.

Hansen, J. C. (1985). *User's guide for the SVIB-SII.* Palo Alto, CA: Consulting Psychologists Press.

Hanser, L. M., & Grafton, F. C. (1983). *Predicting job proficiency in the Army: Race, sex, and education.* Arlington, VA: United States Army Research Institute for the Behavioral and Social Sciences.

Hanson, M. C. (1976). *Guide to career planning and development.* Livermore, CA: Lawrence Livermore Laboratory.

Harmon, L. W. (1975). Technical aspects: Problems of scale development, norms, item difficulties by sex, and the rate of change in occupational group characteristics—I. In E. E. Diamond (Ed.), *Issues of sex bias and sex fairness in career interest measurement.* Washington, DC: National Institute of Education.

Harrell, T. H. (1992). The Sixteen Personality Factor Questionnaire. In J. J. Kramer & J. S. Conoley (Eds.), *The eleventh mental measurement yearbook* (pp. 830–831). Lincoln, NE: Buros Institute of Mental Measurement, University of Nebraska–Lincoln.

Harrington, T. F., & O'Shea, A. J. (1992). *The Harrington/O'Shea System for Career Decision-Making manual.* Circle Pines, MN: American Guidance Service.

Healy, C. C. (1974). *Career counseling in the community college.* Springfield, IL: Charles C Thomas.

Healy, C. C. (1978). Review of the American College Testing Career Planning Program. In O. K. Buros (Ed.), *The eighth mental measurement yearbook* (Vol. 2). Highland Park, NJ: Gryphon Press.

Healy, C. C. (1989). Negative: The MBTI: Not ready for routine use in counseling. *Journal of Counseling and Development, 67*(8), 487–489.

Hemphill, J. K. (1965). Review of the Survey of Interpersonal Values. In O. K. Buros (Ed.), *The seventh mental measurement yearbook* (Vol. 1). Highland Park, NJ: Gryphon Press.

Herr, E. L. (1989). Kuder Occupational Interest Survey. In J. S. Conoley & J. J. Kramer (Eds.), *The tenth mental measurement yearbook* (pp. 425–427). Lincoln, NE: Buros Institute of Mental Measurement, University of Nebraska–Lincoln.

Hilton, T. L. (1982). Career Development Inventory. In J. T. Kapes and M. M. Mastie (Eds.), *A counselor's guide to vocational guidance instruments* (pp. 118–122), Falls Church, VA: National Vocational Guidance Association.

Holland, J. L. (1975). The use and evaluation of interest inventories and simulations. In E. E. Diamond (Ed.), *Issues of sex bias and sex fairness in career interest measurement.* Washington, DC: National Institute of Education.

Holland, J. L. (1985). *Making vocational choices: A theory of careers* (2nd ed.). Englewood Cliffs, NJ: Prentice Hall.

Holland, J. L. (1987a). *The occupations finder.* Odessa, FL: Psychological Assessment Resources.

Holland, J. L. (1987b). *The Self-Directed Search: Professional manual.* Odessa, FL: Psychological Assessment Resources.

Holland, J. L., & Astin, A. W. (1962). The prediction of academic, artistic, scientific and social achievement. *Journal of Educational Psychology, 53,* 132–143.

Hoyt, K. B. (1972). *Career education: What it is and how to do it.* Salt Lake City: Olympus.

Jensen, A. R. (1988). Review of the Armed Services Vocational Aptitude Battery. In J. T. Kapes & M. M. Mastie (Eds.), A counselor's guide to career assessment instruments (pp. 58–62). Washington, DC: National Career Development Association.

Johansson, C. B. (1975). Technical aspects: Problems of scale development, norms, item differences by sex, and the rate of change in occupational group characteristics. In E. E. Diamond (Ed.), *Issues of sex bias and sex fairness in career interest measurement.* Washington, DC: National Institute of Education.

Johansson, C. B. (1977). *Manual for the Temperament and Values Inventory.* Minneapolis: Interpretive Scoring Systems.

Johnson, R. W. (1978). Review of the Strong-Campbell Interest Inventory. In O. K. Buros (Ed.), *The eighth mental measurement yearbook* (Vol. 2). Highland Park, NJ: Gryphon Press.

Jones, L. K. (1981). *Occ-U-Sort professional manual.* Monterey, CA: Publishers Test Service of CTB/McGraw-Hill.

Jung, C. G. (1971). Psychological types (H. G. Baynes, Trans., revised by R. F. C. Hull). Volume 6 of *The collected works of C. G. Jung.* Princeton, NJ: Princeton University Press. (Original work published 1921)

Kaplan, R., & Saccuzzo, D. (1993). *Psychological testing.* Pacific Grove, CA: Brooks/Cole.

Katz, M. R. (1978). Review of the Career Maturity Inventory. In O. K. Buros (Ed.), *The eighth mental measurement yearbook* (Vol. 2). Highland Park, NJ: Gryphon Press.

Katz, M. R. (1982). Career Maturity Inventory. In J. T. Kapes and M. M. Mastie (Eds.), *A counselor's guide to vocational guidance instruments* (pp. 122–126). Falls Church, VA: National Vocational Guidance Association.

Keyser, D. J., & Sweetland, R. C. (Eds.), (1984). *Test critiques I.* Kansas City, MO: Test Corporation of America.

Keyser, D. J., & Sweetland, R. C. (Eds.), (1985). *Test critiques II.* Kansas City, MO: Test Corporation of America.

Kirn, A. G., & Kirn, M. O. (1975). *Life work planning.* New York: McGraw-Hill.

Klemp, G. L., & McClelland, D. C. (1986). What constitutes intelligent functioning among senior managers. In R. J. Sternberg & R. K. Wagner (Eds.), *Practical intelligence: Nature and origins of competence in the everyday world* (pp. 31–50). New York: Cambridge University Press.

Kluckhorn, C. (1961). The study of values. In D. N. Barrett (Ed.), *Values in America.* Notre Dame, IN: University of Notre Dame Press.

Kuder, G. F. (1963). A rationale for evaluating interests. *Educational and Psychological Measurement, 23,* 3–10.

Kuder, G. F. (1979). *Kuder Occupational Interest Survey: General manual.* Chicago: Science Research Associates.

Lathrop, R. (1977). *Who's hiring who.* Berkeley, CA: Ten Speed Press.

LaVoie, A.L. (1978). Review of the Survey of Interpersonal Values. In O. K. Buros (Ed.), *The eighth mental measurement yearbook* (Vol. 1). Highland Park, NJ: Gryphon Press.

Levin, A. (1991). *Introduction to the Strong for career counselors.* Palo Alto, CA: Consulting Psychologists Press.

Linn, R. L. (1982). Differential Aptitude Tests/DAT career planning program. In J. T. Kapes and M. M. Mastie (Eds.), *A counselor's guide to vocational guidance instruments* (pp. 37–42). Falls Church, VA: National Vocational Guidance Association.

Lofquist, L. & Dawis, R.V. (1984). Research on work adjustment and satisfaction: Implications for career counseling. In S. Brown and R. Lent (Eds.), *Handbook of counseling psychology* (pp. 216–237). New York: John Wiley and Sons.

Lowman, R. L. (1991). *The clinical practice of career assessment: Interests, abilities, and personality.* Washington, DC: American Psychological Association.

Lunneborg, P. W. (1978). Review of the Strong-Campbell Interest Inventory. In O. K. Buros (Ed.), *The eighth mental measurement yearbook* (Vol. 2). Highland Park, NJ: Gryphon Press.

McCaulley, M. H. (1990). The Myers-Briggs indicator: A measure of individuals and groups. *Measurement and Evaluation in Counseling and Development, 22,* 181–195.

McKinlay, B. (1971). *Validity and readability of the occupational information access system "QUEST" Questionnaire.* Eugene, OR: Career Information System.

McKinlay, B. (1990). *Developing a career information system.* Eugene, OR: Career Information System.

Meyers, C. E. (1978). Review of the Social and Prevocational Information Battery. In O. K. Buros (Ed.), *The eighth mental measurement yearbook* (Vol. 2). Highland Park, NJ: Gryphon Press.

Miller-Tiedeman, A., & Tiedeman, D. V. (1990). Career decision making: An individualistic perspective. In D. Brown & L. Brooks (Eds.), *Career choice and development: Applying contemporary theories to practice* (pp. 308–338). San Francisco: Jossey-Bass.

Mitchell, J. V. (Ed.) (1983). *Tests in print III.* Lincoln, NE: Buros Institute of Mental Measurement, University of Nebraska–Lincoln.

Mitchell, L. K., & Krumboltz, J. D. (1990). Social learning approach to career decision making: Krumboltz's theory. In D. Brown & L. Brooks (Eds.), *Career choice and development: Applying contemporary theories to practice* (pp. 145–197). San Francisco: Jossey-Bass.

Mueller, D. J. (1985). Survey of Interpersonal Values. In D. J. Keyser & R. C. Sweetland (Eds.), *Test critiques II* (pp. 759–763). Kansas City, MO: Test Corporation of America.

Murphy, K. (1984). Armed Services Vocational Aptitude Test. In D. J. Keyser & R. C. Sweetland (Eds.), *Test critiques II* (pp. 481–489). Kansas City, MO: Test Corporation of America.

Murray, H. A. (1938). *Exploration in personality.* New York: Oxford University Press.

Myers, J. B., & McCaulley, M. H. (1985). *Manual: A guide to the development and use of the Myers-Briggs Type Indicator.* Palo Alto, CA: Consulting Psychologists Press.

National Occupational Information Coordinating Committee, U. S. Department of Labor. (1992). *The National Career Development Guidelines Project.* Washington, DC: U. S. Department of Labor.

Overton, T. (1992). Social and Prevocational Information Battery (SPIB). In J. J. Kramer & J. S. Conoley (Eds.), *The eleventh mental measurement yearbook* (pp. 834–836). Lincoln, NE: Buros Institute of Mental Measurement, University of Nebraska–Lincoln.

Parsons, F. (1909). *Choosing a vocation.* Boston: Houghton Mifflin.

Payne, D. A. (1962). The concurrent and predictive validity of an objective measure of academic self-concept. *Educational and Psychological Measurement, 22,* 773–780.

Pennock-Roman, M. (1988). Differential Aptitude Test. In J. T. Kapes & M. M. Mastie (Eds.), *A counselor's guide to career assessment instruments* (2nd ed.). Alexandra, VA: National Career Development Association.

Pietrofesa, J. J., & Splete, H. (1975). *Career development: Theory and research.* New York: Grune and Stratton.

Plake, B. S. (1985). Review of Basic Skills Assessment Program. In O. K. Buros (Ed.), *The ninth mental measurement yearbook,* Vol. I (pp. 147–148). Highland Park, NJ: Gryphon Press.

Prediger, D. J. (1978). Review of the New Mexico Education Test Series. In O. K. Buros (Ed.), *The eighth mental measurement yearbook* (Vol. 2). Highland Park, NJ: Gryphon Press.

Prediger, D. J., & Johnson, R. W. (1979). *Alternatives to sex-restrictive vocational interest assessment* (Research Rep. 79). Iowa City, IA: American College Testing Program.

Prediger, D. J. (1980). The marriage between tests and career counseling: An intimate report. *The Vocational Quarterly, 28,* 297–305.

Prediger, D. J. (1987). Validity of the New Armed Services Vocational Aptitude Battery Job Cluster Scores in Career Planning. *Career Development Quarterly, 36,* 113–25.

Rabinowitz, W. (1984). Study of values. In D. J. Keyser & R. C. Sweetland (Eds.), *Test critiques I* (pp. 641–647). Kansas City, MO: Test Corporation of America.

Ravitch, M. M. (1985). Review of Basic Skills Assessment Program. *The ninth mental measurement yearbook,* Vol. I (pp. 148–149). Highland Park, NJ: Gryphon Press.

Reid, N. (1986). Testing the test: Wide Range Achievement Test: 1984 Revised Edition. *Journal of Counseling and Development, 64,* 538–540.

Reynolds, C. R. (1986). Wide Range Achievement Test (WRAT-R), 1984 edition. *Journal of Counseling and Development, 64,* 540–541.

Ricks, J. H. (1978). Review of the Career Development Inventory. In O. K. Buros (Ed.), *The eighth mental measurement yearbook* (Vol. 2). Highland Park, NJ: Gryphon Press.

Robinson, J. P., Shaver, P. R., & Wrightsman, L. S. (1991). *Measures of personality and social psychological attitudes.* New York: Academic Press.

Roe, A. (1956). *The psychology of occupations.* New York: Wiley.

Rounds, J. B., Jr., Henly, G. A., Dawis, R. V., & Lofquist, L. H. (1981). *Manual for the Minnesota Importance Questionnaire: A measure of needs and values.* Minneapolis: Vocational Psychology Research, University of Minnesota.

Sarason, S. B., Sarason, E. K., & Cowden, P. (1977). Aging and the nature of work. In H. J. Peters & J. C. Hansen (Eds.), *Vocational guidance and career development.* New York: Macmillan.

Schrank, F. A. (1984). The Temperament and Values Inventory. In D. J. Keyser & R. C. Sweetland (Eds.), *Test critiques I* (pp. 660–662). Kansas City, MO: Test Corporation of America.

Sharf, R. S. (1992). *Applying career development theory to counseling.* Pacific Grove, CA: Brooks/Cole.

Siegel, L. (1965). Review of the Survey of Interpersonal Values. In O. K. Buros (Ed.), *The sixth mental measurement yearbook.* Highland Park, NJ: Gryphon Press.

Snodgrass, G. (1980). *Career Self Assessment.* Unpublished manuscript, Southwest Texas State University.

Spranger, E. (1966). *Types of men* (5th ed.) (Vol. 3) (P. J. W. Pigors, Trans.). New York: Stechert-Hafner. (Originally published, 1928.)

Steinhaurer, J. C. (1978). Review of the Strong-Campbell Interest Inventory. In O. K. Buros (Ed.), *The eighth mental measurement yearbook* (Vol. 2). Highland Park, NJ: Gryphon Press.

Stoker, H. (1993). Standford Achievement Test. In J. J. Kramer & J. C. Conoley (Eds.), *The eleventh mental measurement yearbook* (pp. 863–865). Lincoln, NE: Buros Institute of Mental Measurement, University of Nebraska–Lincoln.

Strong, E. K., Jr. (1943). *Vocational interests of men and women.* Stanford, CA: Stanford University Press.

Super, D. E. (1950). Testing and using test results in counseling. *Occupations, 29,* 95–97.

Super, D. E. (1953). A theory of vocational development. *American Psychologist, 8,* 185–190.

Super, D. E. (1970). *Work Values Inventory: Manual.* Boston: Houghton Mifflin.

Super, D. E. (1990). A life-span, life-space approach to career development. In D. Brown & L. Brooks (Eds.), *Career choice and development: Applying contemporary theories to practice* (pp. 197–261). San Francisco: Jossey-Bass.

Super, D. E., & Crites, J. O. (1962). *Appraising vocational fitness by means of psychological tests* (rev. ed.). New York: Harper & Row.

Super, D. E., Osborne, W., Walsh, D., Brown, S., & Niles, S. (1992). Developmental career assessment and counseling: The C-DAC model. *Journal of Counseling and Development, 71* (Sept./Oct.), 74–79.

Sweetland, R. C., & Keyser, D. J. (1991). *Tests: A comprehensive reference for assessment in psychology, education and business* (3rd ed.). Austin, TX: ProEd Publishers.

Tenopyr, M. L. (1989). Kuder Occupational Interest Survey. In J. S. Conoley & J. J. Kramer (Eds.), *The tenth mental measurement yearbook* (pp. 427–429). Lincoln, NE: Buros Institute of Mental Measurement, University of Nebraska–Lincoln.

Thomas, L. E. (September, 1972). Life planning workshops in community colleges and four-year universities. In D. Aigaki (Chair), *Career development*. Symposium presented at the meeting of the American Psychological Association, Honolulu.

Thompson, A. P. (1976). Client misconceptions in vocational counseling. *Personnel and Guidance Journal, 55*, 30–33.

Thorndike, R. L, & Hagen, E. (1959). *10,000 careers*. New York: Wiley.

Tiedman, D. V., & O'Hara, R. P. (1963). *Career development: Choice and adjustment*. New York: College Entrance Examination Board.

Tuckman, B. W. (1978). Review of Basic Occupational Literacy Test. In O. K. Buros (Ed.), *The eighth mental measurement yearbook* (Vol. 1). Highland Park, NJ: Gryphon Press.

Tyler, L. E. (1961). Research explorations in the realm of choice. *Journal of Counseling Psychology, 8*, 195–201.

U.S. Department of Defense. (1979). *Armed Services Vocational Aptitude Battery counselor's guide*. Ft. Sheridan, IL: Military Enlistment Processing Command.

U.S. Department of Labor (1970). *General Aptitude Test Battery manual, section III*. Washington, DC: Government Printing Office.

U.S. Department of Labor (1991). *Dictionary of occupational titles* (4th ed., revised). Washington, DC: U. S. Government Printing Office.

U.S. Department of Labor. (1978). *U.S. newsletter*. Washington, DC: U. S. Government Printing Office.

U.S. Department of Labor. (1992–1993). *Occupational outlook handbook*. Washington, DC: U. S. Government Printing Office.

U.S. Department of Labor. (1979a). *Guide for occupational exploration*. Washington, DC: U. S. Government Printing Office.

U.S. Department of Labor. (1979b). *Occupational aptitude pattern structure*. Washington, DC: U. S. Government Printing Office.

Viernstein, M. C. (1972). The extension of Holland's occupational classification to all occupations in the *Dictionary of Occupational Titles. Journal of Vocational Behavior, 2*, 107–121.

Walsh, J. A. (1978). Review of the Sixteen Personality Factor Questionnaire. In O. K. Buros (Ed.), *The eighth mental measurement yearbook* (Vol. 1). Highland Park, NJ: Gryphon Press.

Walsh, W. B. (1972). Review of the Kuder Occupational Interest Survey. In O. K. Buros (Ed.), *The seventh mental measurement yearbook* (Vol. 2). Highland Park, NJ: Gryphon Press.

Walter, V. (1984). *Personal Career Development Profile*. Champaign, IL: Institute for Personality and Ability Testing.

Weiss, D. J. (1978). Review of the Armed Services Vocational Aptitude Battery. In O. K. Buros (Ed.), *The eighth mental measurement yearbook* (Vol. 1) Highland Park, NJ: Gryphon Press.

Westbrook, B. W. (1978). Review of the New Mexico Education Test Series. In O. K. Buros (Ed.), *The eighth mental measurement yearbook* (Vol. 2). Highland Park, NJ: Gryphon Press.

Westbrook, B. W., Cutts, C. C., Madison, S. S., & Arcia, M. A. (1980). The validity of the Crites model of career maturity. *Journal of Vocational Behavior, 16*, 249–281.

Westbrook, B. W., & Mastie, M. M. (1973). Three measures of vocational maturity: A beginning to know about. *Measurement and Evaluation in Guidance, 6*, 8–16.

Westbrook, B. W., & Parry-Hill, J. W., Jr. (1973). *The construction and validation of a measure of vocational maturity* (ERIC document 101 145). Raleigh: Center for Occupational Education, North Carolina State University.

Williams, R. T. (1992). Adult Basic Learning Examination (ABLE). In J. J. Kramer & J. S. Conoley (Eds.), *The eleventh mental measurement yearbook* (pp. 21–23). Lincoln, NE: Buros Institute of Mental Measurement, University of Nebraska–Lincoln.

Williamson, E. G. (1939). *How to counsel students: A manual of techniques for clinical counselors*. New York: McGraw-Hill.

Williamson, E. G. (1949). *Counseling adolescents*. New York: McGraw-Hill.

Willis, C. G. (1982). The Harrington-O'Shea Career Decision-Making System. In J. T. Kapes and M. M. Mastie (Eds.), *A counselor's guide to vocational guidance instruments* (pp. 57–61). Falls Church, VA: National Vocational Guidance Association.

Witt, J. C. (1986). Review of the Wide Range Achievement Test. *Journal of Pyschoeducational Assessment, 4,* 88–90.

Womer, F. B. (1978). Review of the California Achievement Test. In O. K. Buros (Ed.), *The eighth mental measurement yearbook* (Vol. 1). Highland Park, NJ: Gryphon Press.

Wylie, R. C. (1963). Children's estimates of school work ability. *Journal of Personality, 31,* 203–224.

Zimbardo, P. G. (1979). *Psychology and life.* Glenview, IL: Scott, Foresman.

Zunker, V. G. (1977). *Dimension of Lifestyle Orientation Survey.* Unpublished manuscript, Southwest Texas State University.

Zunker, V. G. (1994). *Career counseling: Applied concepts of life planning* (4th ed.). Pacific Grove, CA: Brooks/Cole.

Zytowski, D. G. (1978). Review of Wide Range Interest-Opinion Test. In O. K. Buros (Ed.), *The eighth mental measurement yearbook* (Vol. 2). Highland Park, NJ: Gryphon Press.

Name Index

Subject Index

TO THE OWNER OF THIS BOOK:

We hope that you have found *Using Assessment Results in Career Development*, Fourth Edition, useful. So that this book can be improved in a future edition, would you take the time to complete this sheet and return it? Thank you.

School and address: _____

Department: _____

Instructor's name: _____

1. What I like most about this book is: _____

_____

2. What I like least about this book is: _____

_____

3. My general reaction to this book is: _____

_____

4. The name of the course in which I used this book is: _____

_____

5. Were all of the chapters of the book assigned for you to read? _____

   If not, which ones weren't? _____

_____

6. In the space below, or on a separate sheet of paper, please write specific suggestions for improving this book and anything else you'd care to share about your experience in using the book.

_____

_____

_____

_____

_____

_____

_____

_____

Optional:

Your name: _____ Date: _____

May Brooks/Cole quote you, either in promotion for *Using Assessment Results in Career Development*, Fourth Edition, or in future publishing ventures?

Yes: _____ No: _____

Sincerely,

Vernon G. Zunker

- -
FOLD HERE

- -
FOLD HERE

Brooks/Cole is dedicated to publishing quality publications for education in the human services fields. If you are interested in learning more about our publications, please fill in your name and address and request our latest catalogue, using this prepaid mailer.

Name: _____

Street Address: _____

City, State, and Zip: _____

- -

FOLD HERE

BUSINESS REPLY MAIL
FIRST CLASS   PERMIT NO. 358   PACIFIC GROVE, CA

POSTAGE WILL BE PAID BY ADDRESSEE

ATT: *Human Services Catalogue* _____

Brooks/Cole Publishing Company
511 Forest Lodge Road
Pacific Grove, California 93950-9968

- -

FOLD HERE